Do Travel Writers Go to Hell?

Do Travel Writers Go to Hell?

A Swashbuckling Tale of High Adventures,
Questionable Ethics, and Professional Hedonism

THOMAS B. KOHNSTAMM

THREE RIVERS PRESS
NEW YORK

Three Rivers Press and the Tugboat design are registered trademarks
of Random House, Inc.

Library of Congress Cataloging-in-Publication Data
Kohnstamm, Thomas B.
Do travel writers go to hell?: a swashbuckling tale of high adventures, question-
able ethics, and professional hedonism / Thomas B. Kohnstamm. —1st ed.
1. Kohnstamm, Thomas B.—Travel writers—United States—Biography. I. Title.
G154.5.K65A 2008
910.4092—dc22
  [B]   2007041066

ISBN 978-0-307-39465-1

Printed in the United States of America

Design by Mauna Eichner and Lee Fukui
Illustration by Zohar Lazar
Map © 2008 by Fodor's Travel, a division of Random House, Inc.

10 9 8 7 6 5 4 3 2

First Edition

PARA MEU AMOR, TÁBATA SILVA

Author's Note

For better or for worse, this book recounts true experiences. In order to distill the chaos of life down to a clear narrative, it was necessary to omit certain events, rearrange and compress chronology, and combine a few of the characters. I have changed most of the names and identifying details of the characters in this book to protect their privacy. Much of the dialogue and many emails have been re-created, but all are based on real conversations and correspondence.

Contents

├ –

I'd seen too many puzzling things
to be easy in my mind.
I knew too much
and not enough.

LOUIS-FERDINAND CÉLINE,
Journey to the End of the Night

Sound crazy? Well it isn't.
The ends justify the means; that's the system.

ICE-T,
New Jack Hustler

Life is mysterious
as well as vulgar.

ROBERTO BOLAÑO,
Last Evenings on Earth

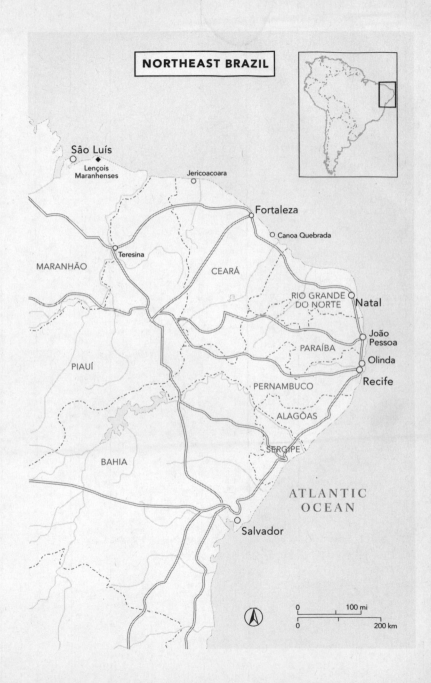

NORTHEAST BRAZIL

Sâo Luís
Lençois
Maranhenses
Jericoacoara
Fortaleza
Canoa Quebrada
Teresina
MARANHÃO
CEARÁ
RIO GRANDE
DO NORTE
Natal
João
Pessoa
PARAÍBA
Olinda
PIAUÍ
PERNAMBUCO
Recife
ALAGÔAS
SERGIPE
BAHIA
ATLANTIC
OCEAN
Salvador

0   100 mi
0   200 km

Predeparture

My name is Thomas. For as long as I can remember, travel has been a part of my life.

Over the years, I've tried to fight it and to break the hold that it has over me. I have made numerous attempts to return to civilian life: to get a job, a home, open a savings account, invest time or emotion or money in something stable—but the road has always pulled me back in. I have never owned a car or a television, or purchased a significant piece of furniture.

At a certain point, I recognized that I was powerless in the face of my travel addiction and did the best thing that I could do under the circumstances: I went pro.

This book is about that conversion. It chronicles the events that took me from bourgeois working stiff with a repressed travel habit to a full-time mercenary travel hack, with all of the good, bad, and surreal that it entails. This is not a sunny look at some dream job, but an unvarnished examination of what it really means to be a professional travel writer scratching out an income in the beginning of the twenty-first century. It is the true story of the life as I have experienced it and the effect that it has on the travel information that makes it into the readers' hands.

Let's get one thing straight from the beginning: I am not some resentful burnout who is trying to settle scores or slight those who would not hire him. I have (almost) made ends meet as a professional travel writer and have enjoyed positive working relationships with numerous editors and publishers. I've written country guidebooks, regional guidebooks, city guidebooks, phrasebooks, Internet travel content, travel essays, and both magazine and newspaper pieces. I've also done publicity work, interviews, and speaking engagements for travel publishers. I've packed more into recent years of my life than would have been imaginable with any other career. I've spent weeks on yachts for free; been comped hotel rooms, meals, astronomical bar tabs, ski passes, paragliding classes, and scuba diving trips. I've drunk Scotch and eaten salmon carpaccio with the ministers of tourism of Argentina, Chile, and Brazil, and spent the night with more exotic, fetching ladies than the average man deserves. I have also made remarkable friends in the process, some of whom you'll meet in this book.

Regardless, this book is not a polite evaluation of the job or the lifestyle and probably won't do me any favors in the industry. I imagine that stories of sex, drugs, excessive ridiculousness, scams, schemes, fistfights, drunken debauchery, police altercations, and general nihilistic selfishness probably won't sit well with the powers-that-be. While I may push things further than most travel writers, I know of many others who have experienced the same trials and dilemmas to varying degrees. We all do. But, up to now, no one has given voice to the everyday life of the gritty miners of travel information, those who dig up the material that is then polished and sold to consumers as Travel Gospel. No one has talked about the roguish misfits out there with years' worth of nights logged in dingy hostels, pounding the pavement from bars to restaurants to nightclubs and back, doing their best to be, or pretend to be, experts on everything going around them. It has also been my experience that the editors, who are our closest work companions, don't really know how we do what we do. Maybe they don't want to know.

This book is not intended to be an exposé and it is not intended to discourage the purchase or use of travel guidebooks. I almost always take a guidebook with me when I travel, and it invariably helps me in some way that makes it worth its price and worth its weight in my pack. It is my hope that this book will help to demystify the origins of travel writing and show that when thousands of travelers follow a guidebook word-for-word, recommendation-for-recommendation, it not only harms contemporary international travel but can also do serious harm to places in developing countries. Maybe if people see what arbitrary bullshit goes into the making of a guidebook, they will realize that it is just a loose tool to give basic information and is not the singular or necessarily the correct way to approach a destination.

So, travel writing, like any job, has its issues. However, travel writing is particularly disorienting since you are expected to work in a tourist environment that is built for pleasure. You must find a way to make yourself effective in that peculiar limbo between work and play. I imagine that the difference between traveling and professional travel writing is like the difference between having sex and working in pornography. While both are still probably fun, being a professional brings many levels of complication to your original interest and will eventually consume your personal life.

We travel writers live in perpetual motion. Relationships are transitory and fleeting. Friendships, even more so. Home is where you are on a given night. It is at once glamorous and pathetic, exciting and perversely routine. The longer you do it, the harder it is to return to normal life, and one day you wake up and realize that the road is your permanent address. There's no going back. This is the life that I have led, and this book recounts the beginning of that story.

I will pose the question to you: Do travel writers go to hell? Do the impossible projects and deadlines we're assigned and the dismal living conditions we face seem unbearable? Do our actions, often corrupt and selfish in the face of a trusting readership, qualify us for eternal damnation?

You may find some answers in these pages. If you do, I'll let you be the judge.

SEATTLE
AUGUST 2007

One in the Hand,
Two in the Bush

Roebling.
Roe-bleeeng.
Rrrrroe-bling.

Alone in the fifty-seventh-floor conference room, I repeat the mantra under my breath. I sit in a rigid half-lotus position atop the glass table and watch the suspension cables of the Brooklyn Bridge flicker against the night sky. The office air is sharp with disinfectant. I take a slug of rum and return to my mantra.

John Roebling had a calling. Unfortunately for him, after the buildup, design, preparation, and politicking for the construction of the Brooklyn Bridge, the hapless bastard promptly dropped dead. His son, Washington, brought the bridge to completion, but not without picking up a case of the bends and almost dying in the process. Neither man ever wavered from a life of dedication, direction, and diligence.

A lot of good it did either of them.

I remove my battered leather shoes, the toes stained gray with salt from the slushy city sidewalks, and knead my left foot through my sweaty dress sock. Hundreds of pairs of headlights move in a stream back and forth across the bridge.

Yesterday during a meeting in this same conference room, a neckless, pockmarked banker pointed out that the name *the bends* was, in fact, coined during the construction of the Brooklyn Bridge. Hundreds of laborers toiled on the footing of the bridge, eighty feet below the surface of the river. They worked in nine-foot-high wooden boxes known as caissons, which were pumped full of compressed air and lowered to the depths with the men inside. After resurfacing, scores of workers were inflicted with a mysterious illness. Crippling joint pain. Mental deterioration. Paralysis. And for a few, agonizing death. The name *the bends* was taken from the debilitated posture of the sufferers.

It wasn't until eight years after the bridge construction had started that a French physiologist determined the cause of the illness. Contrary to popular assumption, oxygen is a lesser ingredient in the air that we breathe. Seventy-eight percent of air is comprised of nitrogen, which, under normal circumstances, has no effect on the human body. When breathing air at depth, the water pressure converts the nitrogen in the bloodstream from a gas to a liquid, washing it through the veins and arteries. So long as you resurface at a slow pace, the liquid gradually transforms back into a gas and is disposed of by your body.

If the change of pressure is too sudden, the liquid bursts out of solution, fizzing back into gas. Similar to the millions of microscopic nitrogen bubbles that are released when you crack a can of Guinness, the bubbles surge through the bloodstream.

If they don't lodge themselves in your joints, the bubbles charge on the fatal path to your brain. You come up too quickly, you die.

I remove a folded piece of printer paper from my pocket and smooth it open:

> Thomas,
>
> I want to know if you'd like do some writing for our new Brazil guidebook?
>
> If you're interested in jumping ship within the next few weeks for Brazil, let me know right away and I could put together an offer for you.
>
> _____ _____
>
> *Commissioning Editor—South America & Antarctica*
> *Lonely Planet*

Once—maybe when I was first out of school—this opportunity would have been a dream job. It is still seductive, but more along the lines of a cheap one-night-stand. My life is fulfilling in other ways now. I have a steady job, a decent income, a beautiful girlfriend, and an apartment in Manhattan. I finally have everything that I am supposed to have. Besides, between 9/11, SARS, Iraq, Bali, and Madrid, it can't possibly be a good time to dive headfirst into travel writing. But I won't lie: I have always been a sucker for a cheap one-night-stand.

God knows, I can already feel myself coming up too fast.

For most people, November 24 is not a special day. Sure, it hosts Thanksgiving every few years, but I could care less about that. In Seattle, where few things out-of-the-ordinary ever happen and where people strive, often pathologically, to maintain a façade of tranquillity, the day has a different significance.

On November 24, 1971, a balding, middle-aged man boarded a flight from Portland to Seattle. He used the name Dan Cooper. He dressed in a black suit, a black overcoat, black sunglasses, and a narrow black tie with a pearl stick pin. Cooper hijacked the Boeing 727 with a briefcase full of wires and bright red cylinders. The hostages were exchanged for four parachutes and two hundred thousand dollars at Sea-Tac Airport (to put that in perspective, the average cost of a new home in the U.S. in 1971 was $28,000).

DB Cooper, as the press mistakenly dubbed him, demanded to be flown to Mexico. He parachuted out of the plane somewhere over southern Washington State and disappeared. Maybe DB died in the jump. Maybe he got away with the money. Nobody knows. But legend has it that DB was a man so disenchanted with his life that he gambled it all on a way out. The point isn't whether he made it or not. The point is that this little bald man didn't spend one more day pumping gas in Tallahassee or adjusting claims in Denver. He didn't waste one more day wondering, "What if?"

I nominate Cooper as the patron saint of disillusioned men, particularly those who, like me, were born in Seattle on November 24.

The phone rings in the conference room. It is the blipping staccato ring of all office phones. I am jolted back to the reality that I have hours of work ahead of me. The digital clock on the phone reads 9:42 p.m.

Tucking the pint bottle of rum into the waist of my pants, I answer with a cautious "Hello."

"Thomas? WHAT ARE YOU DOING IN THE CONFERENCE ROOM, DAMMIT. I knew I could find you there. You and I need to have a talk," my boss snarls. "I am coming by your cube in fifteen minutes. You'd better be there, with the WorldCom spreadsheet ready for me to look at."

I tiptoe back into my cubicle, successfully avoiding anyone in the hallways. I hold my head in my hands, shirt sleeves rolled up, with cold sweat dripping down my sides. My tacky palms are crisscrossed with hairs from my suddenly receding hairline. After the final sip of a metallic-sweet Red Bull, I chew a handful of gum and look across the tops of the cubicles, scanning for other workers. The office appears empty, except for the faint tapping of keyboards somewhere down the hall.

Welcome to life on Wall Street. With such a character-defining foothold in the career world, I no longer have to make excuses for the life I lead. No longer do I have to explain my direction-less postcollegiate life to incredulous eyes and repetitive questions, like: "What are you doing next year?" "Don't you want to do something with your life?" and my favorite, "When are you going to get a real job?" I am no longer just Thomas, the supposed slacker, backpacker bum, or permanent student. I am Thomas, the employee of _____, _____, _____ & _____ LLP, and I am going places.

I make more money than I reasonably should, putting papers into chronological order (*chroning*, in office-speak). My skill set also includes entering numbers into Excel spreadsheets and working the copier and fax machine. Between those projects, I search for old high school friends' names on Google; play online Jeopardy against my office trivia nemesis, Jerry; and generally while away the hours of my life. Jerry thinks that he is better at Jeopardy than me, but really he's just faster with the mouse.

Yes, I know, I really have it pretty good. There are people starving in Africa. And there are plenty of people here in New

York who would love the chance to be in a cubicle all day and not have to operate deep-fat fryers, drive garbage trucks, suck dicks, or whatever it is they do. The problem is that I am an ungrateful by-product of a prosperous society—the offal of opportunity. I am just another liberal arts graduate who bought the idea that life and career would be a fulfilling intellectual journey. Unfortunately, I am performing a glorified version of punching the time clock, and the financial rewards don't come anywhere near filling the emotional void of such diminished expectations.

But let's face it: rebellion is passé. My parents' generation already proved that—over time—rebellion boils down to little more than Saab ownership and an annual contribution to public radio. The old icons have been co-opted. José Martí is a brand of mojito mix. Che Guevara is a T-shirt. Cherokees are SUVs, and Apaches are helicopter gunships.

The American Dream is for immigrants. The rest of us are better acquainted with entitlement or boredom than we are with our own survival mechanisms. And when confronted with a fight-or-flight scenario, the latter usually takes precedence. Escape is our action of choice: escape through pharmaceuticals, escape through technology, and plain old running away in search of something else, anything else. I rummage through the back of my desk drawer looking for a loose Vicodin or a Klonopin. The best thing I come up with is Wite-Out, but I'm not that desperate. Yet.

I continually revisit the words of some sociologist who I read in college. I think that it was Weber or Durkheim. Either is usually a fair guess. He believed that the modern mind is determined to expand its repertoire of experiences, and is bent on avoiding any specialization that threatens to interrupt the search for alternatives and novelty. Many people would call that approach to life a crisis, immaturity, or being out of touch with reality. It could also be called the New American Dream. Fuck the simple pursuit of financial stability. Here's to finding fulfillment in novelty, excitement, adventure, and autonomy.

Following the cue of one of our office team-building exercises, I come up with the following life goals and painstakingly write them out on Day-Glo yellow Post-it notes:

Ski the Andes
and
surf Sumatra.

Wake up naked
from a rum
blackout
in rural Cuba.

Ride the roof
of a bus through
the Himalayan
Foothills.

Win or lose
a bar fight
in a dusty
border town.

Kick my mind
into the stratosphere
with ayahuasca
in the Amazon.

Sleep with at
least one woman
(preferably more)
from each continent.

One by one, I stick the notes around the edge of my computer monitor. All evenly spaced. They're not the clear career objectives of a John Roebling, but for me, they'll have to do.

My desk phone rings.

"Yes?"

"She found you, huh? I heard you sneaking back to your desk," says Anna. Though she is only two years out of Dartmouth, Anna has a mature professional edge. She is invariably the last person to leave the office at night and goes about her tasks with pleasure, frequently asking for more work. Her try-hard humor and enthusiastic friendliness have inspired suspicion in our more acerbic and cynical co-workers. Anna and I couldn't be more different as employees, but have the camaraderie of workplace outcasts.

"Yuck. I'm happy that it's you and not me who's working for Marilyn. I can't stand that cuckoo," Anna offers.

"Marilyn's just having another personal crisis. Unfortunately, as her assistant, I'm a reservoir tip for her self-loathing." I would like to give Marilyn the benefit of the doubt. She once worked for the National Organization for Women, but soon tired of surviving on a pittance and now occupies her waking hours as legal defense for well-known misogynists and womanizers—misogynists and womanizers with their hands in very lucrative business.

"At least you're not working with Allen," she says.

I tell her I wish that were true. If he hadn't dumped a bunch of work on me, I'd be done and home by now. Allen is like the evil asshole twin of Skippy from *Family Ties*, brandishing his papier-mâché bravado, trying to assert his superiority over me in every interaction. Although he's an attorney (and one of my bosses), we are about the same age. If we had been in high school together, I would have beat his ass. The problem is, he knows that and takes pleasure in harassing me. This afternoon, he mocked me for not knowing a keyboard shortcut in Word and then dropped a stack of file folders right onto my lap. I am sure that he ran back to his office, reminisced for a moment, and treated himself to some rough masturbation.

Sometimes after work I go to my overpriced gym on Lafayette Street and kick and punch the heavy bag, pretending that it's Allen. It's not only a great workout, but a dependable way to unwind.

"Allen *and* Marilyn," Anna says. "Dang. Listen, Thomas, I can stay and give you a hand."

Sometimes, I get the feeling Anna sees me as an endangered species, a manatee who will swim headfirst into a propeller if not protected by outside intervention. Sometimes, I can't believe people like her actually exist on Wall Street. But she doesn't understand that, for me, the pin is already out of the grenade. She has better things to do with her time. She has a career to think about. I kindly decline her offer.

I never planned to end up here. After college, I traveled, stumbled my way through graduate school, and tried to discover what my life was about. While I was busy figuring out nothing, or at least nothing that advanced my career or future, my friends moved to the Bay Area, got entry-level jobs with no real work responsibilities for $75K per year, acquired hundreds of thousands' worth of stock options, and attended ridiculous site launch parties on the tab of venture capitalists. If you weren't involved with a pre-Initial Public Offering startup or the financing behind a pre-IPO startup, you were wasting the greatest economic opportunity since buying stock on margin or selling junk bonds.

It was the dawn of a new era. Technology was guaranteed to unchain us from traditional work roles, from the stuffy expectations heaped upon us by past generations. We would be able to create the careers and lifestyles of our choosing. Business was organized around foosball tables and paintball outings. Deep house music went practically mainstream in SF, LA, and NYC. Ecstasy and hydroponics powered the irrational exuberance and infectious hedonism. Imagination was the only limiting factor. The good times were poised to endure so long as the optimism and energy of our generation endured—faith in the potential and inherent goodness of technology would fill in the gaps. We were to change the course of history. It was the '60s love generation redux, but with vague political goals, lucrative day jobs, and expensive sneakers.

I bided my time on the periphery of this wanton excess, while I did an esoteric advanced degree in Latin American Studies, followed by the world's shortest PhD in the department of Social Policy, whatever that is. I lasted through orientation and two classes in the PhD program before deciding to flee. At that point, being an escape artist was not only low risk, it was encouraged. The other side held the offer of consulting gigs, website positions, and stock options as far as the eye could see.

For some reason, the good times did not last forever.

By the time that I entered the job market, Bush had hijacked the White House, the economy had nosedived, planes had hit the Twin Towers, and hiring was frozen. I mistakenly thought that having an MA would open some doors, but I couldn't even get a callback from office temp agencies.

In early 2002, I washed up as a retail employee at Club Monaco—a slightly fancier version of the Gap—up on 5th Avenue and 55th Street in the middle of Manhattan. Even better, I was assigned to the women's dressing room. A key part of my job was to ask female customers if they needed a smaller size. If they came back to the dressing room with a size 6, I'd ask "Are you sure that I can't grab you a 4?" If they came back with a 4, I'd ask about a 2. It was just that simple.

One day, while I was expertly folding jeans and fitted T-shirts, the assistant store manager, a Jersey boy with LA hair and a fake tan, asked me, "Do you think that you'll ever get your act together and go to college?"

"I have a master's from Stanford and started a DPhil at the London School of Economics," I answered and went on folding.

"Yeah right, man. There isn't even such a thing as a *dee fill*.

You should really try a *jay cee* instead. It helped me to get this job," he stated with the resolute authority of a Club Monaco assistant manager.

I told him that I would consider it.

Every boom is followed by a bust and, in America, someone will always find a way to make money off of the bust—most likely lawyers. When I heard that a Wall Street firm was hiring researchers to work on high-profile, undisclosed cases, I was so eager to get out of retail that I didn't slow down enough to really understand what the job entailed. I was told only that they represented, among other concerns, a little-known firm called Cerberus Capital Management that was buying up *distressed debt*. The fact that the company was named after the three-headed guardian dog of Hades and that the papers referred to distressed debt as "vulture investing" did not raise any red flags.

I was racing toward thirty and most of the once-wide-open doors of opportunity had already slammed in my face. Maybe it was time to take the LSAT or the GMAT and get on with forging a dependable career. These were the new realities. Law seemed respectable enough: something to use your brain, make a solid income; something that I could be proud of at college reunions.

Once hired, I worked with Cerberus on a couple of cases, but I specialized in the assorted legal problems of a once-prominent research analyst who had been the foremost opinion on telecommunications companies, most notably World-Com. Research analysts are supposed to give unbiased opinion to the public on which stocks were worth buying. But during the telecom bubble, some analysts just worked hand in hand with the bankers and the telecom CEOs to promote the companies. The bankers wanted to host the overvalued IPOs, the telecom CEOs wanted positive appraisals so as to boost their share prices, and the research analysts just siphoned off as many dollars and perks as they could in the process.

Everyone was in bed together and the analysts were the pitchmen, cheerleading the cause. Our client, a tall, leathery version of Joe Pesci, once made the cover of *Business Week* on account of his uncanny stock-predicting skills. He later made plenty more headlines for his role in the WorldCom bankruptcy.

He also got nailed for bragging in a rather salacious email exchange with a "close female friend" about how he was falsely promoting shitty stocks and playing the CEO of a well-known telecom "like a fiddle" to help a big Manhattan banker orchestrate a corporate coup.

What did he supposedly get out of it? He drummed up a letter of recommendation and a million-dollar donation to get his twins into a swanky Upper East Side preschool, of course. Everyone worth a shit in Manhattan knows that a good preschool is the gateway to Harvard and high society. Plus it's a great place for the parents to network, so it's no big deal if you need to screw over a few thousand investors—especially the kind of common investors who are naïve enough to actually listen to a research analyst.

The argument in our client's defense went that he was simply role-playing in a cyber-fantasy in which his power on Wall Street was fetishized. Kinky delusions of grandeur, nothing more. My job was to read the thousands of emails between our client and any other close female friends that might be lurking out there. Then I was to write essays summarizing the nature of each relationship, searching for anything that could possibly prove another instance of cyber-fetishism. I had become little more than a professional voyeur. Each night, when I got home from work, I wanted to take my brain out of my skull and scrub it with soap.

Our client ended up being a fall guy for the greater fraud

surrounding the telecom bubble. The real big dogs were so rich by the time that things fell apart that fucking tens of thousands of investors and letting a few of their underlings' heads roll seemed a small price to pay. They simply factored in legal expenses as a percentage of annual operating costs and drank away any sense of guilt while getting head in the Virgin Islands.

I hear a few patters of thick-heeled shoes scampering down the corridor and Marilyn suddenly materializes in my cubicle. My fifteen minutes are up. I can smell the stress radiating off of her. She gnaws at the dead skin on her bottom lip and will not look me in the eye. Her fingernails are chewed to the hilt and one of her knee-high nylons is bunched around her ankle.

She goes straight to my files and starts tearing through them, throwing an empty folder over her shoulder for dramatic effect. She's looking for something that she won't find. I keep my files in what I call the Babylon System, if it can be considered a system at all. I figure that its cryptic nature makes it difficult for them to get rid of me on short notice. Job insurance, so to speak.

I desperately need another drink.

"Where's the Level 3 folder? I can't . . . I can't find it," she says in a trembling voice.

"And is that spreadsheet . . . is it ready?"

"I can get it to you tomorrow. I had something to do for Allen and . . ."

"I don't care what you had to do. . . . I asked you to do something and it needs to be done. NOW."

"But . . ."

"No buts. I can't trust you. I've had enough excuses from you."

I feel small and sold, like a hooker being called ugly by a

john whom she wouldn't even accept a drink from in her private life.

Marilyn seems further and further away. Her voice is flat and distant. I nod along and remember how great the mountains look from Seattle when they take on caps of white snow. A ski bus used to go up to Alpental after school on Fridays and another up to Stevens Pass on Sunday mornings. Even on Sundays, it was possible to get fresh tracks on Schim's Meadow if you just got out there early enough. . . .

"JESUS CHRIST, ARE YOU EVEN LISTENING TO ME? I'm going home. The WorldCom doc and the folder had better be on my desk when I walk in tomorrow morning." Marilyn marches off, never once having made eye contact with me.

I stare blankly at my computer screen. I want to gouge out my eyes with paper clips and gash my wrists with manila folders. Why am I sitting here, aiding and abetting white-collar criminals and merging with my ergonomically correct office chair, when I should be on the beach in Brazil?

Twenty-six or twenty-seven is a time of reckoning, particularly for free spirits or whatever you want to call those who don't fit into the normal expectations. It is the weigh station en route to your midlife crisis. Some of the true free spirits, the Hendrixes, Cobains, Morrisons, Joplins, couldn't make it around the bend. Most just drop off or, like the Steven Tylers, the Ice Cubes and Perry Ferrells, compromise and come around to disappointing results. The few, the chosen, the Keith Richardses, Iggy Pops, and James Browns just keep on going.

I try to find where I would fit into this rubric. My adrenaline stirs, tingling in my gums, heating the skin along my collar. I think of Hemingway: "South America hell! If you went there the way you feel now it would be exactly the same." But,

Lonely Planet in Brazil . . . it's definitely novel. My patron saint, DB Cooper, certainly would have gone for it. Hell, he'd probably commandeer the flight down.

This could be my opportunity to experience the present with no regard to the future—to fully exist in the moment. Like Ronnie Biggs, I will mock conventions and live unencumbered with the responsibilities of normal society. Ronnie, one of the perpetrators of Britain's 1963 Great Train Robbery, escaped to Rio and, much to the chagrin of Scotland Yard, flaunted it openly, hosting tourists for dinner at his house and selling commemorative coffee mugs and T-shirts emblazoned with his picture. I think that he even cut a couple of punk songs about his antics. The U.K. couldn't extradite Ronnie because he had fathered a Brazilian child (a reliable contingency plan that I should look into). Ronnie only returned to the U.K. in his seventies, after he'd had a couple of strokes, so that he could take advantage of the National Health Service's free treatment in prison. He was even flown home on a private jet, paid for by a British tabloid.

Ronnie had vision. But in order to execute that vision, he had to be willing to walk away from it all, to be ruthless with his own sentimentality. What about my friends, my apartment, my girlfriend?

Shit, my girlfriend.

Sydney and I have been together for a few years and we are in love. In many ways, she is my perfect woman. She claims that I am her perfect man. Unfortunately, our relationship is garbage. It takes a long time to swallow the fact that the person with whom you are in love is not necessarily the person with whom you can build or maintain a functional relationship. We are both still trying to choke that down.

I call her at home. The phone rings five times before she

answers, "We're late for Celeste's shower, remember? What are you still doing at work?"

"I'm trying to finish up, trying to find some purpose in my life."

"Not this again . . ." She exhales. "Why can't you just suck it up and get it done and get home—like everyone else?"

Sydney grew up in an Air Force family and skipped from base to base across the States and the South Pacific. At twenty, she washed her hands of military life and moved to the promised land of Manhattan. Aided by a lacerating tongue and striking looks, she clawed her way into the metropolitan world.

"I'm not sure that I want to suck it up. This universal dedication to office life is a fad anyways—it's only been around for a generation or so . . . what do you think if I were to become a travel writer?"

"Considering that you don't have any significant writing experience, let alone a Pulitzer or anything, I don't think it's such a good idea. What if we want to have kids? I mean, it sounds like a great hobby, but I'd suggest you keep your paycheck, because I'm not supporting your ass. . . . Really, Thomas, you're the only fucking hippie I know who wears Marc Jacobs cologne and an Armani watch."

"It's hard to be a conscientious narcissist."

"I feel real sorry for you. Get car service and come and pick me up; we're supposed to be at that shower already. . . . Wait, does this mean that we're gonna have to start going Dutch on dates?"

"I just don't know if I'm going to be able to make it tonight, I've got this—"

"Fuck it, fine . . . I'll go by myself . . . but honestly, I expect more understanding from you. I thought we were in a mutually supportive relationship." Sydney is used to getting whatever she wants from men. That's not to say that she isn't intelligent or capable in her own right, merely that she will resort to her black-belt form of emotional and sexual warfare when necessary.

"I'm sorry. Really, Sydney, I just—"

She hangs up. It has become the standard end to all of our conversations.

I bask in the warm romantic afterglow.

Truthfully, I don't even have comfort in my own apartment. Last week, I came home from work to find a sizable hole from the hallway into the back of my bedroom closet. My room looked like the scene in the movies when the apartment is ransacked in search of the hidden microfilm: drawers overturned, laundry strewn across the floor.

The cops told me that professional thieves, working a neighborhood, will trash an apartment to make it look like the crime was perpetrated by random junkies. They probably stole my dirty underwear, T-shirts, and plastic hamper to wrap the electronics and inconspicuously carry them right out the front door.

I had a state-of-the-art laptop. It had all the bells and whistles, although I really only used it to download music and admire some Internet porn.

I had the new MP3 player that held twenty gigabytes of music.

A two-hundred-CD changer that was already obsolete.

A Palm Pilot to hold all of my important contact info—just in case.

A Zip drive to back up the Palm Pilot. That was already obsolete, too.

They even took the cradle for my flip phone.

I was on the crest of the technology wave. Almost everything that I had was small, sleek, and silver. I almost caught up with the twenty-first century—and suddenly it was all gone.

I remember feeling numb upon seeing my room. I've tried to justify the robbery in my head by reminding myself that the thieves can't be having as much negative impact on society as the people who are paying my income. But sociology doesn't mask the fact that I haven't slept in my room since the break-in. I am the little birdie who won't return to its nest after it's been touched by marauders.

The WorldCom spreadsheet sits open on my screen: miles of grids chronicling business decisions alongside the dates of potentially incriminating emails. I look at my convex reflection in the middle of all my Post-it notes. I appear tired, aging, bored, and, worse, boring. Blood fizzes in my veins. Churning and popping. Bubbles race toward my brain as I start typing an email.

> Dear Marilyn,
>
> I am not going to be able to finish the WorldCom project tonight. Or ever.
>
> I'm off to embrace spontaneity, imagination, and other stuff that doesn't exist around here.
>
> Don't worry about the WorldCom spreadsheet. No matter how many charts we make, they're still guilty.
>
> Sincerely, Thomas

I hit SEND. My mind starts collapsing inward like the fancy building demolitions that they show on PBS. Blasting points on all major support columns. It tumbles in upon itself, compacting into the ground and belching forth a plume of dust.

I don't bother to shut down my computer and I don't sign out at the front desk. It is much easier than I thought it would be. I simply grab my jacket and walk out the door. The three female temps nod to me and go back to knitting their black wool scarves. Hunched over her floor buffer, the Guyanese cleaning lady gives me a wink. No one tries to tackle me or hold me there—I just walk out. The most effective fences exist only in our minds or, at least, that's what I'll tell myself until the next time I have to confront my finances.

My stomach convulses as the elevator races toward the ground floor. Vomit perches itself at the base of my throat, a feline waiting to pounce.

The security guard in the lobby doesn't even bother to look up. I can't breathe until I pass through the building's glass doors and the sober air washes over me. Suddenly the office is just one little set of rooms in a honeycomb of an office building, in a city of such buildings.

I get two calls to my cell from Anna and then a series of calls from Marilyn. The phone is easier to ignore once I throw it into the East River.

Turbulence

62 DAYS UNTIL DEADLINE

"Let's go and fuck up New York City," the Doctor's slurred voice crackles through the pay phone. It's ten in the morning and I've got nothing to lose. He's got everything to lose, but doesn't give a shit.

We'll show New York. We'll show New York for all those times that it has wronged us: lifted $1,250 a month from our wallets for microscopic studios with a view of a brick wall; duped us into following unattainable women for three blocks just to get a better look at their asses; smacked our dreams of being carefree Manhattan socialites with the reality of sixty-plus hours a week under fluorescent tube lighting. We, the Doctor and I, will take this city by storm in an alcohol-fueled blitzkrieg that it has never before experienced.

My job's gone. My phone's gone. My girlfriend's gone, for all intents and purposes, and my apartment's about to go. I'm on my way to eliminating any chance of backing out of my plans to escape the city.

I must admit that cutting my ties with New York was easier than I had imagined. It was depressingly easy. You tell the city that you are having second thoughts about your relationship with it, and the city counters that it never loved you in the first place. It never even really liked you and already forgot your name.

Legend holds that Hernán Cortés, the Spanish conqueror of Mexico, made a heroic decision when he ordered his ships burned at Veracruz. It was a statement to his men that they would make an uncompromising stand against the Aztec Empire. Retreat was impossible. Victory was the singular option. It is the kind of story that gives birth to Successories posters and motivational paperweights. The anecdote is recited by playoff-bound high school baseball coaches and midlevel managers trying to fire up their employees to finish direct-mailing campaigns. Regrettably, the story's a bunch of crap.

Cortés never burned his ships, though he did have them disabled or run aground. This wasn't done as a spectacle, but most likely perpetrated in secret once his men were marching on the Aztec capital, Tenochtitlán. The method of boat destruction may be a small technicality, but the motive behind the destruction is more telling. Cortés—a conniving opportunist in the classic sense—was out for the glory and riches of conquering one of the biggest indigenous empires in the Americas. He did not want to have to answer to his colonial superiors or work within their bureaucratic restraints. More specifically, he was making a tactical split from his nagging superior and brother-in-law, Diego de Velázquez, the governor of Cuba. Cortés knew that he couldn't count on the allegiance of all of his men and he sabotaged the ships so that Velázquez's sympathizers (which loosely included all those who respected colonial rule and followed its established law) didn't get word back to the governor. This was Hernán's chance to embrace his destiny on his own terms. He was tired of being beholden to other people who told him how to take his next steps and how to look at the big picture.

Sure, my undertaking is pathetic compared to laying siege to Tenochtitlán and conquering an empire of millions, but I guess that I take my own little Successories story from Cortés's strategy. I am not trying to burn my metaphoric boats as a magnificent act of decision-making, motivation, and leadership, but am simply trying to take my life down its own path and not have to look back or be responsible to anybody else.

If I am going to be some sort of travel writer, I want to be able to be broke and mess up my life and do whatever the hell I want or need to do without having to answer to my girlfriend or a boss or friends or anyone else. I am done with compromises with others. I will be free of expectations and constraints. I will be free of everything except for the most essential of possessions. I think that it was Tyler Durden who said, "It's only after we've lost everything that we're free to do anything." I will live on my own terms and forge my own path in the universe. I will be Hale-Bopp.

I try to explain my thinking to the Doctor over the pay phone, though I can tell that he's not listening. He's recently out of rehab—classified as *counseling* so as not to compromise his career—and after a few more months finishing up at his Ivy League med school he'll be unleashed on the unsuspecting field of medicine. Why I've called him, I am not sure. He's rather undependable in a time of need. He has enough trouble dealing with his own chaotic life. His standard suggested remedies include consumption of large amounts of drugs, alcohol, and "not being such a fucking pussy."

The Doctor pretends to listen to me for a minute or two

and then answers with his deliberate, bedside-manner tone, "I've got just the thing for you: a fresh handle of Captain Morgan's left over from a med-school party last week. It's free and is therefore a wise choice for your individual health plan. Unfortunately, we're going to have to take a more aggressive course of action on your particular case. I think that a poly-medication approach is our best option. You see, I'm also going to have to prescribe you the eight ball that I'm going to pick up before meeting you in Union Square. With some luck, you're on your way to recovery."

It is evident that the concept of fucking up New York City is like fucking up the Pacific Ocean. We all know who loses in the end, but neither of us is intimidated by self-destruction. In fact, we hold the tag-team championship belt. As I start to walk up to Union Square, I experience a moment of stabbing apprehension. I grab a tall can of PBR from Sunny & Annie deli on 6th and Avenue B and knock it back while walking across Tompkins Square Park. Yes, the Doctor is a medical genius; I'm feeling better already.

As for my faltering romantic life, I didn't intend to end things with Sydney. I really did love her. While I couldn't fault her for being practical or wanting to be with someone with a guaranteed financial future, I didn't know if I was, or could ever be, that person. I explained to her what had transpired at work, and when I made it clear that I would not apologize to Marilyn or return to the job, she told me, "It's me or this dead-end job in Brazil. . . . You need to learn to deal with a real job and learn to deal with being a man."

"What kind of man spends his best years sitting in a chair?" I told her that I was cut out for a different lifestyle.

She responded, "Yeah, like poverty and living in your parents' basement. . . . Thomas, I thought that we were going to get married. I already told my family and friends that you were the one. Don't you think that when I told you how I always wanted a teardrop diamond, with two sapphires mounted in white gold, that I was giving you a major hint?"

"Well, I guess . . . I mean I thought that, ya know, we could wait. There are things that I need to do and I'm just not ready to—"

"You know what. Just stop. I see that you've already made your decision." She forced out a good-bye through gritted teeth and punctuated it with a receiver-shattering slam. I have not heard from her since and she will not answer my calls or emails.

It would be hard to classify me as a die-hard optimist, though I firmly believe that—with the right level of enterprise—an advantage can be wrought from any bad situation. As for ditching my apartment, I had complained to my 1980s supermodel-cum-junkie landlady two times before the robbery that the front door of the building did not close properly and that it was a matter of time before somebody got ripped off. I thought that she might actually care as she lived in one of the building's three apartments. I had written the complaints in emails to her father, who managed the building (she was so smacked out that she rarely answered the door of her top-floor apartment or picked up the phone). After the robbery, I was able to convince her father with a few carefully chosen words that it was better to let me sever my lease and pay only half of my last month's rent than deal with whatever drama I could potentially cause them. Working with my favorite corrupt telecom research analyst taught me the advantages and pitfalls of etching information in the permanent electronic record. I still want to know how someone pounded a hole through the wall in the middle of the day without anybody noticing, but that's in the past.

The physical process of moving out was also aided by the

break-in. All of my valuables were probably in some East New York pawn shop, so I had only a few sentimental things, such as photos, to mail back to my parents' house in Seattle. I boxed up my winter clothes and left them with relatives on Long Island. Everything else I dumped on the street corner, and—though I can't imagine what people could see in some of that stuff—it disappeared within a few hours.

Of the valuables that were appropriated during said robbery, the one thing that was insured was my laptop (through a loophole that I'd rather not admit to in print). As the cost of laptops had gone down considerably in the past few years, I was able to purchase a new computer that was smaller, lighter, more durable, and better for travel than the old one. Sure, I'd lost my entire downloaded MP3 collection (easy come, easy go: the karma of music piracy), my digital photo collection (including some tasteful nudes of an ex-girlfriend), and everything that I'd ever written, but now I had a Panasonic Toughbook. There is nothing tough about writing—the act of writing is about as burly as operating a cash register—but with this Toughbook, I could be a rugged, risk-taking travel writer, corresponding about the Maoist insurgency in Nepal, Yanomami mating rituals, or jungle survival in Papua New Guinea, and I hadn't even left Manhattan yet. I had just received my Lonely Planet business cards in the mail, so I was practically bona fide.

A backpack stuffed with T-shirts, shorts, and the laptop sat in the middle of the hardwood floor of my otherwise-empty apartment. I had been gouged on a rush job for my Brazilian visa and a rush job for my new passport. The last-minute and extremely overpriced flight to Rio de Janeiro would depart tomorrow just before lunch.

The Doctor hasn't bathed or brushed his teeth and is wearing hospital-issue scrub pants with a polyester Hawaiian shirt. He's

shod in an old pair of leather flip-flops that have somehow sur-
vived for as long as I've known him. His mass of curly blond
hair is consistently cut to the awkward point that people hit
when trying to grow their hair out and he keeps it back from
his eyes with a pair of dollar-store plastic sunglasses pushed up
on his head. A tiny safety pin fastens the right earpiece of the
sunglasses to the lenses. Only a place like 1970s Los Angeles
could give rise to such a creature.

Seated on one of Union Square's wooden benches, the
Doctor looks sedate and fleshy with his increasingly full, ruddy
cheeks. The saccharine perfume of yesterday's booze emanates
from his pores, telling of a heavy hangover, but his glazed eyes
betray a stimulated anxiety. I know how bad his hangovers are
and there is no way he would be out right now without having
dipped into the cocaine. The bottle of Captain Morgan's sticks
out of a small black deli bag; the cap is already missing.

While rum is underrated—usually dressed up in cuba li-
bres, mojitos, and lameness like coconut Malibu for spring
breakers and big-hair divorcée alcoholics—it is, in fact, a brilliant creation. Rum and its Latin cousins *aguardiente, cachaça,*
and old-fashioned *ron* (*"mi amigo,* Ron" as the Doctor likes
to say) are the true and noble firewater that inspired generations of pirates to sack port towns, burn them to the ground,
and carry off the booty. George Washington, a bit of a scally-
wag himself, ordered a barrel of Barbadian rum for his 1789
inauguration. Today, rum will accompany us as we attempt
to pillage the western seaboard of this island known as
Manhattan.

On the other hand, allow me a moment to be unfashion-
able and state that I think that cocaine is crap. If you don't believe me and are caught up in the whole romance surrounding
blow, I dare you to hang out sober (or even just drinking) in a
small room of people doing lines. They end up as a bunch of
red-faced, bug-eyed sweaty freaks all jockeying for airtime. It's
true that when you're doing coke, you feel confident, alert, and

sexy, but it's just a matter of hours before you are gurning your face off and are paranoid-delusional with your cock crawling up into your abdomen. You wake up the next morning realizing that you spent the better part of the night finding new and creative ways to excuse yourself to the bathroom, trying to chase the high that you got from your first line and were never able to achieve again.

I'm not saying that I've never done the drug. I've lived in South America. I've snorted it, smoked it, drank it, you name it—everything short of shooting it—and it took me a while to come to terms with the fact I never really enjoyed it that much. The whole cult of cocaine, with all of these bankers, hipsters, and brokers thinking that they're the man with their heavily cut eight balls, is a bunch of misguided hype. Foreign exoticism and our national obsession with performance enhancers have raised the stock of the substance from a cheap plant derivative to a social phenomenon. It's similar to when an Eastern European high roller takes his elegant date to T.G.I. Friday's in Moscow and thinks that he's the shit. And he may be the shit in that time and place. But when he then experiences T.G.I. Friday's at O'Hare, or a coke aficionado gets down to Peru and sees the drug without all of the mystique, it is clear that they've been duped. T.G.I. Friday's is a sit-down McDonald's and the magic powder is a bunch of smashed bush leaves run through chemicals that you could find on the shelves of your grandfather's garage.

If rum inspired characters as extraordinary and enduring as Black Beard, Captain Kidd, and George Washington, who has coke inspired? Andy Gibb, Corey Haim, and Roger Clinton?

"Take your medicine like a good boy." The Doctor holds out a key; the tip is piled high with the pinkish white flakes. My eyes dart about quickly and I lean in to take the bump.

So much for soliloquies.

"Who says I don't care about your well-being?" he asks.

"Who says that I care about my own well-being?" I retort.

I have penciled out a list of pros and cons regarding the Lonely Planet offer and begin to read it aloud. I can tell that the Doctor isn't listening. He's still wasted from the night before and has had an argument with his girlfriend, Sandra. The quarrel degenerated to the point that she punched him in the face, three times. The Doc and I are swirling around the drain in a similar mental state and that's always dangerous, as neither of us is the type of person to say, "No, thank you, let's call it a night."

I continue with my list, my voice trailing off. I am reading in my head as much as out loud.

> Pro: I will cover the Brazilian states of Pernambuco, Paraíba, Rio Grande do Norte, Ceará, Piauí, and Maranhão.
>
> Con: I will then have to write nearly a hundred pages and update a dozen maps.
>
> Pro: It is recommended that I travel in Brazil for four weeks.
>
> Con: There is no way that I can do that much research in four weeks.
>
> Pro: I will have to go to Brazil for at least seven weeks.

I do some quick accounting on the page and weigh the advance offered by Lonely Planet against what will be required of me. Then I add another to my list:

> Con: There will not be enough money for seven weeks of research.

And another:

Con: There will not be enough time for seven weeks of research and nearly a hundred pages of writing.

"Sounds like a fucking sweet deal," the Doctor says and then starts to talk about his relationship drama again. Now it is my turn to tune him out as I try to do some career evaluation. If a trip to Brazil is all I really want, I'd be better off working for two or three months at Starbucks, getting its health insurance, smoking bowls every day, and then using my earnings to go to Brazil on vacation than I would be taking this job. Starbucks employees start at almost $9 per hour, plus medical and dental benefits, and the pay goes up from there. Lonely Planet, a company that sells some six million books per year and calls itself the only independent global publisher, claims that writers' workload-versus-fee averages out to $600 per week. That would mean that working a basic forty-hour week, authors earn $15 per hour. Of course, if you read between the lines of what is expected of the writer for this project, it isn't difficult to see that this job will take closer to every waking hour of my time, from weeks of pretrip preparation up through the deadline. Of course, after the deadline there will be additional stages of edits, queries, map clarifications, and rewrites, which will tack on many extra days, if not weeks. That puts the hourly pay below minimum wage, and U.S. minimum wage is nothing nice. You can also forget about health insurance.

Also, a Starbucks employee has no real overhead, whereas my entire research trip (hotels, restaurants, bars, transportation—including the aforementioned visa, a new passport, and the thousand-dollar-plus last-minute flight that I purchased to Rio) is coming out of the advance. It has already been whittled down to a laughable amount. As for the actual work that I'll be doing, let's not forget that the position requires one to have writing skills, foreign language skills, international travel skills, budgeting skills, plus the ability to endure long periods of rough overland travel in developing countries and long periods of solitude. I have scores of PDF pages that I am supposed to read to learn how to write for Lonely Planet and hundreds of pages of feedback from readers that I am to take into account. It is a lot easier, and apparently more lucrative, to make caramel macchiatos.

Some friends have no idea why I have wrestled with this decision. They say, "It's a dream job . . . you get to travel." And you do get to travel, like a madman. Is it really travel in any pleasurable sense when you have to cover an area that's the size of the West Coast of the U.S. in one to two months of research? The research is over 1,000 miles of coastline to explore by boat, bus, and dune buggy. Along those miles, I am supposed to research nearly sixty towns, villages, and cities: some on islands, some in the mountains, some hidden away in national parks. I will pen nearly 150 hotel reviews and more than 150 bar and restaurant reviews. That doesn't start to tell of the number of places that I am supposed to visit to determine if they are worthy of being included in the book or not. I'll also need to gather innumerable details on parks, hikes, bus schedules, flight schedules, boat schedules, bookstores, hospitals, banks, post offices, Internet cafes, Laundromats, travel agencies, tourism offices, border crossings, activities and shops.

It's true: I could do a quick and dirty research job in four weeks. But imagine having one month to track down information as broad as the prices at Laundromats in Seattle, the details of the Tijuana border crossing, where to find a decent sandwich in Bakersfield, an overview of LA's nightlife, hiking trails in Yosemite, museum hours in Portland, bus schedules in San Francisco, and the location of a decent tourist office in Boise. Now imagine trying to do that in a place with no reliable transportation schedules, dial-up Internet connections (when there are Internet connections, or even phones), thousands of miles of unpaved roads, and heavily accented Northeast Brazilian Portuguese as the language of choice. It'd be nearly impossible, and the quality of the final product would be so poor that I'd never be employed to write again. I have a lot at stake here and must do it right. I can guarantee that the editor who came up with the idea of four weeks of research has never been to that part of Brazil. Seven weeks of research would leave me about a week and a half of pure writing time prior to my deadline. I guess that I will just have to be disciplined on the road and make sure to set aside time to write every night.

I tried to negotiate for a larger fee, a later deadline, and the possibility of royalties. I am denied on all three and, as for royalties, am told that it is "a Lonely Planet book, not a Jackie Collins novel." I ask if they can cover my flight down to Brazil, but am told that writers do not work for the company, they are only freelancers. I must arrange for all expenses myself. Their only concession is that I can earn another small fee if I write the unwieldy "Environment" chapter and the "Wildlife Guide" to go in the front of the book. The two chapters will double my page count and add an extra few weeks of library research. Yes, it sounds like a fucking sweet deal.

So, am I doing this for the pure love of travel, as an *independent dedicated traveler* or whatever Lonely Planet claims its writers are? Am I an altruistic provider of travel information to my global backpacking brethren? Am I doing this as a way to get laid? Judging by my advance, I am surely not in it for the money.

"Three punches?" I ask. We walk west toward the Meatpacking District to embark on a northbound dive-bar crawl that will eventually take us to the hallowed ground of Bellevue Bar in Port Authority.

"Get this, dude. Last night, after we got done boning at her place, I decided that I needed to go out and party. What the fuck were we going to do, just lie around and cuddle? She had to work at the hospital this morning, but that is still no reason to go to bed at eleven o'clock."

"True."

"Well, when she refused to go out, I waited until she fell asleep, got outta bed, put my clothes on, and grabbed her new roommate, Amber, who was watching TV in the living room. Have you seen that chick?"

"Not yet. Isn't she like twenty-two?"

"Whatever, dude, she's fucking hot. Anyways, Amber's moping around because she broke up with her high school boyfriend from Jersey that she's been with for something like seven years. She just moved to the big city and needs to live it up a little and, hell yeah, I'm here to help her out."

The Doctor pauses to take a nonchalant bump of cocaine off of the tip of Sandra's apartment key. He continues, "We drank Patrón and Jägermeister to give Amber a little Manhattan, but not take her too far from Jersey. We tore up Chelsea. She said some shit about not usually drinking on weeknights. She's got a lot to learn, but whatever, she's fucking hot. So, yeah, I staggered back into Sandra's room sometime after four, threw up into an open dresser drawer, and passed out."

"I expect no less from you, Doctor."

"Anyways, I wake up this morning with my psycho girlfriend on top of me, screaming her face off. She's turning all dark red with veins popping around her eyes and neck and shit."

This was hardly an isolated incident. For almost four years she has studiously enabled him, shared notes for the classes he skipped, and reminded him of the appointments that he blew off, but he has finally crossed some threshold with her that nobody believed existed.

He continues, "I was practically unresponsive and really just wanted to go back to sleep and for her to leave me alone for a change. I thought that she was pissed 'cause I booted on her work clothes, but she wasn't even talking about the clothes; she wanted to know if I had cheated on her with Amber."

"And had you?" I ask, knowing that he tries to pretend that he is some kind of ladies' man, but is a serial monogamist who doesn't have the gumption to hit on a woman who isn't his girlfriend of many years.

"No dude, I mean, I'm not saying that I didn't kinda try, but you know . . . and I told Sandra so, but I also mentioned that Amber *is* pretty fucking hot and that earned me three punches to the face and a slammed door before she ran out."

"You are a master of subtlety, my friend."

"So then I rolled over and went back to sleep until your ass called me and woke me back up. Sandra's also called a few times, but I just told her that she is a sadist and that she gave me a black eye. That girl has serious anger management problems."

There isn't a mark on his face. I take a pull of the rum and the warmth radiates through my throat and chest. It percolates in my stomach. My vision destabilizes like lost v-hold on a television and I gasp for a cool breath of air.

We proceed to hit all of the classics: Tortilla Flats, The Village Idiot (the best of the lot), Hogs & Heifers, Passerby (which wasn't technically open, but the kindly Ecuadorian janitor let us fill our own drinks from the tap so long as we paid him in cash), and a chain of nefarious North Chelsea dives with names as nondescript and interchangeable as the bars themselves. We keep the bottle of Captain Morgan's under the table between our feet at the first few bars, but by the time that we get to North Chelsea, we decide that it deserves its own bar stool. It is still swaddled in its black plastic deli-bag papoose. Taking bumps of yay in public off of the taut skin between the thumb and index finger suddenly seems like a socially acceptable activity. The rum is a third gone and the bars have supplied us with tequila shots, frosty pints of beer, and bathrooms where it was possible to take down full lines. The last stop is ahead, that fatherland of old-time Manhattan debauched drunkenness in the last bastion of unadulterated Port Authority filth: the ever-glorious Bellevue Bar.

A block from Bellevue Bar, Sandra calls the Doctor again and he utilizes his self-righteous mellow-guy act. "No, I don't want to talk to you. I don't want to talk to you until you calm down. You gave me a black eye. Yes . . . a *fucking shiner*. You have issues. I have a conference tomorrow and now I am going to have to explain to every single doctor and professor why I have a black eye. You're . . . you're . . . physically abusive."

He listens to her for a second and continues, "No, I don't accept your apology. You should see what you did to my face."

We enter the sordid paradise on 9th between 39th and 40th. I melt into a mildewed upholstered chair, after briefly scanning it for exposed syringes on, in, or around the cushions. The ceiling dimly shimmers with thousands of strands of smoke-stained tinsel. We alternate between large mouthfuls of rum, which now just tastes like strong, syrupy water, and flat pints of Budweiser. "Ramblin' Man" plays on the jukebox. We pass the baggy back and forth.

The Doctor spends some time vomiting in the bathroom before returning with an upbeat smile. "I feel good enough to take my boards right now . . . let's stop pussy-footing and get down to business." Judging from the sun through the front window, it is some point in the late afternoon. The room begins to tilt and slide toward the street. My vision smears all of the neon beer signs and my pulse alternately races and creeps. My head is a lump of numb flesh, a block of pink deli ham, from my nose back to my medulla. The jaw and tongue attached to my face seem to have developed their own anxious personalities. My tongue flicks across my teeth, curls over, runs down my cheek, and back.

Am I really in this bar as some act of self-conscious irony or am I only fooling myself? I feel a lot more like the passed-out derelict in the corner than a swashbuckling pirate. My internal dialogue boils over into an internal shouting match.

Are we fucking up New York or are we just a couple of drunk fuckups?

Fucking up New York? Or drunk fuckups?

Fucking up or fuckups?

Fuckedupfuckups.

What does fucking up New York even mean? The old drunks at the bar don't notice that we're here. Why should anyone else care what I'm doing?

Isn't that what I want—nobody to care? At least I've ceased to think about Sydney for the time being.

The Doctor has a creamy vomit stain down the front of his shirt and bathroom floor scum on the knees of his scrubs.

"Are you sure that you're OK?" I ask.

"The question is are *you* OK? Give me some credit. I was just making up with my girl over the phone. It's all cool now," he declares, reeking of puke. She has invited us to a party with some of their classmates down at a loft in the Flower District. Although the Doctor is unsure if he has fully forgiven her, it is worth it to go to the party because there are free drinks. Say no more. At this point, it is either continue or collapse, and we are not going to be able to continue on our own bank accounts. I have already spent too much money and need every remaining dollar to make sure that my Brazil trip will work out. Like French farmers, we need subsidizing.

He gives me a quick look-over and checks my pulse at the wrist, then at the neck. I can feel that I am a sweating, trembling wreck.

"This man needs another drink, STAT," the Doctor stands up and screams at no one and everyone in the bar. "He's moving to Bolivia and is in need of specialized treatment. I'm worried that he may be getting SICKER, or *worse*, SOBER. FOR

THE LOVE OF GOD, SOMEONE BUY HIM A BEER." No one so much as glances at us. The bartender takes this as his cue to walk to the other end of the bar and stare toward the window.

We opt to walk down to the party. It's only about twenty blocks and after enough rum to take the edge off of the blow, we are again invincible. Cops? Open-container laws? Possession? Let them try to arrest me. A night in the Tombs would be a character-building experience. We lose the plastic bag and the bottle is now carried openly, in all of its naked splendor. I am incapable of drinking and walking simultaneously, so we stop every few steps to knock back a gulp of the Captain Morgan's. I would really prefer a nice *añejo,* maybe a Havana Club Añejo Reserva, but Captain Morgan will do; I can barely taste it at this point anyhow.

About halfway to the party, the Doctor turns to me and pleads in an earnest, steady voice, "Thomas. You know that I wouldn't usually ask this, but I need a big favor . . ."

"Bro, I'm broke. I'm leaving tomorrow. I can't take any more cash out."

"No, man . . . I don't need money . . . I need you to give me a black eye."

"On your face?"

"Where else are you gonna give me a black eye? Listen, I'm in a bad situation. She's gonna think that I'm a liar if I get to this party and don't have at least one black eye."

"Never."

"Do this for me as a friend. Please, as your *best* friend. This is the request of a medical professional."

"Never. Depraved motherfucker."

He doesn't let it be—he never lets anything be. At least every other block along our walk the Doctor turns to me and asks me to hit him. "Just do it," he chides. "Don't be a pussy." "C'mon, loser." "I'll pay you. I swear." "Do me a favor here." "Help a brother out." "Remember how much *I* helped *you* when that hypochondriac chick accused you of giving her herpes?" He had teased me more than he had given me any sound medical advice, so he knew that that one would get a better response.

When I refuse for about the eighth time, he gives himself a shaky uppercut to his own right eye. It is a spirited effort, but doesn't leave a bruise. As we round the corner in front of the apartment, I tire of his groveling and am overcome by a mix of pity, confusion, and anger. It is now or never.

I take a gulp of rum, a short shuffle step, and launch my right fist into his face. His head snaps sideways and he staggers forward, falling to his knees and burying his face in his cupped hands. I hear a low moaning and I start to apologize. I am unsure if he is truly hurt or just laughing. He gets back to his feet, shouting, "YOU MISSED MY EYE, YOU FUCKING RETARD."

I recoil two quick steps. "Dude, I'm sorry, man, I'm not used to punching friends in the face . . ." I brace for a fight, but then opt for a different tack. "Seriously, I think it's close enough. It'll work."

"Better than nothing, I guess. Thanks, DICK," he says. I hand him the bottle; he takes a healthy swig and lets it slide from his hand, shattering on the pavement. The Doctor turns to admire himself in the side-view mirror of a parked truck. "You sure this is going to work?"

"Looks pretty legit to me," I lie. It is much redder than black and blue, but it has potential. "What does she know about facial trauma anyways? She's only in training to become an orthopedic surgeon, right?"

"Good point. But, whatever, I know how to handle this. Trust me."

"Trust you? This is your twisted deal, dude. I did my part. Can we get a drink now?"

"You're right. I owe you one."

That's what I'm worried about.

We climb the stairs to the vast converted commercial space. Fortunately the apartment is large enough that I can stay away from the Doctor and Sandra. Even the thought of the psychology behind all of this makes me nauseous. I head straight to the refrigerator and am pleased to fix myself a cocktail in a glass with ice. There's no rum . . . typical. I guess that it's time to switch to vodka.

"You see? You see what you did, Buster Douglas?" I hear the Doctor griping in Sandra's face.

"I'm sorry. I'm sooo sorry," she bleats.

"All I did was try to be hospitable to your poor roommate and welcome her to New York City and you did this. Well thank you very much, Laila Ali."

He has her in an emotional full nelson and he is going to savor it. A few minutes later, I see him collect a few twenties from her to fund the next step of the evening. Guilt, properly applied, can go a very long way. I feel fairly bad as an accomplice in all of this, but not so bad as to turn down the cash or call it a night.

I wish that I could relate the exploits of the evening during and after the party, but the details are foggy. I know that we were at the party for many hours and I managed to avoid the Doctor and his girlfriend for most of it. I don't think that the cocaine lasted through the soiree loaded with stimulant-hungry Ivy League nostrils. At some point my alcohol tortoise breezed past the cocaine hare. I rarely black out, but I lost a few hours there. Eventually, somebody introduced Red Bull, which pulled me back out of the miasma. Now we have wound up in line at some pseudochic lounge/club in western SoHo, cleverly named after its numerical address.

Everybody has abandoned us. Were other people with us before? I am staring at the tips of my shoes trying to steady myself while finishing off the Red Bull. The Doctor, still with a vomit stain on his Hawaiian shirt, is talking to a guy he kind of knows from LA who is working the door. The promoter has sharp, plucked eyebrows and is wearing a sculpted-wicker baseball hat, which makes him look like an androgynous colonial cricket fan. Still, he is this evening's arbiter of who is fashionable or rich enough to enter the club. It is getting close to 4 a.m. and we need to get into this place soon or go pick up more drinks at the store. There is nobody else in the line and potentially nobody inside the club. I hear the Doctor tell the story about how his girlfriend gave him the black eye or cheek after he deftly seduced her new roommate. The roommate is suddenly an aspiring model from Australia—fresh off the boat, mate.

No, we don't have the correct leather footwear for this kind of establishment, but we are the height of rakish, libertine fashion. Our disheveled appearance is beyond intentional. We are futuristic beings genuinely free of the aesthetic concerns of mortal New Yorkers. The Doctor slips his friend his last twenty and makes a deal that we can enter so long as we get a table, which requires ordering bottle service.

"That guy's a sucker. Played him just like I planned. You want rum or vodka?" The Doctor shouts over pumping house music.

We are led to a leather-upholstered booth in the back room. It is still hard to tell if there is anyone else in the club. I am sure that a couple of highly attractive single women are close by, waiting to meet men like us; men who don't follow conventions; men who are pushing thirty but have the courage and vision to start drinking shortly after breakfast on Thursdays. Isn't it almost obligatory that some woman should sleep with me the night before I depart for South America? Maybe I can tell her that I am going to be a writer. Even without a Pulitzer or significant writing experience, I'm about to do some kind of writing/data-entry hybrid thing. Either way, I'll tell her that I am about to be published and will be on the road in Brazil and then she'll understand the importance of this unique and fleeting opportunity to fornicate with me.

"Rum, vodka, I don't care. I can barely see. What time is it anyways?"

It is 3:25 a.m. according to his cell phone.

The waitress comes to the table and the Doctor shouts, "A bottle of rum for me and my patient. . . . Can't you see that I'm desperately trying to save him from himself?"

She nods and walks off. All business.

The Doctor slouches forward, his neck barely able to support his head. "I'll take care of this. My . . . my . . . uh . . . my school loan is already $200K, so what're a few more bucks? Oh fuck, now I'm really gonna be . . . sick."

The bottle is listed as $200. There is a mandatory gratuity of 25 percent. As we don't look too trustworthy and it is approaching closing, they bring the check along with the bottle.

The Doctor gives the waitress his credit card and goes to the bathroom to vomit some more. The lights start to come on in the bar, a faint glow at first. The waitress returns, flanked by a behemoth of a bouncer, to tell me that the card has been declined. I plead that they wait for my friend or let me go and find him in the bathroom, but there is no waiting or bargaining in this situation. I fork over my debit card and feel myself take one step closer to total financial ruin and becoming one of the old drunks at Bellevue Bar. I am performing without a net and have little room for error. The bouncer stands by our table while the waitress processes the transaction.

The Doctor staggers back from the bathroom and puts on his sunglasses as the lights are turned up to full brightness. "Let's fuckin' go to Vinyl . . . no, OK, Shelter then," he sputters and sways backward. I give him his worthless credit card and try to explain the situation with the bill, but he is no longer responsive. I pull off his sunglasses only to see his eyes tick back like an Atlantic City slot machine.

The bouncers start to clear the club. There is no way in hell that I am going to part with a $250 bottle of rum ($18.99 at the liquor store). I slide it into my pants, tighten my belt so that it holds the neck of the bottle in place, and walk out the front entrance. Within five minutes, the Doctor is forcefully ejected from a side door by one of the bouncers.

I yell at him while he gets back to his feet, though I may as well be shouting at the fire hydrant next to me or the brick wall behind us. He looks through me as if he is staring at some vanishing point down the street. "I didn't think that it was going to come to this, but we are going to have to take drastic measures," he drools. And with that he lobs a sloppy punch into my Adam's apple.

Adrenaline courses through my scalp, the tips of my fingers and toes. It concentrates in a ball of seething, brilliant anger in the core of my chest. I transform into a frothing Scandinavian berserker, unstoppable in my rage. My anger, exacerbated by everything from my career shortcomings to my relationship shortcomings to the fact that the Sonics can't sign a decent center is channeled out through the points of my fists and into the Doctor's big, curly blond head.

He doesn't take it sitting down. Nearly a dozen punches are exchanged and we both take a solid beating. The punches are not the crisp cracks of television and the movies, but dull, meaty thuds of bone on flesh and bone on bone. The bottle is dropped and shatters into heavy shards. I land two clean hooks to his head—even a left jab that has been polished in my fantasy beating of my former boss Allen. The Doctor drops on his side and then rolls onto his back. Although prostrate, he continues to swear at me. I stand over him, fists clenched, in an expanding pool of spilt rum.

I don't want to see how much lower this situation can go and am more than satisfied to recognize this as the bottom. I start to walk off; I have a flight to catch. The Doctor is suddenly back on his feet and chasing me. I run. I run like I used to run when the cops were chasing us at high school keg parties or when, as kids, my friend Greg and I would hit some frustrated middle-aged man's car with snowballs. After a block or two, I look back and the Doctor is nowhere to be seen. It's better this way, better to end this before something really bad happens.

I wake up facedown on my floor with sticky brown liquid all over my ears, cheeks, and nose. It is spread around me on the floor. I am relieved to find an empty quart of chocolate milk in my right hand. It is the low-sugar, organic, low-fat stuff. Regular chocolate milk is so bad for you.

After gathering enough composure to walk across the street to the pay phone, I call the limo service of my former employer. "Yes, we're gonna need a stretch for this occasion, yes, with a full bar." "Yeah, my name's Dan Fielding, Esquire, yes, F-I-E-L-D-I-N-G, account number 7-7-7-5-2-4." "I'm new to the firm, this is the first time that I've used your service. . . . Yeah, that's why I'm not in the database." "No, this isn't my office number. . . . No, it's not a cell number either. I am on a special errand, undercover, for the head of the firm, for national security. . . . No, don't pick me up at the office, pick me up on the corner of Houston and Avenue C in an hour."

The driver is hesitant to let me in when he finds a drunken, tattered, black-and-blue kid smelling faintly of sour milk with nothing more than a backpack standing on the street corner, but he doesn't ask too many questions as the firm's account is legitimate. I try to convince the driver to have a drink with me, but he declines. It is against his religion.

A Vicodin chased with a fresh beverage take the edge off of my surging hangover and the edge off of my consciousness. I watch the cool, gray morning sun as we pass over the Williamsburg Bridge and head across Brooklyn.

While waiting for my flight at JFK, I want to call Sydney, but opt instead to call the Doctor to see if he has sobered up. He answers his phone with an odd mixture of merriment and shock, "Dude, I'm in the hospital right now, I've only got a second to talk."

"I didn't know that you had to work today."

"No, man, I'm *in* the hospital. I'm in the fucking ER . . . as a patient."

"I didn't beat you up that bad, did I?"

"You beat me up? *Really?* Somehow, I almost severed my thumb."

He doesn't remember anything. Was it the broken bottle, a knife fight, sewer rats, razor wire, simply tripping while chasing me down the street? We'll never know. He doesn't blame me quite yet.

My boats have all been run aground and I can't say that I feel any sense of accomplishment. Maybe people need social structure and support. Have I been romanticizing my need to escape my own poor choices? Maybe we need to live within societal norms as they're really in our best interest. I should probably set up shop in some nice town, get a nice job, and surround myself with nice friends and a nice girlfriend and have a nice life.

I stare down the long carpeted hallway at JFK, everyone in transit, everyone in a liminal zone, walking in ones and sometimes twos: heading home, heading abroad.

I am terrified. I am exhilarated. I am unfettered.

Detoured

Although I have no idea what I am to be doing for this guidebook, I am not new to international travel or the world of backpacking. My parents were obsessed with travel and they journeyed around the world for two and a half years shortly after getting married, in 1967. Years later in Seattle, when my mother was a schoolteacher and my father was a photographer employed by the University of Washington, they both had some flexibility over the summers. They would take my brother, James, and me traveling for part, if not all, of it.

We lived modestly at the north end of University District where it transitions into Lake City, a shabbier area consisting mainly of used-car dealerships and self-storage units. We were the last family I knew to still have a black-and-white TV and the four of us tooled around in an orange VW camper van with Lone Ranger and Japanese robot puffy stickers covering the side windows. We were not poor, but we were not wealthy by any means. Regardless, my parents always found a way to take my brother and me on the road. As far back as I can remember, we took summerlong overland trips up and across Canada or through Europe, and we even popped into North Africa a few times. We traveled by car, boat, train, and camel—traipsing through Moroccan kasbahs, bunking in Swiss mountain hostels, camping along the Mediterranean, and renting houses in crumbling Croatian fishing villages.

I first traveled by myself at the age of seventeen. I worked at the Folklore Festival of the Pyrenees in Jaca, Spain—a few miles from the French border. I lived in a narrow hostel room with three roommates: a guitar-strumming Spaniard named Carlos who was stopping through as a pilgrim on the Camino de Santiago; another Spaniard, Diego, who was a die-hard Morrissey fan with the telltale hairstyle, and who insisted on taking his siesta naked and had his mother wax his armpits for him; and Josef from Munich, a lively, ponytailed Bavarian who was traveling around Spain in a *Ghostbusters*-esque 1960s Mercedes ambulance. It was gutted and refurbished with futons and posters of Buju Banton and Claudia Schiffer and stacked with mountain bikes and sail boards.

My job, as an official volunteer at the Folklore Festival of the Pyrenees, was to translate the daily schedule of festival events into English and read it live over the city-wide speaker system. The sound equipment was in a minivan parked on the side of the Plaza Mayor. The first day, I read, "Today at nine a.m. in Plaza Mayor there will be a mariachi group representing Mexico, followed by a Scottish bagpipe band at ten, drummers from Ghana . . ." in my best professional-announcer voice. I was fine until I looked out the window of the minivan and saw people stopping on the street, craning their necks to hear the bizarre, foreign voice broadcasting from the black loudspeakers. I completely lost my cool, choked my words, and had to apologize and start over again with sweaty, trembling hands.

In time, the job got easier, my Spanish improved dramatically, and I made some enduring friendships. Evenings were filled with raucous parties with people from all over the world followed by sangria in tiny bodegas, breakfast at sunrise, and then bed for a few hours before returning to work. At the end of the summer, I traveled in the ambulance across Spain with Josef, a French girl named Anne, a Hungarian named Erika, and another Bavarian friend named Susanne. We stopped in small medieval towns and camped outside of Barcelona. Needless to say, after that summer it was difficult to return to American high school, with its underage-drinking laws and crowds of adolescents huddling around clandestine kegs of Milwaukee's Best. Something had changed in me—permanently.

After my junior year of college, I found myself at a crossroads. I had traveled every moment that I could afford to since being in Spain. I had studied abroad in Buenos Aires for a semester, and that was to be my last hurrah before launching into a sensible career. I was majoring in Government and Legal Studies, had just nailed a strong A in Constitutional Law I, and had lined up a law internship in the Bay Area. I was ready to go ahead with it when I heard about a position working as a guide for American high school students doing some sort of summer volunteer work in Latin America.

There was almost no pay or obvious next career step, but there was a free flight included and I could stay in-country after the students returned home. It wasn't a purely selfless undertaking on the students' part or mine—most of the kids wanted to be able to claim some sort of community service in their college applications. I wanted to continue to travel.

An entire book could be written about my experiences as a guide and group leader over the following three summers working in Costa Rica and Ecuador. In any case, I ended up even farther away from the sensible career choice that I had once imagined. I continued to link one trip into the next, with only short respites to visit my family and try to earn extra money in order to travel more.

I found that I excelled as a traveler. I was a natural, of

sorts. Maybe such a skill is only about as useful in "the real world," the career world, as being a good drinker or good in bed, but it was something that came easily to me, and that I was proud of, nonetheless.

The conversion from guide and road warrior to the embryonic early form of travel writer was serendipitous and sudden. I was in India staying with a family for a month and visiting my brother, who was at the time an exchange student studying Archaeology in the southern city of Madurai. I lived with a kindly octogenarian couple. The diminutive man, who stood no more than five foot five, had been the regional director of animal husbandry and would regale me with stories of performing surgery on bull elephants with no anesthetic. Everything was great about the family, except that they went to bed at 8:30 p.m. and padlocked all of the gates to the house by 8. My natural bedtime falls somewhere between 1:00 and 3:00 a.m., so I ended up with an unusual amount of free time on my hands. There was nothing more than a single lamp and a bed in my room. I had three books to my name: *Lonely Planet India*, *One Flew Over the Cuckoo's Nest*, and *The Beach*. I read each cover to cover—a few times. I stayed up and smoked joints rolled in emptied-out beedies and imagined what would happen in the limitless future.

While flipping though the publishing list in the back of *Lonely Planet India*, I noticed that they had only a single phrasebook for all Latin American Spanish. After my time in Costa Rica, I knew that Central American Spanish and, say, Argentinean Spanish were practically different languages. I came up with the idea to write a phrasebook specific to Costa Rican Spanish (complete with surfing, dating, and partying terminology). I had no big ambitions for the phrasebook; I even thought to do it as an add-on section to the Costa Rica guidebook. My honest aim was only to scrape together enough money to go on another trip or two before finding that eventual, elusive career or maybe going to graduate school. I contacted Lonely Planet through their customer service email and, within a matter of weeks, sold them the book from an Internet café in Tamil Nadu. I had just turned twenty-three.

Timing was a huge part of the sale. It was 1998. We didn't finalize the contract until early 1999 and I worked on it on and off through the spring of 2000. The economy boomed in those years. People had lots of disposable income and travel guidebook publishers couldn't turn out books fast enough. Costa Rica was taking off as a destination at that time, evolving from a place visited by surfers and biologists to the go-to American tourism spot in Central America. I believe that if I were to send a similar email to the customer service department these days, I probably wouldn't even receive a response, let alone a book deal.

But back then Lonely Planet was a raw, growing, and evolving company. It was bursting with ideas and possibilities, but also appeared to be bloated and inefficient—a clumsy teenager not yet in full command of its newfound size and bulk. It still held onto its alternative and gutsy persona of its early years, but was clearly no longer a mom-and-pop business. While I declined to write a translation for the suggested *Where can I find a methadone clinic?*, they insisted that the book carry translations for phrases like:

> *Do you sell syringes?*
>
> *I take (cocaine) occasionally.*
>
> *Please don't stop!*
>
> *You can't sleep here tonight.*

The whole project suffered from maddening inefficiencies, miscommunication with the editors in Australia, slow payment, and arcane formatting systems. Manually alphabetizing a dictionary was one of the most tedious things I've had to do thus far in my life.

In spite of such issues, the book became a big success. "A punt pays off" was the title of a celebratory email regarding the book that the editor later copied me on. In the fall of 2000, Lonely Planet gave me the opportunity to move from phrasebooks to guidebooks, but I had already started a master's degree program in Latin American Studies at Stanford. The U.S. Department of Education offered me a full fellowship, plus living allowance, so long as I studied Portuguese. Travel writing was deemed a fleeting youthful dalliance and I opted to push ahead with academia and eventually move into the adult career world.

Some months before I left for Brazil, while avoiding the work that I needed to do for my favorite vulture investors and crooked research analyst, I fired off an email to Lonely Planet, saying that I would potentially be interested in doing some writing on the side. It was not much of a serious thought, more like an escapist fantasy. I had forgotten that I had even contacted them when I got a random call from their Australian office suggesting that I knock out a sample chapter to see if I was capable of writing for their guidebooks. I spent a few evenings writing about my neighborhood, Alphabet City, made sure that the sample was under the word limit, and sent it off. I was later told that the sample passed muster, but it was some time before I would hear from them again. Then, suddenly, I received the Brazil offer and was looking at a couple of weeks to upend and change my entire life.

In order to prepare myself for this new, half-cocked career choice, I began to read a selection of contemporary travel literature. It was something that I felt like I was supposed to do: research material to properly build inspiration. I must have read or skimmed about two dozen different books, and I have to admit that most didn't do anything for me. The majority of travel books fall into three basic groups:

1. There are the earnest writers who become enlightened through contact with the simple, honest lives of Mexican peasants or the unparalleled tranquillity of the Tuscan countryside. A more holistic approach to life is discovered and the universe is balanced. In order to properly enjoy such writing, one should be dressed in an eco-print Polarfleece, drinking fair-trade coffee and relaxing to a *Putumayo* world music CD.

2. On the opposite side of the spectrum are the smug writers who mock how backward plumbing and transportation are anywhere outside of North America. *Those foreigners are so whacky and their toilets are, too! Isn't that hilarious?* With a veneer of foreign exoticism, fourth-grade bathroom humor and petty prejudices are given a new lease on their comedic lives. Such writers should give Orlando or Long Island a try for their next vacation, as both have abundant new cars and functional flush toilets with soft two-ply paper.

3. Last but not least are the Charlie Bronson guys who attempt solo ascents of mountains without telling anyone where they're going, are forced to amputate their appendages with a spork, and then expect us to appreciate their triumph of human spirit. They are so overcome by emotion that they must write a book about it.

Paul Theroux once remarked that travel writing is really about the person who's traveling, so maybe it's just contemporary travel writers whom I can't relate to. There are other things out there. Better things. Classics. There is Chatwin. There are others: Hemingway and Kerouac; both can be considered travel writers.

I could only hope to be like a Chatwin, Hemingway, or Kerouac (excluding the AIDS, self-inflicted gunshot wound, and drinking-yourself-to-death parts). They were true writers coming to terms with the struggle of the people, the living history, the challenges of their generation—all while reflecting on the universal human condition with nothing but a journal, a drink, and pen in hand.

Alas, my situation doesn't come close to Chatwin's, Hemingway's, or Kerouac's. I will be a first-time guidebook writer and, at best, a secondary character in a Carl Hiaasen or Elmore Leonard novel. That's not to say that I am not serious about this project. I am dead serious about it. It is my big break with Lonely Planet, my opportunity to do something huge, to influence other travelers. I will wring the life out of the project with my bare hands. I will learn about hotels, restaurants, and bus schedules, but will somehow do it in a way that will help us all to understand humanity and our common needs and desires a bit better. It could even improve international relations and help the developing world.

That's the plan, anyway.

My first morning in Rio, I lie naked on a narrow cot as my vision comes into focus. The ceiling fan spins torpidly, off-axis. The paint peels from the ceiling along the outline of gray water stains. This is not Alphabet City. A soft bulge of foam rubber strains out of a crack in the vinyl-coated mattress top. My face is surrounded by a tangle of sweaty blonde hair—blonde hair attached to nearly six feet of a catatonic woman. My arm spills across pale white skin, tacky to the touch. Tropical humidity weighs in the room and slits of late-morning light stab through the louvered wooden shutters. Even at this hour, it's pure, sadistic radiation.

My brain is swollen too large for my skull—blood pumping in, backing up against my eardrums, nothing going back out. I don't much appreciate these moments of intermission in an extended drinking binge. I take measured, even breaths and my mind starts to gain forward momentum. The threadbare sheet has been kicked to the floor. To its side are two spent condoms with a trail of red ants running in and out, scurrying to their lair somewhere between the cracks in the cement floor. I concentrate on the faint buzz of their frenzied work.

The naked woman next to me is Inga: a Lufthansa flight attendant whose life intersected with mine somewhere between JFK and Rio. We are near Copacabana Beach. Subjects of last night's *cachaça*-infused discussion include future plans to visit her family's cabin in the Alps, the tastefully eccentric union of a stewardess and travel writer, and the importance of raising bilingual children, particularly those who speak German and English. If it isn't love, it is well on the way to being love, or at least we'll both try to keep up appearances for another day or so.

I need to clean up those condoms, now. We've made significant progress in uncheapening our relatively cheap sexual experience. Bugs and semen will not aid in our suspension of disbelief.

People, when dislocated from their customary surroundings, can free themselves from preconceived notions of how they are supposed to act. Abroad, that which is formerly unacceptable can become commonplace. That which is normal at home can be disregarded as an outdated practice of the past. It's not

"When in Rome, do as the Romans do." People actually tend to do as they've always wanted to do—no one (at least, no one they're going to see again) is watching or passing judgment on them, and they are allowed to reimagine themselves and re-create their own reality.

When a human becomes unbound from his or her place, it also affects the perception of time. The senses are inundated with new sights, smells, and sounds. The flow of new, often-shocking details make us more like wide-eyed children than jaded adults. There is more concentration, recognition, and appreciation given to details throughout the day. With no tether to a place and no base of reference, relationships and plans become hyperaccelerated. New best friends are made and then never seen again. Romances develop with the bottle-rocket trajectory of the *Challenger*. For my generation, the first that has always had a computer at home and that considered video games a normal childhood pastime, life on the road is one of the few things that actually overwhelm our tolerance for stimuli and shock us into the here and now.

As for Inga, I didn't intend to end up here with her, nor did she intend to end up here with me. Such is the unpredictable nature of travel. She had plans to come to Rio with her former boyfriend, who was a copilot. "All the young stewardesses want the copilots," she told me. "The pilots are very old and have many years of making love with many stewardesses." It turns out her copilot was making progress toward getting his wings, as he already had a girlfriend on every route. She declared that she is going to enjoy her trip regardless of him and wants to "make crazy party" in Rio. She is a new woman here.

Common sense would dictate that our liaison is casual and fleeting. Why then talk of bilingual children and visiting her family in Austria? I'd like to believe that it was all hopeful banter, stemming from excitement, possibility, and sexual intoxication—not any sort of calculated fraud on either of our parts.

Two people who have just stepped out of relationships are an incendiary combination. It takes a certain type of person to be completely casual about casual sex, and perhaps neither of us fits that profile.

I would argue that sex is a reasonably easy goal; it is intimacy and love that are far more elusive. Yet this form of disposable intimacy and love is also far more dangerous than the simple physical act of sex. My connection to Inga may be as close to true intimacy as pro wrestling is to punching your best friend in the face, but whatever it is, it feels right—at least for the moment.

It all started innocently enough. She was taking a few days' vacation in New York before heading to Carnaval. We met while waiting to board the plane at JFK and I didn't see her again until the baggage claim in Rio. She was tall and slender and had the scrubbed, healthy look of a youth spent in the crisp air and green slopes of the Alps. She was actually born and raised in Vienna, but my preconceived notions of Austrians all involve hiking, the Winter Olympics, and Red Bull.

We chatted idly about travel while waiting for our backpacks to be birthed from the belly of the plane and reemerge down the slippery metal ramp. She told me right off that she had not been planning to travel alone on this trip, that as a stewardess she was always doing stuff alone, on a schedule different from the rest of the world. This trip was supposed to be different.

"And you?" she asked. "What is it that happened to your face?"

My jaw was so swollen that I couldn't bite properly. "Misdirected frustration, I think . . . probably my own." I answered. Fortunately her bag appeared on the carousel before I had to explain myself any further. She fought through the crowd, grabbed the backpack, and bid me farewell. "Maybe we'll see each other around," she said. The hours were ticking off against my deadline. There was no time for distractions. I needed to get on a flight to Recife or Fortaleza in the Northeast in the next couple of hours if possible. Inga and I departed gracelessly. We did not hug. We did not shake hands.

My backpack was one of the last to arrive in baggage claim. I decided to take a quick look around the airport for an ATM before I went to try to arrange my flight north. At the cash machine, I ran into Inga again. She was distraught as she couldn't withdraw any Brazilian reais. "I was having many problems in New York with this card, but was thinking that it was corrected by now," she said. "I don't know what to do."

"Well, that works out perfectly. I'm taking a cab to Copacabana or Ipanema. You can ride along with me and try out some different banks when you get there." I felt the words spill out of my mouth even as my brain tried to justify the decision.

It made sense to split a cab—a smart, responsible, dare-I-say-chivalrous thing to do. Plus, a night in Rio would help me to decompress a bit, get used to being in Brazil, and get used to being a travel writer. I'd arrive in the Northeast rested and ready to kick ass on the guidebook. In Rio, I could begin developing the new and improved version of me: taking things one step at a time, methodically, like my mom always suggested.

I can't really determine if there was any flirtation or not during the ride along the highway and through the tunnels out to the beach. Inga and I were both trying to play it cool: comparing her stories of working flights between Germany and North Africa with my tales of days as a guide in Costa Rica and Ecuador. We discussed places we'd like to visit in the future. Libya will be the place to go. Albania. Suriname. Mozambique. As we talked, the peerless landscape of the Cidade Maravilhosa, Rio— the Marvelous City—raced by in a deluge of shimmering office buildings, mammoth housing blocks, and the iconic peaks draped with tropical green and favela shantytowns. There was some potential between Inga and me, but everything in our interaction was casual up to the point that we arrived at the ramshackle Villa Copacabana hostel.

We showed our passports to Sueli, the girl who worked at the desk in the small reception room with no windows. She was comfortable talking to travelers and gave us her well-rehearsed story about her life and how she works fourteen days straight at the Villa with two days off between shifts. She was surprised to meet an American. They get few American backpackers in Rio and I am now the second currently at the Villa—a true rarity.

Then Sueli asked me the question. I should have prepared an answer, but had put it off, as usual.

"Do you two want to stay in the dorms or get a double room?" she asked.

Quiet.

I heard myself breathing. "Dorms, *maybe*. I dunno. I mean"—I looked at Inga—"what do you think?"

"Doesn't matter to me."

"OK . . . you sure?"

"Yeah"

"Uh, let's just go for one room then. It'll save money, you know. Plus, you know, dorms can be tricky with valuables and stuff." I maintained eye contact with Sueli.

We signed some paperwork and I settled the bill. Inga said she would split it with me after she got money from the bank. We made our way down the smoky, meandering corridor past a windowless common area, a grimy kitchen with three cheerful Australian surfers boiling ramen in blackened pots, shared bathrooms, and dorm rooms that looked like they had been appropriated from a reformatory school.

In the back of the building there were three or four double rooms built around a communal cement terrace, a nightmare of exposed rebar boxed in by crumbling concrete walls, and crowned by a rainbow of broken bottle bottoms along the top of the wall, protecting us from the next property. We entered our room, which consisted of two narrow cots with fake-leather mattresses fixed to the frames; a musty, listing armoire; and slatted wooden window shutters with chipped blue paint. The ceiling fan fought to chop through the moist air.

We opened the windows to breathe life into the room and busily put all of our things away in the closet as if we were new homeowners. We organized and reorganized all of our stuff. I set some folded shirts on one bed to see where she set her things. *The other bed* . . . were we each claiming a bed or did she think that I already claimed the other one for myself? I was not sure what to do next, so I refolded some pants. Again, things went quiet. Were we committed to having intercourse at some point or were we simply two progressive travelers sharing space and friendly support on the road? She is Austrian after all. I didn't really know what that meant. I was sure that Austrians are advanced enough that men and women travel together all the time and there is no necessary sexual element. Or maybe they are progressive enough that they have sex like flossing or cutting their toenails and consider it a normal human function not worthy of undue emotional stress. Should we kiss? Hold hands? Perhaps this situation called for something more subtle, like slowly brushing her hair out of her eyes with the back of my hand.

I remembered being on the English-speaking island of Bastimentos, off the Caribbean coast of Panama, years before. I had just graduated college and traveled for two days with a female grad student from Chapel Hill. The grad student and I were staying in separate rooms. There was no connection between us at all, though she was a fine travel partner. One of the older guys around town asked me about my relationship with the girl and then admonished me, "What is wrong with you white boys? Do you call that civilized? If I stay in the same *hotel* with a girl and there is no sex, I cannot close my eyes all night. No sleep. Nothing, mon." He was angry at me. I told him that I wasn't interested in her sexually, that things were platonic.

He recoiled, "*Platonic*? You mean you a . . ."

"No, I mean with her. I'm not interested. We're more like friends."

"You mean *you's* here by yourself on the islands and *she's* by sheself and you's not interested because she's your friend? All I hear is that the white man's smart, that we should try to act like the white man. White people be plain crazy."

I started to worry that I suffered from a chronic form of nice-guy complex, a socially induced castration from a youth spent in the Seattle Public School System—where excessive PC progressivism rounds the bend of the political spectrum and comes dangerously close to puritanical fascism. Riding a bike without a helmet, jaywalking, failure to recycle, and suggestive eye contact with a female are shameful, criminal acts worthy of self-loathing, guilt, and, perhaps, corrective counseling. Had my fear of offending others led me to deny my natural male impulses? I bet that Bukowski never had this issue.

Inga and I stood for another minute, abstractly discussing how exciting it was to be in Rio, as she picked at her cuticles and I looked out the window at the neighboring wall. We decided to try her card at a bank and then go to Ipanema Beach, get some drinks, and enjoy the sun. I changed into my board shorts in the men's bathroom down the hall. She changed in the bedroom and put on a bikini under shorts and a T-shirt. Flip-flops replaced my Rod Lavers, and we were off.

The Villa was just a few blocks' walk from the center of Copacabana Beach. Copacabana is 8th Avenue on the Tropic of Capricorn: 10,000 people per square mile, the scent of sex, scandal, and seediness in the air. Believe it or not, those things aren't even the best attractions: Copacabana also happens to be wedged between precipitous limestone peaks and 2½ miles of ashtray-fine sand. The pairing of tropical nature and heavy urbanization makes for an uneasy yet somewhat functional couple.

We walked along the paved beach walk—the *calçadão*—which backs the length of the shore in Rio's South Zone. With twisted mosaic masonry patterns and punctuated with *barracas* (kiosks) selling coconuts, popsicles, and ice-cold beer, the *calçadão* is the main artery of the city's beach areas. The ribbon of pavement throbs with a steady flow of tourists, joggers, beachgoers, drug dealers, street performers, hookers, sex tourists, families, street kids, athletes, models, people who should not sport a bikini (both men and women), Austrian stewardesses, and misplaced American men playing at being travel writers.

Inga and I eventually arrived at the famed Ipanema Beach, but not before Inga's card had been rejected at four banks. Banks with the Cirrus system. Banks with the Plus system. The special ATM for international cards at Banco do Brasil. We even waited at one and pled with an English-speaking manager. No success.

I watched the blistering midday sun fade into a smoldering blaze through the windows of the air-conditioned bank. You know how you are able to hold off on going to the bathroom until you are in view of the toilet and only then do you almost lose control? That's exactly how I felt regarding the beach across the street that was calling to me. I needed desperately to get out of the bank and could wait no longer. But I could not abandon her, particularly when there was still a strong possibility of sex. So, I did what any reasonable man who had already torn through half of his feeble advance—on a project that he hadn't technically even started—would do: I loaned her money. A fair amount of it. Only until she could figure out the banking issues or her mom could wire her some cash, of course.

It was time to relax, to rid myself of North American anxiety, enjoy being in Rio, and hang out with a stewardess in her slinky red bikini with golden pinstripes. I needed to do this in order to gain the perspective that is necessary to write a guidebook—the traveler's perspective—and not from the angle of some wired, freaked-out Manhattan office employee who has just stepped off a plane.

The grainy, golden sand of Ipanema squeezed up between my toes as the sun, still potent in the late afternoon, jackhammered down on my ivory winter skin. The legendary double peaks of Dois Irmãos (two brothers) loomed over the end of Ipanema and stretched into ever-longer shadows across the beach. We drank cans of beer, talked about travel, talked about nothing, and played a flirting game where she threw sand on my chest and we pretended that it was cute. The sun rolled behind the peaks, the drinks alleviated the exhaustion and hangover, and we kissed to coronate a new beginning in a new land. I wanted this to be Day One of a calendar with no history.

We returned from the beach and wandered into the cacophony of a party in the hallway of the Villa that spilled out onto the back terrace. Travelers—some tanned, some sunburned, all sweaty and all in shorts, T-shirts, and bathing suits—filled small plastic cups with beer from large bottles of Skol. There was also a bottle or two of *cachaça*, Brazil's sugarcane firewater—similar to rum, but half the price and twice the hangover. I could smell the sharp tang of dry brick weed emanating from the back of the crowd.

South American brick weed has an unmistakable scent. The stuff is heavily treated with chemicals (some say petroleum), pressed into thin bricks under a truck or some sort of hydraulic machine, and then smuggled over from Paraguay or rural Brazil below loads of domestic produce in commercial 18-wheelers. It's usually 25 percent seeds and stems, but it's better than nothing.

English, as in most hostels, is the lingua franca. The party also echoed with some pidgin Portu-ñol (Português combined with Español, this region's Spanglish), mainly from a few guys trying to hit on the four or five scantily clad Brazilian women with impressive hair extensions. For the record, I speak a form of Portu-ñol, not pure Portuguese. I should speak better—and maybe I did after spending some months in Rio a few years back—but my Portuguese has bled back into my Spanish. When I am lacking a piece of Portuguese vocabulary, I default to Spanish and definitely have a bit of a Spanish accent. I imagine that I sound somewhat like Walter Mercado, the Puerto Rican astrologer who made a mockery out of himself in Brazil with his "*Ligue já*" (Call now) television commercials. Walter, who looks like a cross between your mom and a lamé cape–wearing space oracle from an early Star Trek episode, was a Latino version of Miss Cleo, with her fake Jamaican-esque "Cahl me now."

Aside from the provocatively dressed women, the only other Brazilians are a bespectacled couple from São Paulo, who were celebrating their graduation from engineering school. The rest of the crowd is a motley crew of international backpackers, Carnaval-goers who haven't made it home yet, and an odd assortment of strung-out long-term hostel residents, washed up from God-knows-where.

"KANPAI. KANPAI," a Japanese girl shouted excitedly in the face of one of the Aussie surfers. "How you say *kanpai* in Australian?"

"I dannae. Down the gullet?" he responded with a long smile before the two finished their cups of beer. She sloshed much of hers down the front of her shirt, but laughed it off and went to refill them both.

Someone had an old yellow Sony Sports Walkman hooked up to two small battery-powered speakers, and they were playing Brazilian drum 'n' bass tapes with a solid dose of static. Two fluorescent floodlights shimmered off the jagged points of the broken bottles atop the dividing wall.

The beach areas of Rio don't cater particularly well to budget travelers. Ipanema has some nicer hotels and relatively higher prices. Copacabana exudes a faded glory in which its once high-end hotels have been repopulated by mouth-breathing package tourists—many in search of little more than sex, cheap alcohol, and drugs. A single block is dominated by what may be the largest prostitution pickup joint in the Americas, HELP. Most of the international backpacker hostels have been pushed inland. A budget-conscious hostel in the heart of Copacabana, such as the Villa, is the perfect magnet for a rotating cast of fantastically eccentric misfits and ruffians.

Inga and I were engulfed by the crowd of partiers and over the next hour or two met a potpourri of scoundrels. A Norwegian named Knute handed me a beer and asked me where I was from, followed by where I'd traveled to and where I was going . . . the traveler's standards. He was young, with an elfin Scandinavian quality, and was brimming with excitement to be in Rio.

"This city is my kind of place," he said. "Back in high school, I was an exchange student in Los Angeles for a year. It was great. The sun. The girls. The fucking drugs. Rio's like affordable LA without all the big highways and shitty American laws. It's definitely not Oslo." In LA, Knute had tasted the world beyond Scandinavian homogeneity and had dated a Salvadoreña girl and discovered the joys of crystal methamphetamine. He spoke lustily about meth, like an aficionado of fine cigars or haute cuisine. "We would go to the cook's apartment in West Hollywood in the mornings before school and buy the crystals while they were still warm. D'ya fucking believe that, man?" It conjured images of white-gloved Keebler Elves pulling trays of meth from the hearth. I mentioned to him that in the States people don't usually brag about their love of meth. You keep it to yourself like a DWI or an old case of genital warts. But he was unfazed.

Knute had been traveling for the past two weeks with an Aussie he had met in Bolivia. I didn't know his real name, but referred to him as Mr. Yay—out of respect for his all-consuming obsession. While the other Aussies at the Villa were salubrious-looking young fellows who apparently spent as much time in the waves as on land, this one's sunken eyes and pallid complexion spoke of sleepless nights, a pitiable diet, and chronic masturbation. "Have you tried the coke here yet?" Mr. Yay asked me. "It's fucking brilliant. You can select by strength: good stuff, more mild stuff, you name it. It's all over the place. Shit, you can even get it from the evening guy who works the front desk. That's service, mate." I see why he and Knute are friends. If you think that Americans and Europeans are cocaine crazy, try Australians. Finding cocaine in Australia must be like spotting a wallaby on the loose in Fresno.

Like most Australians and Kiwis, Mr. Yay was on an around-the-world ticket. Once you leave Australia, you have to make it worth your while and visit as many places as possible. He was heading west and had come across northern Africa (hash) to Spain (hash and attractive, available women), had flown directly to Bolivia (cocaine), and had now descended to Rio (cocaine and attractive, available women). He had been in Copacabana for more than a week and had not been to the beach yet during daylight. He bragged that he had never actually seen the Atlantic Ocean except from an airplane.

The hedonistic energy of the party at the Villa was intoxicating in itself. Nobody had to answer to any bosses, parents, neighbors—anyone. Nobody had an alarm set for the next morning. Few even knew what day of the week it was. We were all in Rio by choice and had paid good money to be here. Therefore, it was our duty to ourselves to have fun. I, of course, was in a different situation, and was supposed to be researching and writing, but that was something I would have to deal with the next day. I've studied some anthropology, so let's just label what I was doing *participant observation*.

A few of the people at the Villa had been riding the traveler's scene for too long. If you do much backpacking, you know the type: they would be bankrupt and possibly homeless in their own country, but can scrape by in a developing country on small infusions of hard currency from home, either through family gifts or short bursts of gainful employment.

Andreu, a rail-thin Catalán in his mid-forties, had been in South America for a decade, mainly in Bogotá, Caracas, and now Rio. He said that he used to have an apartment in Ipanema, but sold off all of his possessions and had been staying in a dorm bed in the Villa for a year and a half. He had the wiry, beef-jerky physique of someone who prioritized nightlife over food. I noticed bits of eyeliner around his eyes, not properly washed off from the night before. I'm sure that there are creative ways for a desperate foreigner to make ends meet in this town.

Inga introduced me to Max Buckman, an aspiring model from Hamburg who had come down for Carnaval and decided to stay for a while. They were talking rapidly in German as they thumbed through his portfolio, which he just happened to have with him at the party. I asked Max about the Chinese character tattoos on his shoulders. "They mean world peace, or love, I think," he answered. "I have the Om on my back. I got them in

Berlin. Very cool, yes?" He had met an Argentine girl named Sylvia. Dark skinned, with a black fashion mullet and a sweeping geometric tattoo across her shoulders, she was young and was staying in one of the big hotels with her parents. The parents apparently didn't mind that she was around the corner in a dive hostel getting fucked by a Euro on a plastic-mattressed dorm bed. She spoke only Spanish. He spoke only German and English. They seemed to be doing all right.

I usually try to avoid other Americans when I'm abroad. It's not because I have some travel superiority complex or think that I am better than my countrymen, and I don't buy into the belief that American travelers are inherently less savvy than others (I've met some embarrassing assholes from pretty much every country out there). But in places like Costa Rica that are now rammed with Americans, being around people that you could have met out on any given night at home can detract from the depth of your travel experience. There are few Americans in Brazil and I was pleased to meet the one other American staying at the Villa. He introduced himself as, "Bob . . . Bob Fishman from LA."

Bob was short and slender with a dark goatee, rueful cow eyes, and curly hair pulled back into a black bandana. A few gray strands in the beard and lines around his eyes betrayed his true age, but he wore overstuffed skateboarding shoes, knee-length board shorts with a floral pattern, and exuded a Peter Pan quality that led me to call him Bobby, no matter that he was almost forty.

I initially misjudged him as the quiet type, because he was all wrapped up with a Filipina photojournalist who was here to take shots of street kids for a French NGO newsletter. Bobby and the girl had been together for three days and were acting like they were on their honeymoon. When his ladyfriend walked off to get more drinks, he confided in me, "She told me that I'm a beautiful man . . . nobody ever told me that I'm beautiful before. *And* she gave me a foot massage. This one's different, dude." Her English was not so good and I wondered if perhaps she'd been lacking a more specific adjective than *beautiful,* but I was happy for him just the same.

Bobby had not set foot in California in almost fifteen years, since he claimed to have found himself in trouble with a Ukrainian bookie over some gambling debt. "I usually tell people that I was betting on basketball, but the truth"—he lowered his voice—"the God's honest truth is that it was women's tennis. Fucking Navratilova ruined my life, dude. I put my money on our Texas homegirl Zina Garrison after the ass-kicking that she'd handed to Graf. Next thing I know, Garrison tanks and I am off to Seoul in the middle of the night with nothing but a backpack. Anyways, I was in Seoul for a decade, but I had some issues in Korea, did a stint in Dubai, and now I own a vending-machine business in Chile, you know, like vending machines in all the new office buildings in Santiago. We put in the machine and I pay somebody to restock it, take my cut, and that's it. Good income for almost no work. Santiago sucks ass, though. Bunch of philistines—just like Pinochet wanted." Bobby shifted back and forth from one foot to the other, and drank straight *cachaça* from a Dixie cup between sentences.

"Have you ever considered going back to another part of the U.S.? Like New York?" I asked.

He looked at me with steady eyes down the length of his cup. "Are you kidding me? I fucking hate New York. I'd rather go back to LA and get my head chopped off by Fat Igor the bookie than live in New York. That's the only city in the world where crime falls and the quality of life improves and everybody complains even more. It's a city of angry little trolls. I mean, Santiago isn't paradise—it's pretty much the Indianapolis of Latin America—but it is a good place to do business. That's the only reason I live there. I'd like to do some expansion into Rio. And that's why I'm here now. Research. All business, no pleasure, man . . ."

"How long will you—"

"No idea. I like being abroad. Out here where things are unclaimed. Look at those favelas all around Rio. Do you know what the views must be like from up there? I want in on that real estate. You know how I can get in on that? Fucking New York, man. Are you kidding me? The U.S. is like Europe—a closed game. The best that you can do in the States is beg for scraps off the table of people who already own everything. Out here, though, you can really make something happen."

Inga and I started to get drunk and loosely made plans to take the cable car up to Sugar Loaf mountain the next day, maybe go to a soccer game at Maracanã stadium: standard touristy stuff, but that's what she wanted to do, and who was I to say no to a beguiling stewardess? We then rounded up a crew including two rosy-complexioned Irish girls with beers glued to their hands, a few Israelis, and the one Hungarian, and headed out to some unnamed, cavernous nightclub. Bobby did not come out as he and the photojournalist were in need of some private time. Knute and Mr. Yay said they had to do some business with the kid at the front desk, but would meet us in an hour or so.

In all of our camaraderie, more shots were purchased at the club. Everyone kept asking if Inga and I lived together in the States or in Austria. They all asked how long we'd been together. Admitting that it was for only five hours made us both uncomfortable, but, regardless, momentum and alcohol were on our side. I bought a round, followed by a round from Knute. Max, my favorite German male model, came through with a gaggle of shots after that. The next thing I knew, Inga and I were kissing heavily in a booth along the wall.

I remember tracing my fingers along her hand, while her

arm rested across my knees. We waxed drunkenly about the great possibilities of our relationship, our voices distorted by the bass from the massive speaker system. I have vague memories of sex back at the hostel. Outlines of skin in the darkened room. Snapshots, really. It was passionate. It was kind of intimate. I never even learned her last name.

I roll off the bed and crouch naked on the floor to pick up the condoms. My back peels off the cot like gauze off an old wound. I feel some sense of possession over the contents of the condoms and do not want to share them with a colony of tropical ants. As I pick up the condoms, a stream of room-temperature semen dribbles between my thumb and forefinger and down the back of my hand, tiny ants awash in the fluid. I throw up, but am able to trap it in behind my pursed lips. I hold it for a second, regain control, and choke it back down.

I toss the condoms into a small plastic wastebasket that is gummy with the remnants of years of discarded condoms and cigarette ash. I wipe the back of my hand on the sheet, pry one of the louvers open with my finger, and peer out the window across a maze of concrete and cinderblock walls. Inga lies splayed across the slender bed. She has a shaved pussy with a touch of bumpy razor burn that makes it look like a split, plucked breast of poultry. I wonder what year shaving became de rigueur. Probably 2001 or 2002. Maybe earlier in Austria.

According to Plan

59 DAYS UNTIL DEADLINE

"**P**arachute Artist" is a name given to a certain type of travel writer, particularly itinerant guidebook writers. Tony Wheeler, the founder of Lonely Planet, defines a parachute artist as "someone who can drop into a place and quickly assimilate, who can write about anywhere." You must be able to wake up in Thai Hill Country, Kaliningrad, the Ganges Delta, Tegucigalpa, Mombasa, or Port Moresby and quickly wrap your head around the place. You must determine its character and capture the so-called zeitgeist in a way that can be explained in a 300-word section introduction and 250-word city and regional introductions—even if you've never set foot on that continent before. You must find the best accommodations, activities, restaurants, and practicalities; write pseudosagacious, balanced reviews on all of them; and then flip the channel to the next destination and do the same thing all over again. Efficiency is of the essence.

I know the alternative dimension inhabited by backpackers.

Efficiency is not part of the lexicon. Although I am supposed to be writing about them and for them, I must avoid fully being one of them. I can justify another day or two to acclimate and figure out the Inga situation and will then need to focus exclusively on work.

Inga wakes up and things are far from relaxing. We are finding it difficult to carry on a conversation. I am not sure if it is the hangover or simply the realization that we have little in common. Back in NYC, it would have been a perfect day for a DVD, 800 mg of ibuprofen, and a bottle of Pedialyte. I never would have moved off of the couch. Our room is hot and damp and actually inflames feelings of hangover discomfort. We are not going to make it to Sugar Loaf today. We are not going to make it to Maracanã. I don't know if I'll survive the morning.

I do get out of the hostel to check my email and make sure that everything is in order. The editor seems to have gone AWOL and isn't answering my emails. This is probably standard as they don't want to do too much hand-holding on your first project. I'm sure that they don't want to establish some sort of dependency issue. I have a 5k email missive from the Doctor, who thinks I have anger-management problems. He writes that I am a sadist and tells me he never wants to speak to me again. I take my time walking back to the hostel. Inga is watching TV with a couple of Germans in the common area. We say hello. I lie back down for a few hours of uneasy rest.

I don't get any real sleep, but before I know it, the sun is already setting and the party has started back up outside of my window. Inga slinks in the corner with a bottle of water in hand, looking like someone who has just been resuscitated with a defibrillator. Eventually, most of the crew from the night before decides to go out to dinner. Inga and I consider just grabbing a sandwich and going to bed, but push ourselves to join the group and move along to dinner at an open-air, touristy place down on Avenida Atlântica, behind the *calçadão* on Copacabana Beach.

We sit facing each other at a long table. I hear conversations around me, but cannot participate. Mr. Yay's telling Inga about his time in Bolivia: "Every time that the church bell chimed in the plaza, we would pass around a whole plate of coke with the lines cut out on it. We had a silver straw and everything, mate. We just snorted coke round the clock for two days and it was about the price of going out to dinner and a movie back home. Complete Tony Montana. I tell you, I'd move to Bolivia in a second and live in that hostel for the rest of my life. A fucking great country."

"Sounds awesome. What are the people like?" she asks.

"I don't know. My dealer was a French guy who lived in the hostel. He's got it figured out, I'm telling you."

A waiter accidentally dumps a gravy boat of what appears to be Hollandaise sauce down the back of a woman's suit jacket at a neighboring table. I watch it happen in slow motion—I see it about to happen, but can't muster any reaction until after it's all over. I am sipping a beer to stay awake, but it isn't helping. The food is your average Italian-style international fare. Pastas, pizzas, nothing particularly Brazilian. I push my fork mindlessly into the *frutas do mar* linguine with bits of shrimp and squid in olive oil.

The conversations buzz all around me: exchanges about sports, food, drinking, drugs, and DJs in different countries. I can't participate and stare out to the *calçadão* to admire the throngs strolling up and down the beachfront, shouting, laughing, shopping, drinking. A capoeira performance gathers into a *roda* (circle) between us and the sand. Capoeira is a dance and martial art originally developed by Afro-Brazilian slaves. While it is usually a competition between two "players," the street show is dressed up with extra acrobatics and handsprings to impress the passersby. The shirtless *capoeiristas* wear less-than-traditional Adidas warm-up pants and sneakers as they feint and dodge spinning kicks and leg sweeps. They then move on to doing high jumps and flips over a friend clutching an upturned kitchen knife. It has nothing to do with capoeira but is a crowd-pleaser just the same.

There is excitement all around, but I am here only in physical form. When I really think about it, I am not sure that I like Inga. Yes, I am attracted to her, but I don't think I feel anything more than that. I am attracted to many women; this is hardly groundbreaking. I don't know. I am probably being too negative. Maybe I am reacting more to the perceived notion that she stands in the way of me getting my job done. She's tempting, but I stand in my own way more than anything else.

I look down at my plate and there is a red-and-white horse pill, an oversized gelcap, gently nestled next to my pasta. My memory is a bit foggy, but I am sure that it was not on the menu and not there but a minute ago. I look around the table and everyone seems engaged in small talk.

Mr. Yay, who sits diagonally from me, catches my eye and motions with a subtle upward raise of his chin.

"What is it?" I ask under by breath.

"Just take it. I picked it up in Egypt. It's like coffee . . . but better," he replies in a near whisper.

While Yay may not be the most trustworthy character I've met, he does seem to be a reasonably qualified amateur pharmacist. I put the pill back with a mouthful of beer and continue to try to eat my pasta and to stay awake.

After dinner, most of us head back to the hostel. The pill does nothing against such formidable fatigue. Inga goes to bed and is sound asleep within minutes. I go to brush my teeth and end up talking with Knute and an Israeli girl named Karla on the back terrace.

Mr. Yay makes a grand reentry to the sedate evening crowd bearing the gift of a liter of cheap tequila, which we soon start nursing straight from the bottle. I start to feel better and start to feel some inspiration for the work ahead of me. Karla looks like she has spent much of her postmilitary time doing yoga and traveling. She's tanned and lithe with pronounced muscle tone in her arms and exposed abdomen. But she is no fitness-club girl; she has a curling scar across the knuckles of her left hand and a number of South Pacific tribal tattoos on her arms, gulps straight tequila, and discusses the finer points of motorcycle maintenance with Knute. I, on the other hand, can barely program an alarm clock. Her loose-fitting pants and tank top with the ubiquitous Om symbol hint of time spent in Indian ashrams. She is in the process of moving to Australia, putting the Middle East behind her.

My stomach feels a little off. I shouldn't be drinking. My jaw feels tight. I should just call it a night and go lie down, but I am still restless—worried, no excited, well OK, a bit worried, too, about work and money and the editor and Inga and Sydney. I have a lot on my mind. What am I still doing in Rio? I tell Yay that the pill didn't do much for me.

"If you think you can handle it, mate." He laughs and flips me another. "You look like you're already getting a little edgy. Watch yourself. I don't wanna have to peel you off the ceiling."

"Thanks. You're growing on me, dude," I tell him.

I am about to take the pill when Bobby Fishman, my enterprising American friend, storms onto the terrace, visibly distraught. "Dude, SHE BROKE UP WITH ME. What the hell?" He is on the verge of tears. He sits down between me and Yay and puts his head in his hands. "I thought that it was for real this time. She said that she can't get tied down, that I'm getting too serious, too fast. *Can girls even say that*?"

"It's OK, man," I assure him. "I think that Inga and I are heading in the same direction. I mean yesterday, I thought that, I mean I didn't know what I was doing but, don't worry, man. You'll be OK."

"Wait a minute, what the fuck are you on, tweaker? You didn't let Quigley Down Under over here give you one of his Egyptian specials, did you?"

"Well, maybe. But it didn't do anything, I was just gonna have another, 'cause, ya know, I'm trying to relax, trying to figure things out. Sorry to hear about you and the girl, these things are tricky, man. Like Inga, maybe she'll . . ."

"You can't compare your twenty-four-hour stewardess fling to what we had. I just feel sorry for the next girl. I'm gonna end up treating her like shit. Every time I put my neck out, I get FUCKED and go back to being a defensive prick. Love is stupid and pointless, but a year or two later, I fall for it all over again. Fuck it; I'll take it ALL out on the next one. I don't know who she'll be, but I feel goddamn sorry for her."

"Bob, you've got to chill out," Karla cuts in. "It sounds to me like you need some serious professional help."

"Sounds to me like you need to seriously mind your own fucking business," he says, swallowing back tears and looking her up and down. There is a moment of tense, awkward silence. It is obvious to everyone that Karla is capable of slapping the shit out of him with a few highly refined *krav maga* moves. I guess that he knows it, too, because he gets up, kicks a beer bottle off the side of the balcony, and storms down the hallway, out the front door and into the night.

Karla sits still and meditates on it for a second, then decides that Bobby is having a moment of weakness and pain and deserves kindness the same as anyone else. She must forgive him and extend her assistance regardless of what he said. We discuss the situation and decide we should go find him and bring him back to the Villa. He is surely on his way to the beach and Rio is not a safe place to be out alone in such a state.

We amble down to the beach, but can't find him. We walk nearly the distance of Copacabana's paved *calçadão* while working on the bottle of tequila, but still no luck. The crowd on the *calçadão* has diminished into pockets of late-night partiers drinking on the beachfront, hookers trolling for johns, and random wandering stragglers. The tequila becomes easy to drink. I am not tired at all. I feel like I could keep walking all night. The others don't feel the same way. Eventually, we set up shop at a plastic picnic table on the intersection of the *calçadão* and the street that goes back to the Villa. We position ourselves strategically so that we may spot Bobby in case he passes by.

I ask Yay if he has taken one of the pills, too. "Jesus, no," he says. "I don't touch those things anymore. Why do you think I'm giving them all away to you?"

We talk about beaches and bikinis and spandex. Karla rants about what she sees as the poor fashion sense of Brazilian women. "They don't know how to do *baggy*. All the clothes are tight and way too obvious." I emphatically deny that it's really a problem. As a matter of fact, there is an attractive black girl at the table across from us who looks awfully good in her tight, obvious outfit. We make eye contact a few times. I look away or she looks away, but our eyes cross again and again. I feel an automatic guilt about the flirtatious eye contact, but finally engage her directly, and this time, she doesn't look away.

"I'm gonna go and talk to this girl," I announce. Yay has rolled his pants up to his knees and is walking out in the ocean somewhere in the darkness, his first experience with the Atlantic. Karla and Knute seem to be sitting closer to each other every time that I look at them.

I walk over and sit down, somewhat surprised by my own confidence, but emboldened by her disarming eye contact and lazy smile. We talk, flirt. Her name is Gabriela; she is from the Catete neighborhood on the other side of the tunnel. My Portuguese is rusty but serviceable. The alcohol helps with the self-consciousness of stumbling through a conversation in another language. Gabriela and her cousin are having some beers and singing along to the old bossa nova songs being pumped out of the *barraca*. They are drinking their last beer and then plan to go home. Unless we are up to something good, of course. She asks quietly, "You don't have any . . . any cocaine? To keep going." She laughs awkwardly.

"No, but I have this . . ." I hand her the other pill from Yay.
"What is it?"

"It's like coffee, but better."

She takes it without asking anything else. A kindred spirit.

Yay comes back to the table. His jeans are wet and full of sand. "What happened to you?" we ask.

"I didn't think there'd be any waves out there. I thought the Atlantic was just a little ocean, but shit, mate, I got wrecked," Yay moans. "If that's nature, I can do without it." He wants to go back to the hostel and change. Knute and Karla are interested in returning to the hostel for other reasons. Bobby will have to fend for himself.

Once again, chivalry calls . . . and, as always, I answer. Gabriela and I walk her cousin to the bus, and I offer to chaperone Gabriela on further late-night adventures along the beach.

The next thing I know we are making out in the street and she is pulling violently on the back of my shirt, stretching the neck to twice its size, and biting at my tongue. I am sorry to say this is even before we have put her cousin on the bus. We bid the cousin farewell and go back along the beach to look for another party. My Portuguese is coming back to me, flowing, linking phrases—I feel an overall sense of well-being and confidence in my language abilities and my presence in general. I am a force to be reckoned with. We spot a crowd of about fifteen Brazilians circling one of the beer kiosks on the *calçadão*. Gabriela ends up talking to another guy for a long time, although it could just be for a minute or two. I am unsure. I guess that his Portuguese is better than mine. He has a better tan, too. I think about leaving. I need to move. Need to walk. I have work in the morning, don't I? At the last moment, Gabriela returns, grabs me by the hand, and leads me to the beach. She takes off her clothes down to her bra and underwear and asks if I want to go swimming with her. We leave all

of our valuables, wallet included, right at the end of Copacabana, hidden under one of the small rowboats on shore.

She asks if I have a condom. Of course I do. That is the responsible thing, and I am all about responsibility. "Bring it with
you," she commands. We swim a few yards out into the ocean
and start making out again, our mouths seasoned with salt water. Our legs tangle as we furiously tread water. She climbs into
an empty anchored rowboat and beckons me aboard.

There is no waiting. We get right to it as I pull off her wet
underwear and come down on her like the Mongol horde de-
scending from the hills. I have never been a big fan of speed. I
never had much of a tolerance for stimulants, not even coffee,
but sex on speed is a worthwhile experience. Tens of thousands
of gay men can't be wrong. It starts off like a nude Greco-
Roman grappling match and quickens its pace until it is not en-
tirely unlike watching porn in fast forward.

We try to stay low in the boat and not make too much
commotion, but lose track of our surroundings. We twist and
contort to accommodate ourselves between the two benches
that divide the bottom of the rowboat. She is aggressive, bor-
derline violent, and pushes and pulls at my face and shoulders,
scratching my back and even slapping me across the face.

I grip the oarlocks. I sense that my naked ass is rising and
falling above the edge of the boat and look over my shoulder to
see a group of senior citizens—in sweatsuits and running
shoes—who have paused in the middle of their early-morning
walk to figure out why there is a white ass rising and falling in
the boat. When they see me looking back at them, they start
clapping. Should I mention this to Gabriela or just run with it?
I opt for denial. Less responsible, but necessary under the
circumstances.

Just then, I see a man paddling up to the boat on a surfboard. I scramble to find my underwear, but it's too late—he
reaches over and grabs me by the ankle. "*Pôrra*. What the fuck
are you doing? This isn't a sex motel, it's my *boat*. *Que saco*."

We pull on our underwear and swim back in, with the irate boat owner following on his surfboard and keeping a close eye. The aged crowd watches from the shore. Fortunately all of our belongings are still under the overturned rowboat on the beach. The owner wants the equivalent of $50 to make up for the hourly rate in his vessel. Gabriela proves quite the astute negotiator and talks him down. He settles on a cold can of Skol. He is more than happy when a second beer is offered. We sit and drink with him and laugh about it. The fact that we were naked in his boat goes from shocking to acceptable to hilarious. He says, "*Puta que pareu*, I've owned that boat for years and am still waiting to have sex in it." He buys us a bag of microwaved popcorn. I buy another round of beers. The sun is fully up and I can feel my face starting to burn.

I walk Gabriela to the bus and get her phone number and a surprisingly sweet kiss good-bye. A perfect relationship: beginning, middle, and end without time for things to go wrong or get ugly. I think that I might love her.

I get back to the Villa and Inga is out. I lie in the room and unsuccessfully attempt to sleep for a few hours. The party starts again on the terrace in the middle of the afternoon. Inga is in the crowd, but refuses to look at me. I am going to need to move to a different room in the hostel, but first I have to use the bathroom. As I am taking a piss, I hear a groan and glance over my shoulder to notice a foot sticking out of the shower behind me. Slumped on the floor of the shower, behind the mildewed curtain, is Mr. Yay. He is unconscious with vomit all over his shirt and on the walls of the stall. He has a bloody nose and a nearly empty bottle of tequila between his legs. It is the kind of shower that you shouldn't use without flip-flops, but he seems fairly comfortable with his open mouth resting against the cool, blackened tiles.

I try to help him to his feet, but he is pure, limp body weight. I can barely keep myself upright at this point. I run into Knute and Karla. He puts his arm around me, beaming. "That girl was *foine*," he says, with his best put-on LA accent. It is good to have friends like Knute—he's the kind of person who will give moral support for your behavior, no matter how outlandish. I suspect that Karla finds my actions tactless and crass, mainly because she calls me "tactless and crass." I tell her that I was possessed by Eros, that it was hardly my fault. "You were possessed by amphetamine and alcohol," she answers. "It was all your fault." Good woman. Solid head on her shoulders. Knute and I track down Max and the three of us pull Yay from the shower and put him on his side in a lower bunk with a garbage can in front of his face.

I stumble back to the crowd, but am repulsed by the party, the people, the alcohol. Inga is smoking a cigarette and talking to some dude about some shit. She pretends that she doesn't see me at first but then confronts me by the door to our room. "You know I would have been worried about you if Karla hadn't told me that you were off with some whore woman," she says.

"I wasn't with a whore woman."

"It doesn't matter to me. I've met someone else, too."

"Congratulations."

"Are you wanting to know who he is?"

"Not really. Can I get by you to get in the room?"

"Sure, do what you want. You can go fuck yourself."

I go into the room and start organizing my stuff. I am going to move to a different room for the night. I should have chosen to stay in a dorm room in the first place. It is one thing getting involved with random women, but cohabitation with strangers is always a bad idea. First thing tomorrow, I'm going to the north, regardless of cost. I may have to max out my credit card, but I will get there. As I am folding clothes and transfering them from the armoire to my backpack, Inga barrels through the door. There's a sinister smile on her face; her presence fills the room.

"Where do you think that you're going?" She laughs.

"I think it's pretty clear that we're not working out. I've gotta go. I'm not even supposed to be in Rio right now."

"Good. I came to tell you that I met somebody else."

"You already told me that."

"Fredrick and I have spent the whole day together on the beach, not that you noticed. He is more of a real man. More my type of man."

"Am I supposed to know who Fredrick is?"

"Yeah, he is from Australia. You were with him last night on the beach."

"Mr. Yay? His name's *Fredrick*? Yeah, I'm happy for you two. He's a catch." I continue to pack feverishly.

"You know what's wrong with you?"

"No. Please tell me."

"You think that the world is all about you, you and your dumb, little problems. And then you just act cool, so cool, like nothing matters, but you're just a little boy running from your problems, and running from being an adult."

"Thanks for the psychoanalysis. Are you OK with me staying here in the same hostel for the night or would you prefer that I go elsewhere?"

"If you stay here . . . I might beat you." Her eyes are glassy, maniacal. She smells of tequila.

"*OK*. Well, how about the money that I loaned you before I go? I'm sure that *Fredrick* can help you now, and I really need it so that I can get my work done."

She laughs again, raising her voice, "Forget it. What are you going to do? Nothing. You asshole."

"You're absolutely right. Nothing."

Minutes before, I had come across most of the cash in the closet while I was packing my things. It is now in my front pocket. I figured that I'd ask if she would pay me back. If she said "yes," I was going to let her keep it, but if she tried to play tough, it'd be mine. She gave me a pretty clear answer.

"I thought that you were going to be different, that this was a new start. You're just as bad as my last boyfriend. I don't know why I'm even surprised."

"I'm sorry to disappoint you. I'm not even your boyfriend. Listen, I had no intention—"

"Are you a lawyer now? Just so cool. Like this is nothing."

My packing job is hasty and disorganized. There is nothing that I hate more than to have a disorganized backpack. I push on the top of the pack to try to fit in the remaining shoes, notebooks, and clothes. "I knew I shouldn't have gotten involved with a twenty-two-year-old," I mutter.

That does it. Time for my beating to commence. An arcing haymaker demonstrates her displeasure over the dissolution of our relationship. It catches me square in the eye—a far superior shot to my favor for the Doctor. The second one misses and the third lands awkwardly, though not painlessly, on my cheek. I fall back on the bed and she straddles me, readying herself to punch again, but I get her by the wrists.

"Get your fucking hands off of me, LET GO OF ME!" she screams.

"You just punched me in the face. I'll let go when you calm down."

"What are you going to do, hit me? COME ON, FUCKING HIT ME."

"I AM NOT going to hit you."

"FUCKING HIT ME!" she screams again, her eyes rolling up and back in her head in some sort of alcohol-and-adrenaline–induced psychotic trance. I am ready for the whole hostel to charge the room and drag me out into the street for perceived domestic abuse, philandering, theft, deficiency of character, and poor moral standing.

Technically speaking, I am a feminist in so much as I believe men and women are equal. If a woman is going to throw

closed-fisted punches in your face, I would say that it's discrim-
inatory not to defend yourself, if not retaliate. Males tend to
have superior upper body strength, but this female was bred on
schnitzel and *Weissbier* and is a good two inches taller than I
am. However, I do realize that I'm the one who drove this situation to a head, and also that I do not want to end up in a
Brazilian prison. Moreover, I prefer not to punch anyone, particularly stewardesses, except as an absolute last resort. I keep
a grip on her wrists for a few more seconds, until I can feel her
adrenaline subside. I grab my backpack, unfastened and spilling over, and run for the front door.

Though skipped over in the movie version of *The Beach*, much
of Alex Garland's famed travel novel is about a young man's
search for authenticity outside of his own culture. The narrator, Richard, admits that he wants to observe harsh poverty
abroad. He wants to see something raw and primal, something
that you can't experience in a culture of insurance, HMOs, and
welfare. *The Beach* is also a critique of modern "guidebook"
travel, and the narrator seeks in vain to find a utopia, a place
culturally uncontaminated by other tourists. However, Garland's narrator has almost no contact with Thai people beyond
being offered "banan' pancakes" during breakfast in hostels.
He meets up with two French backpackers and heads off to a
national park to immerse himself in a commune of like-minded
Westerners whose idea of roughing it includes a Nintendo
Game Boy, an endless supply of weed, and a motorboat.

But I understand what happens to Richard and many other
backpackers: it's an easy trap to fall into. You go to another
country and rather than trying to understand the nuances and
textures of that culture, you end up spending your time with a
roving band of people like yourself. Fuck the whole backpacker

scene. Even the people who consider themselves master travelers, who have been to hostels all over the world, are often just neocolonial naïfs. They just want to find a destination where they can stretch their dollar, euro, yen, or shekel into affordable hotels, more beers or easy-to-find drugs, or bragging rights for having done something more extreme or more intense or more authentic than their friends. That pretty much describes the scene here and I am glad to be making a quick exit.

On the way out the door of the Villa, I run past a tall, dark Brazilian woman dressed in a white skirt, white tam, and sleeveless shirt. She's attractive, with long, slender limbs and chocolate skin that glows under the bare bulb on the front porch.

"What's the rush, *maluco*?" she asks while picking up one of the shoes that I dropped.

"Female issues."

"Did you cheat on her?" she asks, narrowing her eyes.

"No. Well, I mean, yes, I did. Kind of." I feel a sudden contempt radiating from her, summoned empathetically from the sisterhood of wronged women. "But you don't understand, see, I only knew her for about a day and we didn't really have much in common and I met a nice Brazilian girl and then we got in an argument and then she punched me in the head."

"Punched you? Did she give you all those bruises?"

"No. Those are from a friend of mine."

"I see."

"It's been a bad few days."

"She wasn't Brazilian, was she?"

"Austria . . . uh, from Austria."

She gives me a quizzical look.

"I don't know the word in Portuguese . . . a gringa."

She relaxes. "Brazilians are jealous and like to make a little drama, drama like on *telenovelas*, this I know. But when you gringos make drama, it is always big drama, fights, wars."

"We try to keep it interesting."

"Why interesting? We don't need more interesting here. We have enough violence, poverty, and drugs. But we deal with it. We cope. Gringos, you have everything, but you like to make things crazy." She smiles.

"Human nature, I guess."

"No, I think gringo nature is different. America is good to make money, but I've seen your movies and TV, all serial killers and rapists and rapist killers and baby rapist killers, and they need special science detectives to solve all of it. I'd rather just stay in Rio and get killed by a stray bullet. I'm from the Northeast. We have our problems, too, but it is a lot more relaxed. I'm going back soon."

"Where to?"

"Recife. I have some modeling work to do up there."

"Really?" I ask, intrigued. I've certainly had enough women on my hands for one night, but this one seems particularly interesting. "I am going to either Fortaleza or Recife tomorrow. Wherever I can get a flight. Let's try to cross paths."

We hurriedly exchange email addresses. She walks out to the sidewalk with me, helps me to get my stuff into a cab, pats me on the head, and advises me to stay away from gringas in the future.

A taxi driver and I cover practically every block of Copacabana, checking out every hotel that I can possibly afford. There is some sort of festival this weekend, a last gasp of Carnaval. Because of this, affordable hotels with vacancy are as elusive as a competent English orthodontist. I finally settle on Motel Caligula. With a steady stream of visitors in and out of the door, it must have some vacancy, and it looks shabby enough to actually fit in my price range.

"Do you want the deluxe or the simple room?" the matronly receptionist asks me.

"How much?"

"It's all per hour. If you want to stay for the whole night, you have to pay per hour until checkout. You can only stay overnight in a deluxe." The nightly fee is the equivalent of $90, much more than I'd like to spend. However, given the night's events, this is clearly an emergency, and a time to use my credit card. I go into my backpack to get the card from its hiding place in with my socks.

No credit card.

I check again.

I check three times.

Touché. Inga was more crafty that I thought. She must have grabbed it right before I repossessed my money from her.

I fork over my remaining cash and receive the key with a rolling pin–sized Doric column attached to the key ring. My room smells of bleach and has a round bed with a single white sheet, a television with four channels of pornography, a mir-rored ceiling, and a sunken shower with a heart-shaped red soap. I am hesitant to put my head on the off-white pillowcases, which smell like the head sweat of an old wool baseball hat.

I opt instead to walk down to the beach and clear my mind. I make a quick international call from a pay phone to cancel my credit card. The pristine beauty of the Atlantic Ocean under moonlight cleanses my soul. I breathe the fresh air, let my toes dig into the sand, and soak in the natural splendor. I bring all this drama on myself, I decide. The universe is still inherently good, and with more prudent behavior on my part, all will be fine. I smile at a couple of kids walking toward me along the beach. How good, pure, and uncomplicated it is to be young.

I look to my side and notice what appears to be a homeless man working on about five grams of cocaine, the white lines jaggedly laid out on a torn square of cardboard. It is a shame for the kids to see that, for it to corrupt their innocence, their optimistic ideas about life. The kids get closer to the man. Be-fore I can say anything, they start talking with him and then tearing into his huge lines of blow. For a few minutes I watch them put it away as if they were in the '86 Mets dugout.

One of the shortest kids, maybe nine years old, wears a hat made out of a balloon animal (yes, like a clown makes at a birthday party). He walks over to me with a plastic garbage bag full of empty cans and asks if I'd like to learn some capoeira. He takes a drag off the open end of a one-liter Pepsi bottle that has an inch or so of clear liquid sloshing around the bottom. I tell him that I already know some capoeira, that I had started practicing the martial art a few years back when I lived in California. The poor kid. I decide to humor him. We do a *ginga*, the basic step of capoeira. The right foot moves back and the left arm comes up to protect the face. Then the right foot returns forward and the left foot goes back with the right arm up for defense. The kid doesn't know what he is doing and looks pretty much as you'd expect a shirtless nine-year-old on cocaine and paint thinner with a yellow balloon hat to look.

"Is that a dog on your head, little man?" I ask.

"No, it's a giant puma robot. Now you have to buy me a beer."

"How about a soda?"

"Beer or five reais for the capoeira class. Now."

"Buy the kid a drink, you fucking Yankee," someone says from behind me in English. I turn to see Bobby, slouched over a table with half a dozen or so empty cans of Brahma in front of him.

"Let's drink to the pursuit of the new American dream—getting the fuck out of America," Bobby announces, as he cracks open a fresh can of Brahma and hands it to me.

I outline the Inga debacle for him and he laments, "I don't know what to do about women. I really don't. You want them; they don't want you. They want you; you don't want them. People want to dominate or be dominated, that's it. Fuck all this love, caring, and satisfaction crap. I should never get involved with girls anyways; they don't fit in with my lifestyle."

I tell him that I'd heard that vending machines and romance were a tough mix.

"You are too much of an American, my friend. It's about thinking *outside* of the box. Do you really think that all I do is sell Cheetos from vending machines? Does that seem to you like the highest pinnacle that I could climb to?"

I give him some everything-has-its-own-relative-value speech that I'd gleaned from being a social sciences student at a liberal arts college . . . success is a matter of—perspective . . . it all depends on what you want out of life . . . the usual.

"Ya know, dude, I may not look it, but I'm thirty-seven. What do you think I'm doing staying in a shitty backpacker hostel?"

"Meeting young Filipina photojournalists. I mean, that's an acceptable reason—for me, anyways."

"No. I'm scouting new markets."

"Like what?"

"Think outside of the box. What do you think?"

"I dunno, dude . . . vending machines in hostels?"

"Try again."

"Chain youth hostels? No, wait, international phone cards?"

"Getting colder."

"Amateur porn?"

"I've dabbled in that, but there are generally poor profit margins. No, man, I'm a professional entrepreneur, like an artist, except business is my medium. The main creative venue that I've been developing is the business of MDMA."

"You sell ecstasy?"

"Look, I'm no fucking college-campus dealer or the dude in the corner at a rave. *I'm taking this shit global*," he answers. "I have sellers all over. The entire middle level of the trade can be handled efficiently by mail and email. The pills look like any other pills, not much different from Tylenol. Dogs aren't trained to sniff for them and they sure as fuck can't catch them in the millions of parcels coming through the mail every day. You only have a fraction of the competition that you find in the coke market, plus a more polite clientele, and less dangerous people involved in distribution. Half of the drug gangs in the favela here, like the ones who run the coke trade, have never seen a hit of E in their lives. Not yet, anyway."

"But the margins can't be that great. You can't charge twenty bucks a pill to people in Rio or in Santiago like you can in the States, you know? Can you?" I ask, though I am unsure of the precise definition of *margins*.

"I have no interest in selling to the public here. Expats and backpackers, they're my market; they eat the shit up and will pay as much as they would at home, if not more. Backpackers will spend all day hunting for a hostel that is ten dollars instead of fourteen, but will gladly throw down cash for a grip of pills, the chance to roll their face off in some waterfall with a few Swedish chicks or whatever. Good drugs are something that people will always splurge for when traveling. It's part of the experience-of-a-lifetime mentality. You see, my market is the Gringo Trail. You know, the Lonely Planet crowd."

"Dude, are you rolling right now? I can barely see any white in your eyes."

"Maybe I am, but that's beside the point." He orders four more beers from the *barraca*. "What I have is a niche market for what is still a relatively high-demand, low-supply pharmaceutical here in Latin America. I don't want it to get too big. I want it to stay a nice, manageable, inconspicuous size. I don't personally sell this shit at all. I hand-select people who can communicate with travelers, people who know their world, so the customer isn't scared that they're gonna get stabbed or ripped off or whatever. I'm here in Rio looking for representatives . . . so to speak. I'm establishing franchises, taking a page out of the Howard Johnson handbook."

Bobby isn't wearing a linen suit. There's no Jan Hammer soundtrack in the background. He is more like the skinny, agitated guy in an old Beastie Boys T-shirt by the refrigerator at a house party ranting about the decline of popular music.

"So, the girl, then?" I ask. "She was out of left field, huh?"

"A man's got to balance somewhat of a personal life, too. The falling-in-love part has got to go, though. Fuck it, dude. Thomas, you seem like a good listener and a reasonably smart guy. Let me break it down for you: I fly to Amsterdam a few times per year and get the stuff in bulk straight from the chemists—very civilized, educated, and nice people; friends of mine, none of the mujahideen or Shining Path thugs that you have to deal with at the source of heroin or cocaine. I sell in midsized batches to my representatives at ten bucks a pill—or less, depending on the quantity—and they can resell for whatever they want. I'm on my way to holding down the backpacker scene in Santiago, Rio, and Buenos Aires. I might also go for Cuzco, but there are a lot of Israelis and Frenchies already doing business up there. I'm not gonna fuck with São Paulo 'cause there just aren't enough travelers and it's too big of a clusterfuck."

I watch as he grinds his jaw, flexing it back and forth, and ask more about his distribution process from Santiago.

"All mail, dude. I'd never cross a border with so much as a single pill. Never. I mail all of the shit from Amsterdam to Santiago and make sure that it clears safely into my warehouse before I set foot in Chile again. If there's any problem, I just set up my home base elsewhere. That's basically what happened with Seoul, though it was really a little more complicated than that. I have no attachment to Chile beyond the vending-machine business, which is really just a nice way to launder cash that requires minimal work on my part. As for the communications aspect of my job, I set up email accounts under fake names and then my representatives ask me to send them prints of photographs from some trip or another. I know that you young fuckers just email photos around, but I am still a print photo man. A photograph is twenty-five pills. Four photos are a hundred pills. Doubles of four photos are two hundred, and on up as you like."

"What do you pack them in—coffee grounds or dryer sheets or something?"

"It's not weed or coke, man, that's the beauty of it. I use FedEx envelopes with the pills stuck to a page in rows, like those colored candy buttons that kids eat. The FedEx package looks like an envelope with photos in it. Sometimes a few of the pills do get cracked or smashed, but you can just powder the pills and then put them in empty gel caps. I don't recommend it, but you can cut them then with ephedrine, cornstarch, or baby laxative, you know, whatever."

He pauses a moment and then starts to emotionally downshift, his eyes increasingly tense. "I mean, honestly though, Thomas, what is wrong with that girl? What is wrong with me? We could have been good together."

"I'm here for you, man. At least she didn't kick your ass. Look at my face."

"You already looked like that."

"Well, it's worse now. It's a nice reminder of why I can't be getting mixed up with girls, either. I may not be building an international ecstasy ring or anything, but I am trying to write the definitive guidebook to Brazil."

"*I can tell*. You look busy, man. Fuck it, stick around here and we can make more money together than you could make writing a thousand guidebooks. Seriously, look at this town, how sensual it is. It's got the music, the beaches, the women, even some decent DJs. It might be the best potential market for ecstasy on the planet, and it is just taking off now. Stay down here. Travel guidebooks will be completely replaced by the Internet in a year or two anyways. Goddamn waste of time if you ask me."

"Dude, I've never sold anything in my life, except, like, bags of mixed nuts for the Cub Scouts. I mean, I don't have a personal problem with what you're doing, but I am more or less philosophically opposed to sales. It's just not in my character. And I'm already working, I mean I haven't earned anything yet, and I haven't actually written anything yet, but I am trying to become a travel writer, you know? I've got crazy shit to do in the Northeast. I've got to get on the road."

"First off, young man, you're still cranked. You need to slow down and start taking better care of yourself. Second, Thomas, my friend: selling illegal things is much easier than selling bags of mixed nuts. As a matter of fact, illegal things practically sell themselves. You're here, right now in Rio. Enjoy it. Hang out. Why do you have to rush off?"

Bobby shakes my hand with a crushing two-hand grip. His hands are slender but his hazy, drug-fueled sense of solidarity is commanding. He squeezes with sweaty palms, not wanting to let go, letting the faux empathy of MDMA pump through his cranium and down into his hands. He looks deep into my skull. "We're gonna have us some fun."

I am usually good at sleeping on a plane and have fully mastered the head-down-on-the-tray technique, but on this flight, I am unable to sleep. Creeping paranoia. Gnawing anxiety. Impending diarrhea. These are all factors.

Although Bobby never did convince me to join in his life of crime and entrepreneurship, he did convince me to stick around for enough drinks that I don't remember returning to the motel. I do know that the sun was up when I bid him farewell. I wandered back to the Caligula, gathered my belongings, and wasted no time in getting a cab straight to the airport. It was either that or wake up three years down the line, living on a bunk in the Villa Copacabana, talking about the old days of backpacking and wearing bits of last night's eyeliner.

I made it to the airport as the rest of the city was just starting to wake up and, after some hectic negotiation, was able to drum up a standby ticket for a flight to the midsized Brazilian city of Fortaleza. My territory for the book runs from Recife north and then east along the coast to São Luís. Fortaleza is right in the middle. I thought it would be nice to establish a base there and explore the surrounding region, instead of doing it as a straight trip, which would entail far too many trips inland and ultimately screw up my itinerary. I can store my papers, extra gear, and whatnot in Fortaleza and won't have to schlep everything with me. Plus, I've been there once before.

The flight shouldn't be taking this long. The plane has already made two stops along the way—passenger pickups, like a school bus. These delays, combined with my time trying to hustle the ticket at the airport, paying in cash, and waiting a few hours for departure, have turned the trip into a whole-day affair. The first time that the flight descended for a stop at a smaller airport, I was convinced that we were making some sort of emergency landing. There was a swamp or a desert or something below the plane for as far as the eye could see. We were fucked. I tried to get control of the pounding of my heart. Instead of my doomsday scenario, we simply swapped some passengers and took off again. I should have known better, as I have been on flights with stages before. But it mattered little, as this time we were heading right into a fierce-looking storm front. The guy next to me had a manicure and was drinking *cachaça*. The smell of the raw alcohol was going to make me rip open the emergency door and hurl myself out of the plane, even if we didn't crash. So, I opted to hide in the bathroom.

Someone knocks on the bathroom door from time to time.

Someone asks me in English if I am "OK in there?" No sir, I am not. I lean forward and rest my forehead against the coolness of the mirror. I peel off my sweat-drenched shirt and wash my face and chest down with lukewarm water from the minisink. I try to blot myself dry with rough paper towels from the dispenser, but the water has run down my sides and saturated the waistband of my boxers and the top of my jeans. I roll up toilet paper and stick it between the elastic and my skin. That should do the trick.

In the lavatory, I stare at myself in the mirror and shake my head: laughing, just staring. My pupils are dilated and I can see every pore in my face, every capillary in the bloody whites of my eyes, every protruding hair that is where it shouldn't be. There are bits of sand on my scalp, bits of sand between my toes. The bruises are a plum purple, set against a pinkish sunburn that has declared victory over my nose and cheeks.

unamoscaenmisopa@_____.com is scrawled across the back of my hand in ballpoint. For those who no speaka the Spanish, that's: aflyinmysoup@_____.com. The blue ink bleeds out into tiny azure starfish that pool in my pores and hair follicles. Bobby made me promise to commit his email address to memory and not share it with anyone else. He told me not to write it down, but I guess I don't trust my memory much at this point.

Shortly after midnight, the plane touches down at Fortaleza's airport. It is not the open-air tropical airport that I remember arriving in back in 1996. There is a food court. There is duty-free. Car-rental kiosks. Tourist offices. A roof. Should I introduce myself at the tourist office? Will they know who I am? The office is closed, so I will have to announce my arrival at a later date.

I spring for a taxi into town as there is no way in hell that

I am going to screw with public transportation at this hour—
particularly in my panicked state of hollow-screaming-
staggering-drooling exhaustion. Minutes from the airport,
Fortaleza reveals itself beyond the façade of modernity at the
terminal. The taxi rolls along partially completed highways and
above nondescript neighborhoods of low, boxy buildings. In the
distance is another enclave of development: a knot of glassy
high-rises, whose glittering upper balconies show a city aspiring to climb out of the morass of Third World urban sprawl.
Tourist dollars at work. I can't help but think of Miami or
Puerto Rico a generation back.

Fortunately, I was able to finagle a discount at a decent hotel near Meireles Beach. After a couple of quick phone calls
that I made while waiting for my flight at the airport in Rio, an
old friend put me in touch with his Brazilian friend whose family runs a tour agency out of Salvador. He hooked me up with a
reservation at a reliable business hotel. I will be staying under
the "friends and family" discount. Though I fantasize about
press junkets and free hotel rooms, Lonely Planet has a stated
policy that their writers can't accept discounts or freebies. The
reputation of the brand is authority and integrity. This point
runs as a Publisher's Note in the front of each book:

> Why is our travel information the best in the world?
> It's simple: our authors are independent dedicated
> travelers. They don't research using just the Internet
> or phone, and they don't take freebies in exchange for
> positive coverage. They travel widely, to all the popu-
> lar spots and off the beaten track. They personally visit
> thousands of hotels, restaurants, cafés, bars, galleries,
> palaces, museums and more—and they take pride in
> getting all the details right, and telling it how it is.

I figure that accepting that discount through a friend has
nothing to do directly with my affiliation with LP and is there-

fore within the rules. It won't really affect my all-important sense of objectivity. My financial situation is already bleak and this discount will help immensely. Furthermore, the hotel can be my initial base of operations, and from there I will figure out the next stage of this project.

I arrive at the reinforced, gated door of the hotel and the night watchman checks me in. The small lobby is covered with tiny blue square tiles, the type usually reserved for a bathroom floor. The ceiling has some sort of carpeting on it.

The watchman says that there is no reservation for me and that he doesn't think that there are rooms available. I plead that he checks the files, the computer. There must be a note about my arrival.

There is nothing.

I wanted to do all of this undercover as Lonely Planet suggests, but will resort to using the ace up my sleeve if necessary. "I am actually the writer for Lonely Planet and am going to be writing about Fortaleza and about hotels in Fortaleza. Do you think that maybe you could check again? This is pretty important." This is a touristy town and the LP book is the definitive guide; it can make or break many hotels. I know this and he knows this. I stare him in the eyes.

I don't want to lose my objectivity on this particular hotel, but sometimes arms need to be twisted, or at least the hotel needs to know who they are dealing with. At this level of over-tiredness, I have extenuating circumstances. I await his response, his apology, my room.

He looks at me with heavily lidded, red eyes, "Never heard of it. What is it?"

"It's a guidebook and is very important to the tourism industry."

"Well, I can probably arrange a room for you if you come

up with a gratuity for me. Or you can go elsewhere. But I don't recommend walking around here by yourself at night. Either way, I'll need to discuss with the manager tomorrow about a longer stay."

I awake from my slumber to a horrific ringing. It is Marilyn on the telephone and I am still in the conference room on the fifty-seventh floor. THERE ARE SPREADSHEETS TO BE DONE.

No . . . it's the front desk at the hotel. It is already check-out time. My clock says 9:00 a.m. This can't be. I only just started to get some sleep. Why, dear God? I would give my left testicle to be able to stay in this bed. I tell them to just charge me for another night. They tell me that a business group is arriving from Teresina and that they need my room. They have reservations.

I ask to speak with the manager.

He is the manager.

"I have a reservation," I plead. I am even supposed to have a discount. "I don't mean to be immodest, but I'm the writer that they were told was going to be arriving. I'm the one who works for *Lonely Planet*."

"We don't give discounts except for groups of three or more, or long-term stays. Are you sure that you are at the correct hotel?"

I can't handle any drama or confrontation at this point. I tell him that I'll be out by eleven. I make the instant coffee with the little coffeepot in the room. This will probably be the last time that I have this much luxury on the trip, and I'm going to take full advantage of it. I flip on the television and watch a presenter in a full-denim outfit with a Portuguese Don Pardo voice. He simultaneously talks about Jesus, advertises mobile phones, and has audience members sing karaoke of Brazilian pop songs while flanked by a row of gyrating women in thong bikinis. The women have their faces painted like cats, complete with pasted-on whiskers. Maybe I can learn from this. Does this show encapsulate the contemporary Brazilian experience? What does it all mean?

I sip my instant coffee on the balcony and then organize and repack my bag. Stuck inside a box of Trojans, I find my recently canceled credit card. I remember now that I hid it in there, just in case Inga tried to grab it from me. Maybe she wasn't so crafty, after all. The details are cloudy, but it is clear that I fucked myself, fucked myself real good. I look at a rusted amusement park across the street and three blocks down to a mostly obstructed view of the beach. The breeze is damp and salty. The amusement park queues Britney Spears's "Toxic" for the second time in a row on its loudspeakers, while screaming kids bounce on the orange inflatable moonwalk crowned with a giant inflated lion head. I finish the coffee and vow that from this point on, I am turning the corner on this project.

Following the last version of the LP book, I will go to Iracema Beach. I'll find a decent place that I can check into on a weekly rate and get on with my life. According to the book, Iracema is the city's traditionally bohemian quarter. Once home to poets and intellectuals, it is now a hangout for backpackers with a lovely beachfront promenade that comes alive at night. The guidebook promises decent hotels and hostels and a friendly vibe. I remember partying there at night when I was last in town, but don't remember much else.

I walk to Avenida Beira Mar (Seashore Avenue) and stagger down the length of it towards Iracema, doing battle with the morning heat. I am keenly aware of the friction and sweat between my skin and my backpack. On the edge of Iracema, near thermal breakdown, I seek shelter in a shop to eat a bowl of *açaí*, the dark purplish Amazonian berry that is prepared to look a bit like a black Slurpee. It is pulped, frozen, blended with a jolt of guarana syrup, sometimes some banana or other fruit and—at least in these parts—served in a bowl lightly topped with granola. The flavor is sweet, hearty, and rejuvenating. Complementing the caffeine from the guarana, the *açaí* startles me into consciousness with a frigid pulse through my teeth and into my frontal lobes. I lean forward in the chair and attempt to let the back of my shirt dry.

I soldier on to Iracema and wander through the neighborhood and down to the metal pier that extends out from the beachfront. I watch a few surfers ride the muddy beachbreaks that roll alongside the pier and then start the hotel search on foot. Am I at the wrong beach? Did the other writer visit here in the last twenty years? Are you fucking kidding me? Milton Dias and Luís Assunção last drank and penned poetry here in the 1950s, which leaves about a half century for this place to become a rotten tourist ghetto. Imagining Iracema Beach as a welcoming bohemian corner of Fortaleza is like pretending that the present-day Haight-Ashbury doesn't have a Gap and bands of panhandling, meth-addled teenagers.

Iracema is named after José de Alencar's nineteenth-century Indianist novel. The novel is named after Alencar's protagonist: the beautiful, innocent Tabajara princess Iracema, meaning "honey lips" (possibly also an anagram for *America*), who marries the Portuguese conqueror Martim and gives birth to the first true Brazilian, a child named Moacir.

Iracema was the first book that I read in comparative literature class as a grad student in Latin American Studies. I guess that I had higher expectations for the book's namesake. Poor José. He was trying to tell an optimistic story of what was to come for Brazil. He seems to have passed along his idealism to the last Lonely Planet writer who came through here, but nobody else.

Within a few minutes I take in some of the highlights of the area: Rats on the beach. Teenage hookers in spandex. Old Italian dockworkers apparently on package sex tours. Block-sized themed nightclubs drowning in beer-company advertisements. I can't deal with this right now.

The popular beach towns at Jericoacoara or Canoá Quebrada are both within a day's trip from town. I can head straight for the bus station and be in one of them by nightfall. At a smaller beach town, I can find refuge among the sand and the freaks. No, I want to get away from the freaks, the backpackers. Maybe I'll go to a village up the coast where there is no tourism: a quaint fishing village with dunes and a pastel-colored colonial church, a town where the single guesthouse is quiet and the owners have an attractive daughter with mocha skin, a clean smile, and a strong back. No, I need to stay put and work. Fortaleza is the lynch-pin city of this region. I will stay here and figure out what I am doing and how I am supposed to do it, and then venture farther afield, when I am properly armed to do the job. I need refuge to establish a base of operations.

I am taking notes on all of this in my journal. Standing on the street corner, I write:

> Sweating badly. Need help. Need sleep. Need to know what I am supposed to be doing. Fortaleza = 3rd world Daytona.
>
> Alencar was wrong, except for the whole thing about Europeans fornicating with local women.
>
> Beaches now populated by chubby tourist conquistadors from São Paulo gorging themselves on beer, fries, and breast implants.
>
> Did the last LP writer actually visit any of these places?
>
> Why am I here? Was Manhattan so bad?

I am in no position to be picky. Not now. I find a budget hotel that isn't listed in the current LP book. It will maximize my research efficiency if I stay in a place that isn't already reviewed. Then, at least, I'll have the confidence to add something new to the book. I need to add something, anything. It's the third day—or is it the fourth?—and I've yet to be productive.

The room in the hostel is small and basic with a locked metal window that once opened to the street. One wall is a huge system of drawers and closets; the other wall has a twin bed with a foam mattress. It is not quite what I had hoped for, but I am relieved to have four walls and a place to put down my pack.

I can make some progress on my writing in this room. I can organize my chapters, learn the guidebook formatting system, and start to knock out the writing. I'll research by day and write by night. This may just work after all. I look forward to my first evening of writing and decent sleep and now have the peace of mind that I can stay put for a bit. Sometimes it is best to have the decisions made for you, to not be running back and forth in your own head. Having too many options is draining.

While I am tempted to sleep for the rest of the day, I decide to go out, recaffeinate, and get some work done. I am too tired to really research or write, but there are plenty of other things that I need to do first anyhow. I throw back a few coffees and spend the better part of the afternoon seated in a rattan chair at a Cuban-themed café. Eventually, I will write about this place, I decide. I take notes and call it "real," say that it has "character" and a "cool, airy ambience" and dig for other clichés. But I can't get ahead of myself. I must learn what I am supposed to do and how I am supposed to do it. I pore over stacks of printed pages of the various files that I have for the Lonely Planet project. There are hundreds of pages of reader's letters, random emails sent in over the past four years that I must sift through to determine what applies to my areas and what is worth checking up on. Many of the letters have to do with the likes of restaurants in Colombia, a hostel that stiffed someone on an exchange rate in Chile, and a whole bunch of stuff mixed in from the general customer service email in-box. Some are helpful and suggest gems of hotels or restaurants that the writer should check out, but the majority are inane complaints about random hotels, screeds about the out-of-date material in the guidebook, or long, pleading letters asking for a writing position at LP.

Lonely Planet has come up with a new format for this series of books. We must reformat all of the old text into the new style. I had no idea how to use the old style, but there is some new template called Felix that works as an overlay in Microsoft Word, and I am supposed to figure out what takes a Heading 3 or a Heading 4, a light list, a list A, a practicality font, or a Point of Interest (POI). I won't even start to explain about the new mapping guidelines.

This will not be a typical update, as in: Is this restaurant still in business? Are these hotel rates the same? Is this new hostel worth including? No, this will be a complete overhaul of the content; a repositioning of the importance of different sections of the book. A new style for reviews, introductions, practicality listings, accommodations icons. This won't be like sitting down to write *The Sun Also Rises* in Brazil, it'll be like sitting down to write sixty thousand words in HTML code for a travel website. I can hear my heartbeat in my ears and feel that now-familiar sensation of my hopes crumbling around me.

The more that I read, the more proposed changes that I discover. The chapter introductions need to be retargeted, rewritten, improved. The boxed texts need to be replaced. The focus of the entire book needs to be recalibrated. While Lonely Planet was once aimed at backpackers, the new primary market is American and British couples who hold full-time jobs, on a two- to three-week vacation. Yet we still need to appeal to the backpacker base, and the odd top-end traveler (often the former backpacker who is now a business professional, but still likes to travel in an independent manner), meaning that I need to research and write about attractions and destinations that are appropriate for each type of travel, including different classes of hostels, resorts, B and Bs, buses, car rentals, charter flights, ride shares, and more.

Lonely Planet would like 20 percent of the coverage going to budget, 60 percent to midrange, and 20 percent to top-end. I also need to keep in mind what a solo female traveler would want, what a disabled traveler would want, what a gay/lesbian/bisexual/transgender traveler would want, what a vegetarian or vegan would want, and I need to be sensitive to not write with a particularly American point of view. The company does not think that this will dilute the content or voice of the book. As it stands, the last edition is about 70 percent budget hotels and restaurants. There are almost no Internet cafés, websites, or email addresses listed. The prices are all severely dated.

I try to calm myself down. It will all be OK. It's just a steep learning curve. I leave the café and walk around the neighborhood for a while, trying to get a better feel for the layout and trying to convince myself that I will get the hang of this project. Eventually I am able to bend my stress into motivation. I am so overcome by purpose and ambition that I forgo dinner and march back to my hostel. Papers are organized, important things are noted, some even highlighted, and the laptop is switched on. I will study the appropriate PDFs and learn Felix and may even write some of the chapter introductions if I am so moved. All I need is to get my heart rate down, finish another hour or two of this studying, and start putting words on the page.

An hour passes and I am really hitting my stride, taking it all in and starting to get a glimpse of the big picture. I hear a crashing noise near the front of the building. A man enters the boardinghouse, shouts something unintelligible in slurred Portuguese, and slams the door behind him. He walks into the neighboring room. I can hear him as clearly as if he were next to me: his footsteps, him spitting on the floor. I hear his bed creak as he lies down and then I hear him fart, cough, spit some more, and fade off into a steady snore.

What the fuck? I get close to the wall with the closets and realize that it is not a wall at all, but rather a stand-alone shelving unit used to divide a single room into two. A curtain covers the distance from the top of the closet to the ceiling. My new roommate pauses with the snoring, rolls over, clears his throat, and starts snoring again.

I have stayed in some messed-up places while on the road before: crabs in the shower drain, bats shitting on my sheets, my bed folding in half in the middle of the night, a rat in my backpack—you name it—but it is all that much less tolerable when you are trying to work.

I have approximately three sentences down on the page when the light in my room flickers and then goes out. I use the battery-powered light of my laptop screen to find the door to my room. A quick look into the hallway proves that the whole building has blacked out.

This is a sign. I shut off my computer, cover my head with the pillow, and sleep for the next twelve hours. So much for day three—or was it four?

A Day in the Life

I am rarely lonely or depressed when I travel alone—except when I first wake up in the morning. My eyes adjust to the surroundings and I try to figure out where I am and what I'm doing there. One white ceiling with cracked paint is the same as the next. It is also a point in the day when I have too much space to reflect on the events that have led me to where I am, and to think about what else I could be doing with my life. It can take me an hour or more to get the motivation to get out of bed and reintroduce myself to whatever mayhem lies on the other side of the door.

This morning, the last few hours in bed are an attempt to put off facing the overwhelming heat of the day. The liter of water that I keep at arm's length while sleeping is long gone. My dehydration eventually forces me from bed and from my stewing depression. I take a quick shower, dry off, and am instantaneously drenched in sweat again.

I manage to wrap the small, rough towel around my waist and tie it by the tips of two corners. Sitting on the edge of the bed, I read the Fortaleza chapter of the last LP again and try to understand the information and the city as a whole, try to get a sense of what this town is about. Why would someone want to visit this town? Why—beyond being a major city—does it deserve precious column inches in this book and such a prominent spot on the Lonely Planet trail? I haven't been here in years, but I do sense that it's been some time since the chapter received a proper overhaul.

OK. So I guess it's time that I give it one. I tear out the guidebook pages that pertain to Fortaleza and carefully slice out the city map using the nail file on my fingernail clippers. I hate to be the gawking tourist, stumbling down the street with a whole guidebook in hand—those people are amateurs.

I pull it together and start to feel excited about my first full day of research. I dress in a guayabera, loose-fitting shorts, a pair of leather flip-flops, and tinted Persol aviator glasses: my work uniform. The clothes are baggy enough that they don't cling in the heat and have enough pockets to hold all of my papers, pens, and notebook. I wear a bathing suit under the shorts, just in case I end up at the beach.

It is time for what will become my morning ritual. I organize my personal belongings in stacks in and around my backpack (in case I need to leave in a hurry), put the appropriate pages of the guidebook and copies of maps in my pockets and notebook (the map goes in the folding pocket in the back), shackle my laptop to the bedpost, and then hide it between the mattress and the bed frame. This brings a degree of order to the beginning of a day that can feasibly spiral off in any direction. I take a few deep breaths, think of my patron saint, DB Cooper, and am out the door.

Walking down the street toward the beach, I try to reconfigure my gaze, to flip my brain into guidebook researcher mode. My mind needs to be an open receptacle for information, eyes wide open, taking it all in; understanding how one place relates to another, what it all means, and how I would bring it all together in a few precise words. If I look at a restaurant, it is not merely a building, a restaurant, or a place that serves pasta; it is *name-of-restaurant* followed by *telephone number* (if one exists); *email* or *website* (if either exists); *address* (if one exists); *opening hours* (if they exist), and *average prices of an entrée or dish specific to the restaurant* followed by a *summary* of the *type of food, service*, and *something pithy* about the place. It should be humorous if possible, but definitely enlightening in some way. I am a machine. I must think about every restaurant, hotel, and tourist destination balanced against other options in the area and other options that I'll include in the book. Do I already have a pizza place in this part of town? Is there anything beyond pizza places in this part of town? What about nicer restaurants around here? Something with more local flavor, perhaps?

I'll only have the opportunity to visit many of these places a single time, so it is important to get all of the information on the first try and to constantly reposition it in regard to the other information that is constantly being added to the equation that is the Lonely Planet imagining of Fortaleza.

I start with the easy stuff. I cruise through a couple of grocery stores to get information for the "self-catering" section, a holdover for the original, diehard backpacker group that once constituted the main LP readership. Grocery stores here, as elsewhere, are easily identifiable—they're big, well-lit buildings with huge glowing signs out front, shining down on lots of shopping carts. You probably don't need a guidebook to find one, but it's what I'm told to do, so I'm going to do it.

I wander into a massive store bookended by large parking lots. I am confused about the address of the store. The supermarket has main entrances that head out toward three different avenues. Also, I can't find the telephone number or opening hours listed anywhere. I ask one of the cashiers and she has no idea about the address or schedule and says that the store has about six phone numbers. I am directed to a manager who is dusting bottles of rum and whisky in the liquor section. The manager looks me up and down after I ask the questions, probably wondering if I am casing the place for some sort of heist. Why the hell would some gringo care about these details that no locals know, and none of the employees (or the manager) care about? It opens when it opens and it closes when it closes. The store is here, where you're standing, and what kind of customer calls a grocery store on the telephone anyhow? He's eventually able to get me the hours, but mentions that it usually doesn't open on time and frequently stays open later if there are still customers. For the address, he just gives me the name of the street out front. I am not even going to bother to try to figure out which is the main telephone number.

After another similar grocery store experience, I graduate from "Self-Catering" to the "Eating" section, also known as "Restaurants." It is pushing lunchtime, so I will try to hit some places as they get their midday crowds. I plan to steer clear of all but a few of the touristy places and all but a few of the places listed in the last book. I'm going all the way with this one, giving it a full and much-needed overhaul—new restaurants, new flavor, all of it. As Napoleon said, "If you start to take Vienna—take Vienna." I look at the restaurant situation this way: if you are in San Francisco, you don't need a guidebook to tell you to get the chowder in a sourdough bread bowl in Fisherman's Wharf or overpriced pasta in North Beach . . . these things are obvious tourist experiences that are more difficult to avoid than to track down. What you need is advice on where to find the best burrito in the Mission, the best café in Noe Valley, or that quirky Chinese place where the owner orders on your behalf.

It is hard to fathom how many places I will have to visit to determine what stands out here. How am I supposed to eat at all of these places? I have room to choose a dozen or so for the book, and they pretty much all need to be positive reviews. Over the years, guidebooks became unwieldy bricks of information, so now there is an industry-wide attempt to pare down the length as no one wants to carry around an extra three pounds of paper in their backpack. But shorter word counts mean that I can't just go to twelve places that I randomly chose and say "This one's good, this one's OK, and this one sucks." That wouldn't leave enough information to point people in the right direction, which is the avowed purpose of a guidebook. I need to visit a broad cross-section in order to determine the best ones, not just the best food, but the best deal, the best quick eats, the best family spot, and more.

I set my sights on what could be a promising new addition to the restaurant section. It is right off of Meireles Beach, the nicer midrange area that will appeal to the new LP audience. The restaurant appears to be affordable and is easy to get to after a day on the beach. Perfect. I get closer and read the menu posted near the door of the building. I take note of the address and cross streets. They also serve lunch. I don't see any opening and closing hours. Two white-jacketed waiters navigate around me and stroll between rows of plastic folding chairs and tables draped with red-and-white–checked tablecloths. Inside, another waiter sideswipes me as he comes out of the kitchen with a serving tray stacked with cold bottles of beer. The doors swing behind him and I get a glimpse into the kitchen, which looks strikingly similar to the changing room at a public swimming pool. It appears to be sanitary enough.

I guess I should get out of the way, so I head over to a table by the corner and watch pedestrians strolling past, observing them with the keen eye of a wildlife photographer. A Nordic silverback male on the tail end of his mating years parades the street with his fecund, juvenile mate. In order to attract the potential mate, he is adorned in cut-off jean shorts, unlaced work boots, and a yellowing tanktop that reads *Hard Rock Café Bangkok*, all topped by a long, glorious mane of thinning mullet. She is in ripe tropical adolescence and demonstrates her sexual availability with a golden hair weave and a mouth smeared in glistening lip gloss. A bled-out blue tattoo of a crucified Jesus decorates her shoulder and warns that she is to be taken seriously. She nuzzles under his arm, indicating impending transactional intercourse, and the pair proceeds toward their eventual mating destination.

After I spend a few minutes taking in such scenes of beachfront wildlife, a waiter finally arrives at my table. I am decently hungry and can afford to order one pasta dish, but am not sure about an appetizer. I ask the waiter if there is a house specialty or a dish that is more popular than other things on the menu.

I am told to try "the house spaghetti." I end up with a simple Bolognese that looks identical to the dish I see on everyone else's table. It's salty and heavy as lead, but edible. The oily fat from the ground beef pools in rainbow swirls atop the sauce. Fine. I can write about this. But I need more details, illustrative details, with "colour and flair," like I also need practical details: Lonely Planet demands the opening hours, telephone number, drink prices, and more.

I ask the waiter some questions about the menu. He is a stoic sort, whose answers are completely devoid of the details I seek. I look around the room to see if I can pick up any clues from the other customers, the decorations, the music, anything.

The cement room looks like a World War II pillbox bunker crossed with shades of the Olive Garden. I consider asking to speak with the manager, but don't want to set off any alarms with the waiter. Maybe there isn't even a manager here. The chef? I could speak to the chef, but how do I explain this interest to the waiter, who is in the process of serving close to a dozen tables?

Again, I don't want to blow my cover, but I see no other choice than to pass along my card. It says: *Thomas Kohnstamm. Author. Lonely Planet.* I had to bribe someone in the Australian office to get the cards expressed to me in time for my departure. Certainly this will open some doors. The restaurant is a moderate to highly touristy place. They weren't in the last LP book and I'm sure that they'd be ecstatic to be in the next one. I wave down the waiter and pass along the card, asking that he give it to the manager or the chef.

I wait. Once I had the opportunity to go out to dinner with a restaurant reviewer in Manhattan. She tried to stay incognito, but about halfway through the meal the waiter caught on to the fact that she was ordering for our table of four, trying to diversify the order and tasting the different dishes. Suddenly we were supplied with a round of sorbet, a wide sampling of desserts, and a couple of bottles of Prosecco on the house. I don't expect, or want, that kind of treatment, but at least I can try to get the necessary information so I can move along to the next place.

My waiter doesn't come back with a manager. He doesn't come back and say, "Please, don't worry about the bill." There is no sorbet or Prosecco. He doesn't come back at all.

After fifteen minutes or so, I finally wave him back.

"Would you like another beer?"

"No. Thank you."

He starts to walk off, but I stop him. "Did you give my card to the manager?" I ask.

"No."

"Did you still have it then?"

"No."

"Did you give it to someone else?"

"Yes."

"Who?"

"The cook."

"Well, you see, I am writing restaurant reviews for an important travel publication. I'd like to talk to the cook or someone about the restaurant."

"OK." He walks off.

Some minutes later he returns with my bill.

"Did you talk with the cook again?"

"Yes."

"And?"

"He's cooking." He hands me a copy of the one-page menu sheathed in a plastic sleeve. "The menu has all of the dishes on it."

I give up. I have too many other places to visit and lunchtime is already heading toward its close. I look at the other table of Brazilian tourists drinking beer and laughing about shared stories and inside jokes—all eating the house spaghetti or another dish that looks just like it. I start to feel alone again, the consummate outsider, but can't waste time on that emotion. It's time to move on. I copy some basic notes from the menu, pay my bill, and head off to the next restaurant. I will just have to stretch what I know about the place into some sort of review.

It is pushing two o'clock. I walk three or four blocks to a big tourist seafood restaurant on the beach. I take notes on the menu at the door. This place is already listed in the guidebook. The telephone number and address are different from what is in print. I can't afford the prices of the restaurant, not that I could eat anything else after the spaghetti at the last place, but I know that I must go in and check it out to give the restaurant its due.

Once inside, I order an appetizer with crab. The portion is so small that I feel as if I've ordered a single dish in a tapas restaurant. I still have no sense of the kitchen. I grudgingly order an entrée. Although they are a seafood restaurant (and have a huge drawing of a fish on their menus and on the awning of the building), the waiter says that they are short on fish—all fish. They are having some sort of refrigeration problem today. I have to order my fourth choice, which doesn't taste particularly fresh. I am able to get only a few bites of it down. I feel like I should interview a few of the patrons or come back for dinner to give the place another chance. Overall, it was a negative experience, but would it really be fair to axe them from the book? It seems to be a restaurant that survives on tourism, so cutting them out of the LP book could be a significant blow to their bottom line. I vow to come back later and try it again in a day or two to see if things are better. I give the leftovers to a street kid.

After four more restaurants, I start to just look at the menus in the front and do a quick walk through to spy on a couple of people's plates. My feet are cramping. I am the only mad dog walking around in the afternoon heat, and I've already spent more than I planned to spend in a week on food. Looking through my pages of scribbled notes and dots and lines added to the map, I am unsure if I have actually accomplished anything. I am struck by a sense of guilt. Unfortunately, I can't waste time on that emotion, either.

By going back to my hotel room and comparing the hotel list to what is reviewed in the last LP book and a perusal of the city maps, I find an area that I will research this evening after dinner. I try to write for about an hour, check my emails at a nearby Internet café, and grab cheese bread and coffee from a street stand—the only dinner I can afford after my day spent lunching at the restaurants. Then I go back to the room, put on a pair of long pants, and head out to do the midrange and top-end hotel reviews.

Each of the four hotels I visit goes the same way:

- I say that I am looking for a room for two people for one night and ask about rates. I figure that the imaginary second person gives me an easy out. I can say, "May I see another room just to be sure it's something that my girlfriend would like," or, "I have to go discuss this with my friend. I'll come back later."

- I ask about the rates in the high season.

- I ask for a card and/or brochure with the hotel's essential information.

- I ask to see a room.

- I feel the bed, take a closer look at the sheets, look at the bathroom, turn on the shower, and try the fan or a/c if they have it.

- I then ask to see a second and third room. I do the same things in each room. I try not to take notes so as not to set off additional suspicion as to what I am doing.

- Afterward, I stand outside the hotel for a few minutes and try to strike up a conversation with someone who is staying at the hotel. A North American or Western European visitor (aka someone similar to the book's intended market) is preferable, though an attractive woman trumps all. I explain to them that I am a writer and am doing a review of the hotel, and ask if they can tell me about their experience.

- I compare the guest interview to my own observations, run around the corner, and quickly jot it all down into my notebook.

- I take the essential information off of the card or brochure and record it in the notebook, too. The card or brochure is put in my pocket until it can be transferred to my backpack for later reference.

The hotels are reasonably nice. Clean. Cool. Quiet. Expensive. I would love to stay in one of these places under different circumstances, but I just can't afford it and I couldn't possibly take a discount due to my status with the guidebook company. After all, that would compromise my objectivity.

At the fourth—and most upscale—of the hotels, I arrive sweating, unkempt, and in dire need of a toilet. I was reasonably well groomed when I stepped out of my hostel, but after this many hours on the street, I am visibly suffering. I enter the lobby and head straight to the restroom. In the process, I realize that I've picked up a tail, as in a lumbering, suited man who follows me into the john and eyes me suspiciously while trying to busy himself by fiddling with the towel dispenser. I don't have time for this bullshit. I want to take a piss in peace and get on with the review, a review which will, in the end, bring business to this hotel. I wash my hands and head back to the front desk. A sign in English says that they change traveler's checks, so I take the opportunity to break one of my checks before asking to see a room.

The blow-dried woman behind the desk looks me up and

down and asks in English, "You are not a guest at this hotel, are you?"

"No, I'd just like to cash the check and then I'm going to inquire about a room," I respond, while pulling the check from my wallet.

"I see. Well, actually that service is just for guests." I notice that she makes brief eye contact with my friend from the bathroom, who now stands toward the back of the lobby.

"Even if I am about to look at rooms? It says right there that you change traveler's checks."

"Sir, please don't raise your voice."

"I'm NOT raising my voice, I just . . ." A group of three young Brazilian businessmen, about my age, look over from the sofas.

"Sir, you are bothering our paying guests. I am going to have to ask you to leave." She looks back toward my friend and I hear the clack of his leather shoes headed toward me on the marble floor.

I consider some sort of a do-you-know-who-I-am-type of retort, but realize it is pointless and don't want to embarrass myself anymore. I slide the check back into my wallet and walk toward the door, eyes to the floor.

I return to my dilapidated hostel on Iracema Beach. There is a crowd of dreadlocked Frenchmen partying on the front patio. I hobble by and go straight to my room to try to regurgitate the rest of the day's information into my laptop before I lose track of it. I start to type the hotels onto the page. Maybe I'll replace them with better hotels when and if I find them. I enter more of the restaurant information, but I need to do more research before I am sure if these new entries belong in the book or not. I look at what I've produced and determine that it is approximately one twentieth of what I need to do. Not a twentieth of what I need to do for the whole book, but a twentieth of what I need to come up with for Fortaleza.

I am backhanded by the reality that, at this pace, it will take nearly three weeks just to finish this town (and I have sixty more towns to go). Even worse, I will be broke within two to three weeks, even if I stay only in the most inexpensive accommodations. The elaborate transportation and food costs have decimated my budget. I calm my panic by focusing my energies on writing, making progress.

The light again flickers in my room. I look up toward the bulb and the power cuts out altogether. I find my way to the hallway, where someone is heading toward a room with a flashlight.

"Do you know what's going on with the electricity?" I ask in Portuguese.

"Same shit. This happens every night," he says while fumbling for a key: one hand holding a flashlight, the other holding a nearly empty bottle of *cachaça*. I realize it is my beloved neighbor with the flatulence and snoring issues.

I return to my room and try to work by the battery-powered light of my laptop. If I hold my notes at an angle to the screen and position myself behind the screen, I can read them and then spin the laptop around and type some of them down. It works for a half hour or so, until the snoring gets so loud in the other room that I can't concentrate long enough to memorize the notes, even for the few seconds that the process requires.

I consider going out to research bars and nightlife, but am in no mood to be social and don't have the energy to even put my shoes back on.

I opt to switch things up for the next day, to rotate the crops like George Washington Carver. There are a number of smaller towns and destinations in the orbit of Fortaleza that I need to visit for the book. Some of these places just have a short mention in the book; others require more detailed hotel and restaurant reviews. I'd be tempted to blow off visiting some of them, but I'd hate for someone to write into LP with the email that all guidebook writers fear: "On your suggestion, I went to stay at the XXX hotel in XXX town and unfortunately it closed down . . . five years ago."

I wonder about Pacatuba, Maranguape, Canindé, and a few other nearby towns listed on the map, but not covered in the text. Why is one beach town like Mundaú included and another left off? In an earlier email exchange with the editor I had asked about adding new towns to the book. I was told that because of time constraints it was best to just follow the last book as a guide and not be too ambitious about adding new towns, unless someplace was hyped in rival guidebooks. For example, a few hundred words could be reassigned from Fortaleza to some other town, if it was really necessary, but that's about it.

I intend to rent a car and make the day trip out to the town of Baturité, but after a look at the nest of highways going in and out of the city, I decide that I am not much of a driver and head to the bus station. Besides, I need to include all public transportation information in the guidebook. The best way, and maybe the only way, to learn about it is to experience it first-hand, right?

I take a city bus to the terminal. This first stage of my trip sets me back an hour or so, because of frequent stops. Once at the terminal, I decide to take the regional bus to Paracuru, because it's closer than Baturité. As I wait for my departure, I jot down bus schedules. There is no single board that lists all bus schedules. As in the whole of the country and in most of Latin America, the terminal is occupied by dozens of privately owned bus lines, each with its own routes. At the ticket windows they tell me different departure times than the hours posted right next to them. And the drivers seem to have their own, third schedule, which is different altogether. After an hour of research, my mind reaches its saturation point. There is no making sense of this. Not, at least, without some creative revision for the guidebook's sake.

My bus finally departs and is both overcrowded and sweltering. There is a teenage boy sitting on my shoulder for much of the trip. The bus creeps along the road, through outlying suburbs that seem to have been built out of the scrub by workers who simply gave up halfway through. Many have the roofless foundations of a Machu Picchu or Pompeii, the walls slapped together from corrugated tin, cinder blocks, and rebar. The wiry plants and bushes sprout out of as much sand as dirt, and have started to cover the unfinished foundations. The ocean looms to the north. You can't see it from the highway, but you can feel its presence.

After some three hours the bus arrives in Paracuru, the sun already on the wane. I sit at Formula 1 restaurant to relax and survey the scene. After a walk to the beach, run-throughs at a couple of other restaurants, and a few hotel reviews, it is time to catch the bus back to Fortaleza. Nightfall is coming. Three hours later, I am back at Fortaleza's bus terminal. In the station, I eat a quick dinner of *coxinhas* (little thighs), which are shredded chicken and Catupiry (a gooey Brazilian cheese similar to a runny piece of Brie). The chicken and cheese are formed to look like a chicken drumette, sometimes with a toothpick in place of what would be the bone, and then breaded and deep-fried. At under a dollar each, the *coxinhas* fit within my personal food budget. They're individually served on small paper napkins that are soaked through with oil, becoming transparent before I am finished with the food. I use the napkins to smear the remaining beads of oil from my lips and dust away the bread crumbs. I take a quick inventory of the papers in my pockets and then catch the city bus back to my hostel. Another day gone. I am physically worn out and I've added only one of dozens of smaller, somewhat insignificant towns around Fortaleza that belong the book.

As I mentioned before, this is not my first time in Fortaleza. I first set foot in this part of the world in 1996. I encountered many of the same inconveniences and difficulties, but at that time it seemed easier to take everything in stride. Of course, I was actually a carefree traveler then, and now I must remind myself that this is a job, and that work is work, not diversion, even if I am trying to guide other people on how to amuse themselves. In December of '96 I had just graduated from a university exchange program, where I studied history, language, and politics in Buenos Aires. Following a properly raucous going-away party, my girlfriend, Meg, and I boarded a flight for Fortaleza. Overall, Buenos Aires had been a positive experience, but we craved sunny beaches and a warm, welcoming culture that wasn't available in big-city Argentina. Buenos Aires was concrete, clubs, and leather shoes. We wanted sand, reggae, and flip-flops.

We arrived in Fortaleza with the idealistic notions of young students who were busy reading Cervantes, Borges, and Neruda, paired with the history and rhetoric of Castro, Allende, and Guevara. We were fully open to spontaneity and planned to sleep on the beaches and take in the culture of pan-American understanding and camaraderie. When we arrived in Fortaleza, we found that no one could follow our Portu-ñol and that it was nearly impossible to find an ATM or change traveler's checks. Our dreams of sleeping on peaceful, tropical beaches were overshadowed by the faint glow of a McDonald's sign as rats scurried past and crews of adolescents roamed the sand looking for aluminum cans. Yet, even then it was less developed, more naïve, and less overrun with sex tourism and sky-scraping time-shares than it is now.

On the first trip, Meg and I ate street food almost exclusively, when we were able to eat at all. We got tragically sun-burned, almost drowned trying to swim across a river and keep our backpacks dry, and smoked joints rolled in waxed napkins for lack of rolling papers. We slept on beaches, we slept in sand dunes, we got giardia, we got pillaged by mosquitos, but we loved every minute of it. My other good friends from the exchange program in Buenos Aires, Roner Davies and Mack Hardison, who traveled on and off with us on that trip, gave me their guidebook called *Lonely Planet Brazil*. It was a prototype of what the book is now, but it helped to guide us through some of the larger cities in the region. Our trip was cut short when Meg was bitten by a snake in the parking lot of the Maceió bus terminal (we were out there smoking with a guy whom we had met while he was seated on a bench in the station getting a tattoo of Bob Marley), but it still did not dampen our spirits.

Now, I walk much the same path that I did with Meg, Roner, and Mack, nearly a decade ago, but am crumbling under my anxiety for a good night's sleep and the fact that I will soon go bankrupt.

Before I return to my lonely, uncomfortably bed, I go to an Internet café to check my email and see if I have heard from the editor. I am still in the process of figuring out what the fuck I am supposed to do on this project, and I have sent quite a few questions her way, but haven't heard back.

There's nothing from the editor, but among the spam is an email with the subject line "Recife?" I open it and it reads (in Portuguese):

Thomas,

Do you remember me? I am the girl who helped you to the taxi in Rio when you were beaten by the gringa. Where are you? I am going to be working in Recife and

Olinda for the next few weeks and am going to get an apartment. I am looking for a roommate. I have already found a place. I am just looking for another person. If you are in Recife or Olinda please let me know.

Kisses,
Inara

The Gringo Trail

54 DAYS UNTIL DEADLINE

In travel, few things are as enjoyable as the overnight bus trip. Back home it seems an impossible hassle to take public transportation across town. On the road, however, a twenty-hour bus trip is welcome, so long as you get a movie (thereby passing the time if you can't sleep) and have air-conditioning (thereby making it possible to sleep if you can). It also saves you from paying for a night in a hotel.

I've done bus marathons in India, Peru, and Colombia, hauling ass at double capacity on potholed highways full of ox-carts, rickshaws, and other buses playing head-on games of chicken in our lane; I've peered out the window at the burnt wreckage of other buses in Andean mountain valleys below; and I've been searched head-to-toe by sweaty, heavily armed thugs at paramilitary roadblocks. I therefore proclaim myself an international black belt in long-distance bus travel. Any weathered bus traveler understands that—all other variables aside—there are two keys to your comfort on a massive overnight bus voyage:

1. The angle to which your seat reclines.

2. The types of sedative that can be purchased without a prescription in the country of travel. I am no doctor, but a -*pam* or -*zepam* suffix is a good bet.

I had those two essentials in order, but the variable that I didn't take into consideration on this particular trip was my stomach. It began as a mere tremor, but by the time that we were onto the second consecutive showing of Brian Bosworth in *Stone Cold* with Portuguese subtitles, my cramping was unbearable. Did it have something to do with that bowl of cereal and tap water that I had eaten with no utensils the morning before I left Fortaleza? I had a feeling that was pushing it. Or maybe it was the liver in grayish gravy that I accidentally consumed at the bus station buffet. I thought it was beef, I swear. In any case, the Boz's portrayal of undercover cop Joe Huff was a contributing factor. What I had hoped could be resolved with a quick trip or two to the bathroom in the back of the bus turned into hours bouncing down the highway, my head on my knees, pants around my ankles, in a steamy little poo sauna. The nausea and discomfort of being confined to the tiny, vibrating bathroom combined with heat and exhaustion soon overshadowed the pain.

In long-term travel you have to learn how to deal with stomach pain and diarrhea. Some try to be the boy in the bubble: they brush with bottled water, eat only in American-style hotel restaurants, wear swim goggles and flip-flops in the shower, and obsessively wash their hands with Purell. But for anyone who is really immersing themselves in the culture, or is actually on the road for more than a week or two, stomach problems are an unavoidable occupational hazard (as are skin problems, sunburns, and bug bites). You must learn how to toughen up and practice steady control over your mind and body. I perfected all of that holistic, mind-over-matter shit in India. I wasn't enlightened in some ashram or taught by a yogi, but was forced to learn by sitting in the back of a bathroomless bus while something that felt like a ferret tried to gnaw its way out of my large intestine. You learn to deal with it. You have to. A significant percentage of the world's population goes about its day-to-day life teeming with parasites, and they still make do.

Eventually I am able to return to my seat and get somewhat comfortable by lying on my side in a fetal position in the semireclined chair. Some Argentine comedy with lots of slapstick, starring a guy who looks like a cross-dressing Latin Sonny Bono, plays until we coast into the station.

I am not opposed to challenging myself. I am not opposed to risk or pain for the opportunity of a unique experience. I am, after all, the same person who once ate an acid blotter and then spent the day watching *Schindler's List* and drinking Orange Juliuses at a mall full of cowboys in Central Oregon. I am also the same person who decided—while at a Halloween party in Manhattan—that I'd run the New York City Marathon with absolutely no training . . . four days later. I photocopied my friend's race bib, jumped in on the Brooklyn side of the Verrazano Narrows Bridge, and finished in just over four hours with little more than excruciating knee pain, bleeding nipples, and a raw scrotum. No one had told me that it was a bad idea to run 26.2 miles in boxers. It is pushing these boundaries and comfort zones that make you remember how many millions of ways it is possible to experience life, to explore the fringes of our physical and emotional perception.

I often reflect on Terry Cook, the former pro skier known for his one-piece early-'90s ski outfits, his bald head, and his death-defying back flips. His ski movies went as follows: A skier or two would drop off some massive cliff. You could barely believe that anyone would be crazy enough to jump the cliff.

Then Terry would follow. He'd launch off of the same cliff, but would up the ante by laying out a huge slow-motion back flip.

I remember him almost drowning after dropping a hundred feet into loose powder. They dug him out at the last second and he walked away with a grin on his face. A serious Charlie Bronson. Legend has it that Terry did bigger and bigger back flips and jumped off of higher and higher cliffs until he eventually jumped the Donner Pass highway at Tahoe. He was successful on his first few tries, so he repeated it again and again, just for the sake of pushing the envelope. One morning Terry decided to jump the highway and he didn't quite make it. He shattered the lower half of his body. It was bound to happen.

I had thought about this the night before as I sat in the dark hostel, listening to the snores and farts of my neighbor, the creaking of his bed. I could picture it all: dutifully continuing my research in Fortaleza and going without sex for the rest of my maiden voyage as a professional travel writer. That's like a virgin prom, a sober New Year's Eve, and a dignified office Christmas party all rolled into one. On a basic moral level, I am opposed to such square behavior. Plus, my current strategy wasn't working anyway. I opted to push the envelope. I got up and went to the bus station and bought a ticket for the next overnight bus to Recife.

I did, after all, have an invitation to stay in an apartment for a couple of weeks with a Brazilian model. Hanging out in some fucking hostel is not really travel. I could run away from all of that and try to find an "undiscovered beach" with fewer Westerners—a place where the other travelers happen to have logged a bit more time on the road and have a more cynical view of travel. But is that really any better? I opt to do just the opposite, to head straight into the vortex. Travel is truly experiencing other cultures and lands—embedding yourself in them, participating, living. Or so I tell myself.

I am going to go and live for a couple of weeks with a model because it is the kind of travel that LP needs reflected in its books. Simply treading the same backpacker road over and over again does no justice to the writer, the traveler who uses the book, or to the region itself. All it does is contribute to the development of a tourist trail in which thousands of travelers shuffle along the same path, strictly adhering to the book's suggestions, visiting the same small beach towns, and all staying in the same hotels and eating at the same restaurants. This tourist trail is popularly known as the Lonely Planet Trail. *Lonely Planet–style* refers to a style of guidebook-dependent "independent" travel, while *LPification* is when a town is promoted in Lonely Planet and is subsequently flooded with travelers, eventually rendering it a tourist ghetto. Maybe I can mitigate that effect by being more adventurous in my research.

I am going to take it upon myself to reach out beyond the standard tourist experience and find something different, edgy, authentic. This is the kind of stuff that appeals to the core, original LP readership that wants to go beyond the packaged window dressing of the tourist experience and see things from backstage. This is my chance to go off the beaten track and relate my experience with some real "colour and flair." I am not exactly sure what that experience will be. Hopefully it'll be sex that has nothing to do with a guidebook, but I am sure such sex will open my eyes to other interesting details about everything around me. I am up to the challenge . . . not for myself, but for the readership.

I make my way from Recife's multistory, cement bus terminal up to Inara's chosen location—the smaller, colonial town of Olinda. Once a rival city, Olinda is now basically a northern suburb of Recife. There is no multistory, cement station here; the bus merely drops you off on the street below town. Olinda has a fraction of the population and industry of Recife, but it also has charm nonpareil. The cobbled streets of colorful colonial buildings climb like veins up a large hill facing the ocean. From the top of the hill, you can look out toward the Atlantic or back at Olinda's sprawling big brother to the south.

Walking into town from the bus stop, I am approached by a multitude of touts who want to give me tours of the city's historical buildings. It is obvious that this is already a major tourist town, but I will approach it from my own angle and see what else there is to it. Paris and New Orleans are tourist towns, but there's obviously more to them than Notre Dame and Bourbon Street. It is definitely a matter of approach. It is a steep slog up the cobbled hills to the upper area of the city, Alto de Sá. I stop in a bar to kill a few hours before I am to meet Inara at the house of someone named Beatriz.

One icy glass of beer gets my brain running again. I decide to pen the introduction for Olinda. I write:

Olinda is...
The town of Olinda is touristy, but

I must sell it better. I dig into the page of my notebook with the tip of my pen while sipping on the next beer. I then read the corresponding section from the last edition of the guidebook, move the first paragraph to the middle, the middle paragraph to the end, and the final paragraph back up to the beginning. I play with some adjectives, add a couple of sentences to the end for good measure, and come up with:

Beautiful Gorgeous Olinda is While Recife plays the role of an economic industrial center, beautiful Olinda is recognized as its cultural counterpart: a living city with bohemian hippie bohemian quarters, art galleries and museums. The beautiful historic center of Olinda sits on a

> hill overlooking Recife and the Atlantic Ocean. It is one of
> the largest and best-preserved colonial cities in Brazil
> [Note to self: is that true?], with twisting streets of colorful
> old houses and a ~~bunch~~ plethora of ~~frequently ramshackle
> scenic~~ churches in various states of decay and repair. It is
> a tour~~ist trap touristy~~ destination, but Olinda does not
> disappoint, as it remains charming, ~~friendly and fun~~ fun
> and friendly.

Good enough. I guess it can be just that easy. So much for
completely overhauling the information in the book. I can add
more to it later, if necessary. I switch to coffee in order to stay
awake until my meeting with Inara. I brush my teeth in the
bathroom, bringing my backpack with me. I can't trust leaving
it at the table. When you have no home, no foundation, you
sometimes need to find a little place of comfort where you set
down your stuff and establish a fleeting moment of personal
space. You barricade yourself into a corner like making a castle in chess. The restaurant and adjoining bathroom have almost served that purpose, but I am ready for a bed. A door. My
own bathroom.

I have to ask three or four locals before I can find the back
street where I am to meet Inara. The house is set behind a
thick cement wall that takes up a corner on a dead-end street.
I stand in front of a painted metal door studded with rivets. It
has the appearance of a fortified compound. I immediately
start to imagine how I can write about this for the book. The
Dutch razed Olinda in the sixteenth century. If this is some sort
of guesthouse or apartment-hotel, I could write that it is ready
for some kind of Dutch attack. "The outward fortified appear-

ance of this guesthouse is fearsome, but surprises with its personal charm and welcoming environment." It is dumb as fuck, but has potential for the kind of half-assed one-sentence guidebook humor that shows you are writing with "flair."

Inara isn't outside. I am a little late so hopefully she's already inside. I ring the buzzer and wait. An overweight housekeeper with short bleached-blond hair and a missing front tooth answers the door in a white smock. She asks me a couple of questions and lets me into the front courtyard. I stand there for ten minutes, holding my backpack, until I am introduced to Beatriz, a pasty and bloated brunette, clearly a beer drinker. She sports wire-rimmed glasses and an excruciatingly tight ponytail. Her lower half is packed into black stretch pants with her hips exploding over the elastic waistband and her knees flaring out below. She covers her heavy breasts with a boxy white T-shirt that says "Beatriz Fernandes Academy, Personal Trainer."

Beatriz immediately tells me that she inherited the musty, labyrinthine house from her lawyer father. He had, in turn, inherited the land from her grandfather, who—she makes sure to mention—was born in Lisbon, not Brazil. His portrait, that of a wildly sideburned man with a serious set of eyebrows, hangs in the front hall, frowning coolly at passersby. The grandfather has all the look and charm of a nineteenth-century slave owner. The house has stacks of workout mats and small barbells, surrounded by empty beer bottles and piles of mildewed Brazilian gossip and diet magazines.

I ask about the shirt and she tells me that she is a personal trainer, but barely works now because people do not want to come all the way out to her house. People are getting lazy these days. Beatriz herself won't leave the house anymore. There is too much crime. Recife and Olinda are coming apart at the seams. "There is no future for this city," she says, "probably no future for Brazil." I might think that it is a place of beauty, but according to Beatriz there is only a thin facade over the chaos, the drugs, the prostitution, the crime, and scheming. It is best to just keep quiet and stay inside.

"So, you're Inara's friend from Rio?" Beatriz asks.

"Yeah, from Rio. You're a friend of Inara's, too?"

"No, I own the apartment she wants to rent."

"Oh. I see. Is she here yet?"

"No, but you know these people: always late. They're all the same. Will you be signing the papers?"

"Well, we hadn't really discussed that yet. I want to take a look at the apartment first. I kind of need to talk to Inara about it, too."

"She said that you would sign the papers. I won't rent the apartment to an unemployed black, but if you sign the papers and pay up front, I'll do it, OK?"

There is a moment of silence. It is always a challenge as to how to address racism in your own culture, let alone another culture. I opt for the less confrontational "I'm pretty sure that she's employed."

"She's black. She has no legitimate job. She is from Bahia or someplace. Any money she has is not coming from Christian means."

"She's a model."

"Gisele is a model. Nobody wants to see a black model. You think that we want to buy clothes that we see on thieves and hookers? Olinda used to be a place of Christians and European values. Now it's overrun with niggers and whores."

Frankly, her reaction isn't all that surprising. Even though Brazil claims to be a "Racial Democracy," it is not hard to find racism or see how race plays into a thinly veiled, unspoken class system. I'm still thrown off-guard by her forthrightness, however. It is doubly odd to hear this spouted by someone who, in the U.S., would be considered black, too. I guess that race is relative. Maybe it's the British hang-ups about purebreds and pedigree that gave America such an all-or-nothing approach to white or other. Of course, we're still more mixed than the Brits, but in the U.S., if you are 75 percent white and 25 percent black, you're black. In Brazil, you're not black until you're pretty damn close to 100 percent sub-Saharan African descent. I guess that the Portuguese didn't take such a hard line on perceived racial purity. The Portuguese colonizers were a small crew of scabby sailors. They simply didn't have enough female settlers to be so uptight about trying to maintain bloodlines. Brazil was founded on miscegenation—procreating with whomever you could or felt like fornicating with, rather than importing European women to maintain a pedigree. It strikes me that miscegenation had some benefits. I must admit that the average Brazilian is a lot more attractive and robust than the average American. Miscegenation is probably the way to go.

The housekeeper, who is of at least 50 percent African descent, brings Beatriz a beer, switches on the television, and the two settle in to watch a *novela*, one of Brazil's world-famous soap operas. While Brazilians may say things deemed offensive by race- and terminology-conscious Americans, they are still much more likely to actually sit down and spend time with someone of a different race.

Beatriz turns to me. "Join us and watch this. I'll show you the apartment during a commercial. . . . Want a beer, gringo?"

After a few minutes of the *novela*, a solid Brazilian melodrama of tears, betrayal, unrequited love, and product placement, Beatriz leads me outside and through a narrow alleyway that runs along the side of the building. A steep set of cement stairs leads up to the door. It appears as if this was once a maid's or groundskeeper's apartment. The door opens into a tight living room with an attached kitchenette. Everything in the kitchenette is minuscule, including the minirefrigerator, which is kept in the closet. There is a short, hard couch in the living room, an end table, and nothing else. The room leads back into a single bedroom with two twin beds. Each boasts a foam-rubber mattress covered with sky-blue sheets. Only the bedroom has windows, but as the wall between the two rooms does not reach all the way to the ceiling, it allows air and noise to pass easily between the two. There is also a small bathroom with a toilet so tightly packed into the corner that you have to sit side-saddle. Fucking foreign plumbing.

The view out the bedroom windows is of a pulsating hive of other windows staring back at the apartment. People stacked upon people: hanging laundry, lazing in the window, having sex, shouting at friends a few balconies away. There is a telephone pole that features a dozen wires that have been spliced into the main power lines, banditing electricity for anyone willing to risk their life to hook it up.

Maybe this isn't the ideal living situation for someone who is supposed to be working. Days from now, I will probably wonder why I didn't move along to another hotel, to another side of town, someplace where I could focus more clearly. But things are always different in the moment. I am tired, dirty, and sick. I am ready to put down my heavy backpack and am ready to stop having to worry about keeping an eye on my computer. As a travel writer, you have no division between your personal life and your work life. You are supposed to be working twenty-four hours a day. I don't care what your job is, no one can

perform at peak for twenty-four hours a day. Your personal decisions affect your work and your work decisions affect your
life—all day, every day. Sometimes you just have to settle and
then work things out from there.

That's how I justify my hasty decision, anyhow.

Short of visible rats or swarms of cockroaches, I am not going to pass on this apartment. It seems like a fair price. I am
filthy, it is clean. I am tired, it has a bed. My stomach hurts, it
has a toilet. I barely slept the night before. I am already here. I
am not going to walk back to the other side of town and search
for a hostel. I am ready to sign whatever papers and spend a
few minutes in the bathroom before having a long date with
the mattress.

Inara arrives in shiny blue polyester hot pants that look like
they are castoffs from a Wonder Woman costume. Her feet are
clad in espadrilles with straps that wind upward toward her
knees. As she struts in, she pulls behind her two large rolling
suitcases. At a touch over six feet, she is majestic, with creamy,
unblemished legs and a quality ass for a woman of her height.
She either has a new weave or her hair has grown ten inches
since I last saw her in the doorway of the Rio hostel.

There is little room for discussion. We are both here with
our luggage. I have no will to haggle, debate, or even continue
to weigh my options. I sign some papers, pay my half of the
money up front, exchange some brief pleasantries with Inara,
and am asleep within a matter of minutes.

I awaken in the evening to find Inara unpacking her suitcases
on the other side of the room. A silhouette of my body has been
sweated into the blue sheet.

"Good evening. Feeling better?" she asks.

"Maybe. Sorry, I'm a disaster." I look around. My clothes

are strewn about the room. Half the sheet is hanging off the bed. While I'm no prima donna, I'm embarrassed to be in such a disheveled state in front of such an attractive woman.

Inara laughs. "I grew up with five brothers and three sisters . . . all in the same house. I'm used to it," she says.

From what I can gather in my groggy state, one of Inara's suitcases carries all of her belongings and the other one is filled completely with shoes. Wooden heels, plastic heels, clear heels, stiletto heels. Already placed on her pillow are a two-foot-tall knock-off Tickle Me Elmo, with a hard red plastic head and open mouth, and a smaller stuffed Tweety Bird. Tweety is worn and losing some stuffing. He has been dressed in an oversized T-shirt that says PIU PIU, his Brazilian name. Inara puts a collection of thong underwear into a drawer by the handful and fills another drawer with cell phone chargers, papers, and a box of hair pins and beads, which I later learn are a present for her young niece. The majority of her belongings stay in the suitcases, which are then slid under the bed.

I decide to make a point of keeping things casual with Inara. I am not going to take the same path as I did with Inga. I can take inspiration from the skier Terry Cook's pursuit of adventure, but need not follow him in risking the same thing over and over again until it spells my downfall. I must remember that I am working. I must remember my professional mission— though, last I checked, my personal mission was expanding my repertoire of experiences, in which case, she's fair game. OK, clearly this will require further deliberation.

Inara has made a trip to the store and stays in to cook dinner: stewed beef medallions with salted rice, and black beans flavored with bay leaf, garlic, and more salt. Eating at home is a welcome change from the restaurant circuit. Now that we are living together, it gives us the chance to actually have a conversation. She is from a small town in Sergipe. There were nine children in her house, though her father has many other children with other women. Inara does not drink. She has never tried any drugs and considers them sinful. She has never traveled outside of Brazil, though she does speak some Spanish, some English, some Italian, some German, and, inexplicably, is in the process of learning a few words of Finnish.

She lived and worked in São Paulo for a few years before moving to Rio. She is twenty-one and has plans to conquer the world of fashion and modeling.

"Soon I will go to New York, Paris, Italy, but for now I work just in Brazil. São Paulo Fashion Week is *máximo*."

She shows me a two-by-one-inch photograph in a copy of Brazilian *Vogue* from some months back. It's of a tall, slender girl on a runway in some sort of feathered outfit. The photo is so small that I can barely identify the face. The skin tone is different, the cheek bones are higher. I look harder and ask, "That's not you, is it?"

"No, but I know her. Look at this. . . ." She digs under her clothes in her suitcase to find a thin stack of photographs. They are mainly from a vacation that she went on to Porto Seguro a few years back, dancing in lambada/aerobics classes while being sprayed with water cannons at a cheesy beachside club. She produces a photo of her and the girl from the magazine flanking a man in an expensive suit, his arms draped over both of their shoulders. His face has been scratched away until the white base of the photo paper shows through.

"An ex-boyfriend?" I ask.

"Not exactly . . . a promoter."

"Fashion promoter?"

"Yes. He got her in *Vogue*. He promised me the same."

"So you worked with him, too?"

"I did. I met him as a teenager when I went to the beach with some friends. He was from São Paulo and was staying in a fancy hotel. He drank Black Label and dressed like he was in a *novela*. We thought he was very cool."

"How old were you?"

"Sixteen, when I met him. Seventeen when I moved to São

Paulo. He set me up in an apartment living with five other girls. Honestly, Tomas, I'd never even seen a tall building before. He promised to make me famous, that I'd be in magazines, on Globo, in *novelas*. The only thing he ever did for me was to get me a spot as an extra in an old Ja Rule video they filmed in Rio."

"How long did you work with this guy before, um, this happened?" I motion to the scratched-out face on the photos.

"A few years. He was a liar. I work for myself now. I don't need a leach like him. One day I'll be the face of Brazil. Everyone talks about Gisele Bündchen, but she's from the South and doesn't look anything like the rest of us. She should be the face of Germany."

"What are you doing in Olinda then?"

"I'm not doing anything in Olinda. I'm working in Recife, at Boa Viagem Beach. There are some industry parties happening there and a club opening, too. It's a good place to get noticed and make some connections. But for living, I prefer to stay in Olinda. I need something a little smaller—reminds me more of home. So, what's it like being a writer?"

"I'm not sure. I've never written anything of any length before, not real writing, anyway. Actually, I'm not sure that what I am doing now is really writing. It seems more like updating or . . . bullshitting."

"If you're writing, it must be writing, no?"

"There's some writing, yeah, but mostly I'm just running around trying to see things and pretend that I know what I am talking about, so that eventually I can write something about it. I've got to go all the way from here to São Luís."

"In Maranhão?"

"Yeah. Been there?"

"No. São Luís is very far away. You have a big trip ahead. Could be fun, though. So, when did you decide that you wanted to be a writer?"

"I don't know, a few weeks ago, maybe. I've tried out a few different careers over the years, just trying to figure out which

I like best. I had a job working in an office, but I guess that I was bored and I wanted to try something else."

She looks at me blankly and I ask her another question before she can ask how much I was making in the job that I threw away.

"Is modeling what you've always wanted to do?"

"It is my dream. Yes, I've always wanted to be a model. Then again, I never had many other choices. What else is a 1.85-meter girl from a poor family of nine kids going to do?" She laughs. "I haven't even gone to school since I was fourteen. No one is offering me a *boring* office job."

Over the first few days, Inara and I both work long hours. She leaves in the afternoon carrying a variety of outfits and comes home late in the evening or early in the morning. She has all sorts of parties and events to attend.

I try to hole up in the apartment and write, or at least learn how to format everything with the template. There are many acronyms to learn, guidelines to follow, and standards to uphold. This is no longer a freewheeling take on backpack culture. The company these days is clearly not interested in the *I take cocaine occasionally* or *Please don't stop!* type of information. Maybe I arrived at this job a few years too late. The new LP style isn't just about making the books much more midrange, it is also about making them more mainstream. Lonely Planet is going for the biggest audience possible.

Unlike some LP writers and readers, I don't necessarily think that they're selling out. The reality of the situation is that they're only trying to stay competitive and relevant in an increasingly crowded marketplace. Microsoft was once an underground upstart. Hip-hop went from Africa Bambaata to NWA to Sean Combs; rock from Robert Johnson to Led Zeppelin to Creed. It is all part of that same process: you must evolve or perish.

Unfortunately, as with the rebellious college graduate who finally cuts his hair, buys some suits, and gives up bong hits for golf, the struggle to endure often requires a sacrifice of spirit and individuality.

Whereas Lonely Planet used to offer up rather polemical political opinions and frank advice on drugs, sex, and how to cut corners, the books now aim to be as inoffensive as possible, to talk up how fun and exciting each place is rather than reveal any unsavory or controversial realities. They are trying to sell a destination (and thereby the book) more than they are trying to say anything honest about it. Every book claims that the inhabitants of that country are some of the "friendliest in Latin America/Europe/Wherever . . . if not in the whole world." Instead of telling crafty budget travelers how they can slip into the pool at the large resort hotels, as LP once did, they are dedicating a significant number of words to reviewing the actual resort hotels for families and wealthy travelers. Those people buy books. They have cash in their checking accounts and functional credit cards. It is a brave new world for these guidebooks; the only problem is that we writers are still just as poor as the original backpacker audience.

Researching a small, cosmopolitan, and tourist-savvy town like Olinda turns out to be a different and much easier task than researching the likes of Fortaleza. Yes, Fortaleza has tourism, but there is no savoir faire. Though I thought I'd be avoiding the gringo trail by living with Brazilians, Olinda itself sits right in the trail's center lane: a place where Lonely Planet writers are pursued, cajoled, and persuaded.

While doing hotel research one day, I am cornered by the Swiss owner of a hostel who was somehow tipped off that I write for Lonely Planet. He has been listed in all of the guidebooks for over a decade. His business started as a small hostel for backpackers, but after years of a loyal following, fueled by guidebook publicity, he is now upgrading to hotel status, and is on his way to becoming more of a resort facility. A pool has been installed, as has a restaurant of sorts. I am invited to help myself to the amenities.

When I arrive, the Swiss owner offers me a drink. Here in Olinda, everyone who figures out who I work for offers me a drink. He has a comb-over, blackened teeth, and an agenda. A few years ago, another hostel opened with a variation on his hostel-cum-hotel's name.

"Highest form of flattery, no?" I offer.

"Well, my hotel has always been in the *Lonely Planet,* and backpackers would go right to it when they arrived in Olinda. Then a couple of years back this Brazilian bastard opened a hostel, stole my name, and bribed someone at the phone company and stole my telephone number. The one that was listed in the guidebook."

"You couldn't get it back?"

"No, the man with the hostel is related to someone in the telephone company. They're out to get me. Thank God, I already bought up every possible variation of the website name and email addresses."

I have to admit—I kind of like the fact that a local snatched his number. Foreign-owned hostels outnumber locally owned places by a huge margin in the guidebooks. Foreigners understand international standards for accommodations. They know how to market to Europeans and North Americans. They speak English, French, German, Dutch, Italian, and Hebrew. They have a friend at home in Geneva, Copenhagen, or Vancouver who can make them a website—even a website that can take international reservations. They get shills to send letters to all of the guidebook companies recommending that the writer visit the hotel. It is good to see a local get an edge over the foreigner for a change.

"I need you to promise me that you'll change the number

for me in the book. Every year you print the same thing and it is always incorrect."

"Lonely Planet doesn't print every year. More like every four years."

"No, it's every year," he insists.

"Trust me. This book hasn't been updated in almost four years. It's too expensive for them to update it with any frequency."

"No, I've seen the 2003 handbook. I think that I have a copy somewhere. I have called and left messages and sent many, many emails."

"You must be thinking of Footprint. That's a different company. Either that or you have a counterfeit knockoff."

"Are you sure?"

Fucking asshole. He gives me a free drink and thinks that it gives him license to interrogate me. "Yes, I'm sure. They're not the same thing. Footprint's a smaller company, but they do try to update every year. I'd imagine that their writer is doing a lot of his research off the Internet." Footprint has filled some of the vacuum left by LP's desertion of backpackers. Some travelers try to differentiate themselves as cutting-edge and hard-core by claiming that they are faithful to the Footprint brand and would never touch a LP book.

We thumb through a copy of the LP book that is kept behind the desk at reception and discover that the phone number is incorrect in the LP book, too. Maybe the Footprint writer has just been lifting it from the LP book year after year. The owner makes me promise to make the change and lavishes me with a few extra drinks from the bar.

I make my way through half a dozen hotels and restaurants that afternoon, gaining momentum and a higher blood alcohol level at each locale. By the end of the evening I find myself

back at Alto de Sá, where in typical Brazilian fashion a spontaneous street party has erupted. Students crowd the streets
around charcoal grills serving kabobs, beer vendors with loaded
coolers, and two capoeira circles. I am talking to a Brazilian
guy and mention that I played capoeira for about three years in
California, London, and New York. The next thing I know I am
in the middle of the circle attempting a few disoriented spinning kicks and drunken cartwheels.

The guy goes easy on me. People seem to find it amusing
that there is a drunk gringo playing capoeira in street clothes. I
think that I hear some cheers from the crowd. Maybe it is boo-
ing. I attempt a head-high kick and, without the flexibility that
I once had, the upward momentum yanks my other foot out
from under me. I crash onto my side and tear open the palm of
my left hand. There is enough blood all over my shirt that I am
able to make an honorable exit to the sidelines. I get another
beer and the vendor gives me a piece of newspaper to wrap
around my hand to stem the bleeding.

I move on to the nightclubs, switch the newspaper for a
wad of waxed napkins, and start to drink hard. Now and again
a person approaches me to let me know they saw my *capoeira*
spectacle. I don't know if it is a compliment or if they think I
am a buffoon. Probably both. I have been commended for my
buffoonery in the past. I lean against the bar and pen such
semi-intelligible observations in my notebook as: The booty is
round ¡INDEED!

I hit the Preto Velho and Atlântico clubs. More beers are
consumed. My notes become illegible. I am soon buying big
bottles for three girls and the guy with whom I played capoeira.
I am introduced to "another gringo." He looks upset.

"What's the matter, man?" I ask.

"I'm a fucking Brazilian. My parents were from Palestine,
but I was born in Porto Alegre and these people in the Northeast can't get that through their head."

He introduces himself as Azzam. He became a DJ while attending university in the U.K. and is now touring through Brazil, experiencing the Northeast for the first time.

He is pleased that I can pronounce his name. "What the hell, man? This is my country and nobody can pronounce my name. It just doesn't work in Portuguese. My parents never thought about that ahead of time. Works in English, though. A guy in Recife was totally freaked out that I could speak Portuguese and refused to believe that I was Brazilian. He called me an Arab and told me to go home. I'm not sure where that would even be at this point."

We ponder the loss of home and he makes me promise to come see him play at some clubs in Recife over the next few weeks.

Some six hours and an incalculable number of beers later, I head home. Beatriz catches me as I enter the walkway back to the apartment. The sun is fully up and she is paying for a twelve-pack of beer from a delivery boy at the gate.

"Wait. Wait. I need your help with something. Come with me." She is teetering and smells of alcohol. I am ready to run for my door, but she is too quick. I hope this has nothing to do with sex or helping with some sort of house-maintenance problem.

Judging by the assortment of empty bottles in her room, she is on her third half-liter of Brahma. I have an excuse, as I've been up all night. They're getting started. I rest against the doorjamb. Beatriz sits down on the corner of her bed. The maid is seated on a chair in the corner. The room is small. Beatriz has subdivided the rest of the house to rent out to long-term lodgers. The floor space is covered with dirty clothes and towers of the ubiquitous gossip and fitness magazines, capped by empty bottles and a ceramic ashtray spilling over with cigarette butts. Beatriz is in her standard black spandex pants and white training academy T-shirt. The maid wears a smudged apron and is painting her toenails pink.

"Here it is." Beatriz announces while searching through a stack of cassettes. She pops it into the deck and queues up some Whitney Houston. After some frantic searching with the FAST FORWARD button, she locates her song. They clear their throats in unison, open a couple of beers from the new twelve-pack, and start to sing along: "EYE EE EYE WIW AWAYYS LUUV YUUUU." It is a commendable approximation of the language, considering that neither speaks a word of English. Beatriz has a copy of *Dancing on the Ceiling* in her hand. I worry that it is next.

"Tell us now what it means. Translate please." They are overwhelmed with anticipation.

I do my best to explain in Portuguese. I tell them that it is a love song and was on the soundtrack for a movie.

"Yes, with Keeven Coznehr. Very sexy."

"Very. I've got to go, ladies. Got work to do."

"OK. Yeah, and don't forget that I need the other half of the rent by tomorrow."

"How's that?"

"You paid me half on the first day and you haven't paid me the second half."

"That's Inara's half."

"That's between you two. You signed the papers. So I want the money by tomorrow or we have a problem."

I feel as if I've been mugged and find myself wishing that Beatriz had, in fact, wanted sex or help with some sort of house-maintenance problem. I'd gladly pony up and fuck her or snake the bathroom sink to not have to deal with a rent problem and a scheming roommate. I'd even do the maid for good measure, but I have a feeling that they'd prefer the cash.

The Low Road

I have a situation on my hands, and to solve it, I will have to channel the power of Karrass. Not Alex Karras as in the dad from *Webster*, but Karrass as in Dr. Chester L. Karrass, the "you don't get what you deserve; you get what you negotiate" guy, whose ads for negotiation tapes, books, and seminars have graced every in-flight magazine printed in the last three decades. Dr. Karrass is to airplanes what Dr. Zizmor is to the New York City subway system.

I have never attended a seminar by Karrass, nor have I ever read one of his books or listened to a tape, but I can close my eyes, picture his self-satisfied, successful capitalist headshot, and remember that in life, as in business, "you don't get what you deserve; you get what you negotiate." I will call upon the strength of Karrass, march up to the apartment, confront Inara, and rectify this situation.

I find Inara asleep in bed, the back of her forearm draped across her face, shielding her eyes from the morning light that beams through the window. She's dressed in a small white tank top with spaghetti straps, one which has slid down her shoulder far enough to reveal a thick, dark nipple. She has relatively small breasts, but with a firm shape. I have always believed that shape, not size, determines the best breasts.

The temperature is already pushing well into the nineties and her skin glistens with a fine, sticky sweat. Her lips are damp with saliva. I watch her chest rise and fall as she tries to wring oxygen from the humid air.

Inara stirs, notices that I am looking at her, and sends a muffled groan in my direction. She covers her chest and rolls on her side to face the wall, cradling her sinister Elmo doll. The sheet has pulled away and now I am looking straight at her ass, with a slender white thong disappearing midway down between the sculpted halves. I realize that I am not breathing, hoping not to make any noise and ruin the moment. Fuck Karrass. I have already lost. I bet he never figured out how to negotiate with a nearly naked woman.

I climb into my bed, lie on my side, and try to close my eyes. It works for a moment, but I feel like I am sprinting within my stationary body. My pulse surges. "I'm sure that she has no interest in you," I tell myself, hoping to talk myself down. "This is all in your head."

She readjusts her tank top and rolls to face me across the room. We both lie on our sides with our knees drawn up, about eight feet from each other. I think that I can smell her perfume, though it could be my imagination.

"You're just getting home?" she asks.

"Yeah, big night. Lots of research."

"Yeah, me too. Way too much time in high heels."

"Yeah?"

"Yeah."

"OK."

"So, what happened to your hand?"

"Got carried away in the moment."

"A gringa?"

"Not this time."

"Good." She smiles.

"You need anything?" I fish.

"Like what?"

"I don't know."

"Anything?"

"Sure."

"A foot rub?" she asks.

Talk is overrated in the buildup to sexual encounters. Words do little more than occupy the time that it takes to segue from physical distance to intercourse. Usually two people have already decided if they are going to have sex or not—or, I should say, their bodies have decided for them. Eye contact, body language, and semiperceptible scents build the real momentum. Talk, so long as it is innocuous—no matter how corny or pointless it is—keeps personal defenses at bay by taking up the time that it would take to rationalize why you might not want to do what you are about to do. Invitations for backrubs or to look at photographs, music collections, etcetera, are cliché, but they provide the necessary filler.

I laugh. Inara laughs. She looks at me with one eye, the other side of her face obscured by the pillow and her weave. She grips the Elmo doll, its heavy plastic head doubling over the stuffed neck.

I oblige her with the foot rub. She lies on her stomach while I massage her foot, my chest on the bed, knees on the floor. Tweety is seated at the far end of the mattress. We make eye contact. He appears to understand the hysterical nonsense of it all, the impulse that pulls beyond rationality. I start to kiss

Inara on the back of her knee as she reaches down to touch my neck. I am tired and hung over. My nerves are shot. Didn't I come up here with some other purpose in mind?

I get a good grip on the waistband of the white thong with my teeth. It hasn't even been ten minutes since the initiation of the foot rub, when she reaches under the bed and gets a condom from her suitcase. It is unlubricated. She is allergic to artificial lubrication. Using a dry condom is only for the dedicated, the true of heart. It is a precise process that requires significant patience, like getting pandas to mate in captivity.

When we ultimately achieve the right balance between force into aperture and natural female lubrication versus dry latex, and it finally goes in, I am so surprised that I almost finish. I focus on my breathing and regain control. We move together slowly, almost intimately. My chest slides against hers. Her hands slip down my sides. Sweat runs off my forehead. I push Elmo out of the way with my left hand and roll onto my back. She is on top. The pace quickens. Beads of perspiration trail down her chest and streak her abdomen. I'm five foot eleven. I'm not tall, but I'm not short, either. Beneath her, I feel like nothing more than a little pilot fish, tagging along for the ride.

Immediately after the orgasm, my mind starts to clear, to return from testosterone-intoxicated hyperspace. It is the same glimpse of clarity that you get as you come down from a hit of ecstasy and think to yourself, "What was THAT all about?" Tweety looks at me differently now. Is it crazed scorn? Creeping regret? He is saying, "You done fucked up now." The bed is not big enough for Inara and me, let alone the other two. After a few minutes I return to my own bed and consider moving out of the apartment. I am no match for her. She has unfair advantages.

Inara convinces me that she doesn't need to pay—not today anyhow. You don't get what you deserve; you get what you negotiate. And I was negotiating from a weakened position. She tells me she'll be paid soon and will take care of it then. As she is self-employed, she won't grovel for cash advances from sleazy agents and producers, and I shouldn't try to put her in such an uncomfortable position. This isn't America. People don't pay up front for work, not without strings attached. Those are luxuries reserved for a white man in the white man's world.

Inara's friend, Andreia, is in town and needs a place to stay. She doesn't have much money, but Inara argues that she will still help to defray the cost of rent. At first I balk, but the heady mix of fatigue, lust, and now guilt lead me to say that I will at least consider it. Besides, Andreia's contribution will be enough to stall Beatriz for at least a few more days.

Inara and Andreia were once neighbors in São Paulo. Andreia completed a year of university there, though she wasn't able to get the money in order to finish the program. She did pick up enough English and Portuguese coursework to try to become a schoolteacher and wants to try to live away from the bedlam that is São Paulo. She has been floundering for weeks in Recife, with no good job prospects on the horizon, and is hoping to stay with Inara for a bit.

Andreia arrives at the apartment towing her suitcase. I guess that there won't be a lot of time to discuss whether she'll be moving in or not. Her presence instantly defuses some of the tension between Inara and me. Andreia has a peaceful face with a light sprinkling of brownish freckles tossed across her nose and a charming, small gap between her teeth. She looks considerably younger than her thirty-four years, though she dresses conservatively and has a hairstyle that is more mom than model.

"I thought that Recife would be a cheaper and calmer place to live than São Paulo," she tells me. "And it is, but it still isn't cheap or calm enough." She tells us about her inability to find teaching work in Recife. She plans to regroup in Olinda and find some temporary employment until something pans out with a school or she has to return to her family's apartment in São Paulo. She moves quickly to colonize the couch, neatly stacking her clothes, astrology charts, and school binders under the corner table in the common room. She fills the small fridge with packets of hot dogs and a carton of eggs. She has embarked on a hot dog–based protein diet, which is said to help you lose weight through the midsection while gaining weight in your ass and thighs.

Unbeknownst to me when I approved Andreia's tenure as a resident of the apartment, she came as part of a package deal. Otto, her new Israeli boyfriend, does not technically live with us; he just spends the night. Every night. I have no idea where he keeps his personal belongings or if he has any personal belongings.

Four people to a small, one-bedroom apartment creates a tight living scenario, even if we're not usually all there at once. Beatriz is not supposed to know that the other two are staying with us and they must sneak in and out at odd hours. Considering that I am the one paying for 50 percent of the rent, I should be upset, but I am learning to accept this chaos and enjoy some of the unpredictability. Rather than being a hysterical American, I will try to appreciate the moment and figure out the details in the longer run. As they say in Brazil, *sempre tem jeito*, there's always a way. Don't drive yourself crazy over stuff now, there's always a way to work it out in the end.

Although my impulse after sleeping with Inara was to leave the apartment, I realized that I couldn't afford to do that. I also realized that it wasn't such a bad thing to share a bedroom with an attractive woman who is willing to have sex with you, regardless of other complications. Otto. Andreia. The more, the merrier, I guess. Inara and I have sex only one more time. A quickie, or *rapidinha* as they say in Brazil, standing up against the closet door while Otto and Andreia eat dinner in the other room. Inara hikes up her skirt and pulls her underwear to the side. I stand on my tiptoes. Afterward we join the others in the living room and eat dinner seated on the floor, passing around plates of rice, manioc, and chicken thighs cooked with onions. We share a two-liter plastic bottle of guarana soda, which is a bit like a ginger ale with a caffeine kick from the Amazonian guarana berry.

Andreia maps out astrology charts for all of us during dinner. It seems, as I am a Sagittarius, that travel is in my blood. Otto doesn't talk much and is visibly nonplussed when Andreia determines that marriage and children are in his near future. Inara is ecstatic to find out that money is just around the corner. I don't believe in astrology, but hope, at least, that Inara's horoscope is true.

So far, my trip has not gone exactly as planned, not even as could be predicted by the most wildly inaccurate fortune-teller. Either way, at least I have accomplished my primary goal: I am a long way from the late-night, caffeine-riddled hours I spent in my gray Formica cubicle, terrified of the impending petrifaction of my mind.

Andreia starts working in a supermarket, setting up displays and stacking cans in giant pyramids. She wears a tight uniform with a short skirt and offers promotional deals, often for pay-as-you-go mobile phone companies. She makes minimum wage, which is now at 260 reais a month, or about $89 American. That's a touch over $1,000 a year. She has a partial college education.

If something doesn't work out soon, she'll have to go back to her parents' place, even though her parents aren't much better off than she is. I don't know how Otto feels about this. I don't even know how long they've been together. Aside from our brief pleasantries at that post-*rapidinha* dinner, he's been an elusive roommate.

One morning, I awake to find that it is only Otto and I in the apartment. Inara never came home and Andreia is out early to set up displays for a Nestlé *Milho* promotion. Otto offers to make coffee, an offer I have never refused.

He is shorter than I am, with a concave chest, blue eyes, and shoulder-length blond hair. He has a delicate manner of talking that would lead you to believe that he is an NGO volunteer or traveling graduate student.

"So, Andreia told me that you are writing a book?" he asks, while fiddling with the stovetop espresso maker.

"Well, not exactly. I am writing a guidebook."

"Like the Lonely Planet?"

"Yeah."

"Which one?"

"Well, actually, the Lonely Planet. I, uh, work for them," I say.

He pauses for a moment and looks me over. "I hate guidebooks, especially the Lonely Planet," he says. "All you do is teach inexperienced people how to tour around in little groups, imagining that they are doing something independent." Never underestimate Israeli bluntness. I have met a number of people who are anti-guidebook for a number of reasons. First, there are the cynics who hate guidebooks, who simply feel the need to dislike anything that is popular. Others dislike the commodification of independent travel. For others, it is simply a pissing contest to show how hard they are, that they can travel for a year with no guidebook, no plans, no money, no shoes, whatever. They believe that less-savvy travelers—those who rely on guidebooks—sully their experience by inundating supposedly out-of-the-way places and making them less authentic. Beyond the bravado, they have a point, although it does not diminish all the value of a well-written guide.

"Well, I figure that a guidebook has its uses and misuses," I say. "Without a guidebook you spend a lot of time gathering basic information and reinventing the wheel. I mean if you want to make sure not to miss historical sights or if you have to figure out the best way to get from the airport to a hospitable part of town, you're going to have to do a shitload of homework otherwise."

"Nah. I prefer something more like the Brazilian *Quatro Rodas* guide, something local. Otherwise, you are better off with a good map and a dictionary. You should get your information from the people who live in a place, not from some guidebook printed in China."

I can see his point, although I don't find it particularly realistic. Only a small percentage of travelers have the time and skill to travel with nothing more than a dictionary and a map. And, whether you have a dictionary or not, few people have the mastery of foreign languages to get all of the information that they need from conversations on the street. I guess people like Otto, the hardcore travelers and the hardcore cynics, believe that those people shouldn't be allowed to travel at all—shouldn't be allowed to mar the landscape with their ignorance and weakness, unless, of course, they are manly enough to spend two hours tracking down a Laundromat in Portuguese.

As Otto has just eviscerated the value of my job, I want to know what makes him so fucking tough, wandering around Brazil and sneaking into other people's apartments to crash for the night. I can talk shit about my job, but it doesn't mean other people have the same privilege. That's like speaking ill of relatives. I've had my front tooth knocked out (by accident), had my nose broken a couple of times (neither time in a fight), and can hold my own with an Ivy League medical student or a Lufthansa stewardess. Aside from the guys in the mailroom, I could take anyone at my old job—I'm not to be trifled with.

"So what great adventure brings you to my couch?" I press.

"I came to São Paulo as a security consultant." He smooths

his hair back into a short ponytail and ties it with a rubber band.

"Ahhh, a security consultant. What kind?" I ask. Network security? Firewall consultant? His little ponytails screams IT geek.

"Well, I did three tours with the IDF and came out when I was in my mid-twenties. I hadn't really studied, and security was all that I knew how to do. I didn't want to go to university. I had seen too much, had too many intense experiences to return to a classroom. So, I ended up training people, teaching them the specialities that I'd learned in the IDF. You know, business security, personal security."

"IDF, like Israeli Defense . . . ?"

". . . Defense Forces. Yeah. I led a counterinsurgency squad that brought in militants for questioning. We'd get a tip from the field about a safe house or location of a militant, and when night came, my team would enter the house, kidnap him, and turn him over to intelligence. We were good, too. Usually we'd have the suspect gagged and tied before he even woke up. They used to call us the Pony Express, because we never missed a delivery."

OK. I'm willing to admit when I'm wrong about someone, particularly when that someone is capable of breaking my neck. And for comparison, I spent most of my late teens and early twenties studying liberal arts, drinking Natural Light, and traveling whenever possible. I think that the most masculine job I had was as a handyman at a swimming pool, where I occasionally had to use power tools.

"Do you want milk with that?" Otto asks.

"*What?*"

"The coffee. I like mine with lots of milk and sugar. I have a real sweet tooth."

"Yeah, just milk. Thanks. So, three tours?" I ask. "Why'd you leave then?"

Otto fixes a surprisingly good coffee and hands me the one mug that we have in the apartment. He sits on the floor.

"Sometimes, it wouldn't go as planned. I was almost killed during my third tour. A friend saved my life, but lost his arm in the process. That's the nature of sacrifice, man. That's what we would do for each other without a second thought."

"What exactly happened?" I ask, wondering if my jitters are from the coffee.

"We just got surprised in a house one night. I actually let my team down. I should have known better, I should have given the building a more thorough check. My friend saved my life, but paid a big price. It's a good thing he had a Micro." He stares at the wall for a moment, lost in thought.

"A what?"

"A Para Micro-Uzi. It's the best for close-quarters urban combat. It's only about twenty-five centimeters long and weighs two point five kilos with a full twenty-five-bullet magazine. A full-sized Uzi is just too long for tight hallways, staircases, and small rooms. You know, a lot of times these militants were hiding in basements and little rooms in the walls."

Suddenly I feel like the world's biggest pussy. I need not say it; he can read the expression on my face. He obviously doesn't need a guidebook. He could probably survive with only a knife and a piece of flint.

"Step back a minute. You see, I have always felt that other people didn't understand, that they were weak and did not appreciate the reality of our struggle. Struggle was all I ever knew, so it was easy to do these things. I'm not a bad guy. I don't even have much of a temper. Now I see that it doesn't have to be that way, but back then . . . You must understand, my family is from Poland. After the war, those who made it back from Treblinka had nowhere to go. Their neighbors had taken over their houses and had no plans to give them back. Nobody wanted us. Europe is so critical of Israel now, but they were more than happy to send us out of Europe after the war. I mean, I grew up thinking that fighting, that struggle, were necessary ways of life. And frankly, you Europeans and Americans can only be critical of us because your forefathers fought to give you that luxury."

"I see it as a bit more complex, but yeah, I'll admit my experience growing up was pretty different. So you left the military and came to Brazil to help kidnap people?"

"Nah, the opposite. I trained security forces on how to protect their bosses, and how to keep their politicians from getting kidnapped. They were pretty inexperienced." He smirks. "They wanted to spend all of their money on bulletproof limos and fancy guns that they saw in Jean-Claude Van Damme movies, but they had no idea what they were doing. I could kidnap any one of their guys in ten minutes, by myself, with, I don't know, one of these Brazilian tambourines strapped to my chest. Like I said, I was good, but I didn't know how to do anything else after the military. This was my best option. I was also offered work in New York with some businessmen who knew some of the commanders from my division, and also some work in Colombia. Mercenary work. But I thought that this job in Brazil would be the most honest. But, in the end, my work was just helping to protect corrupt thieves and swindlers. I used to believe that I was fighting for something worthwhile."

"So you quit, took off and met a girl? Why aren't you traveling with all of these other Israelis on the road around South America?"

"They're all army friends. All of them. They're all trying to forget about what they've seen or focus on smoking marijuana or going out or surfing, whatever activity they can find to distract themselves. They all follow the Lonely Planet or whatever like a bunch of tourists. I am getting some space from all that. I don't want to travel with Israelis. I don't want to travel with a guidebook. I don't want to have my hand held, or sit around and smoke weed or even speak Hebrew for that matter. I am trying to experience a different life and see that a different life is possible, but without having to forget who I am."

I start taking day trips to Recife and the surrounding areas. Sometimes Otto joins me on the trips. He spends lots of time adjusting and retightening his ponytail and giving me a hard time. He laughs when I stress about research—it's such a paltry concern to a couch-surfing mercenary. Just the same, I feel pressure to know everything there is to know about the area and be the resident expert, even though I've never set foot in most of these towns.

Otto likes to quiz me with multiple variations on the following conversation:

"How long does it take to get to Garanhuns?"

"I don't know."

"C'mon, I thought you were the all-knowing Lonely Planet writer. Fuck, I should be writing this book. Tell me where Garanhuns is, at least."

"Inland."

"Say it with some confidence. Yes, it's inland, but that's not too specific, is it? What's the best place to eat there, anyways? For under ten dollars? What about a hotel?"

We have only a few of those conversations before I start to make up answers and claim a sense of authority that I don't really have. A travel writer is a storyteller after all. You can figure out the details later, but sounding like you know what you are talking about, speaking with authority (even just vague authority) goes a long way.

Garanhuns? "Yeah, a few hours, east. But you can never count on the punctuality of local transportation." That leaves room to cover for most potential errors.

A good restaurant there? "Well, there are too many to say.

But for an authentic experience, I'd recommend sampling the regional cuisine in the central market." Chances are they have a central market and some sort of regional cuisine.

Otto is not the only one with these sorts of question. Other travelers, when they find out that I work for Lonely Planet, ask about good flights from Buenos Aires to Europe, good hotels in São Paulo, how to figure out their visa extension, and any other travel-related query that you can probably imagine. I can dismiss most as outside of my expertise, but the questions pertaining to the region that I am covering for LP are more difficult. I am loath to admit to anyone that I am trying to figure it out as I go along, and continue to find it disturbing when other travelers seem to know more than me. However, I am learning to massage small bits of information into a sense of understanding. As they say, the two most important attributes for a travel writer are a strong liver and a good ability to bullshit.

Recife is only a part of a chapter of my book, but it's big enough to require a guidebook for itself. I make trips to Caruaru, down the coast to Porto de Galinhas, and, eventually, even to Garanhuns. I spend more time on buses and navigating the public transportation system than I am able to spend in any of the towns. Garanhuns is so hot that I am able to do only about an hour of research before retreating to the shade. The days are ticking by and these smaller trips, the constant back-and-forths, are sapping my energy, cash, and morale.

Otto becomes morose and temperamental and decides that he is no longer interested in riding along with me on any of the trips. I ask him what's wrong and at first he claims that he is simply bored, but later he admits that someone had tried to pick his pocket a few days back in Recife. Without even looking at the pickpocket, he grabbed the man's arm and dislocated it at the shoulder. He had scared himself with the resurgence of the anger and the violence that he had been trying so hard to put into his past. After dislocating the thief's arm, Otto realized that he was little more than an adolescent street kid, who immediately burst into tears.

My challenges are more of the organizational variety. I am beginning to think that this approach of establishing a base and reaching out to cover all of the surrounding area is not efficient under my time and financial constraints. It is a Jimmy Carter or Bill Clinton approach: gather and balance all of this competing information from a central seat of power. You talk to everyone yourself and screen every bit of incoming information. It ain't working. I can see now that I am going to have to take more of a Ronald Reagan or G. W. Bush approach, where I set forth a few goals, and run roughshod over everything else. Keep the inflow of information to a few trusted sources. Sure, some details will have to be sacrificed in the process, but this is all in the name of meeting the deadlines and goals that my editor has entrusted me with. I am going to have to do a rush job for Fortaleza and then move straight on to São Luís, and do it all in a single take. I vow to myself to get at least the important details right.

My patience pushes toward its limit with Inara's foot-dragging on the rent money. We discuss the payment again and she claims that she'll have it soon. Talking to Beatriz is even worse. She says that since the apartment is under my name and passport number, she'll have me arrested if we don't pay the rest of the money. She also threatens to lock us out and sell my laptop. I figure that she is bluffing, but don't want to test her resolve. The fact that she even knows that I have a computer proves that she has been sneaking into the apartment and looking around.

I still have another week or so in the Recife area. I am already sick of looking around the big, noisy city and I've only gotten through a fraction of the necessary research. Someone stole my reading glasses during my first visit, and the whole experience pissed me off. Finding an ophthalmologist, getting a new prescription, and picking up and paying for new glasses wasted time that I didn't even have to begin with. I try to be professional about it and not let it color my take on Recife. But lowered motivation to research a city, due to exhaustion, lack of funds, a petty theft, whatever, will inevitably translate into weaker coverage in the book. Lack of professionalism or not, it is just what happens when you have to make hard decisions about which areas get the full treatment and which get short shrift. There is just not a lot of shrift to go around. I am sorry to say that in this case, my tepid coverage will be spread out to thousands of travelers and potential travelers who follow the Brazil guide, all because some dumb asshole stole a pair of glasses that he will soon find make him nauseous, unless he, too, has astigmatism.

Just as quickly as he appeared, Otto disappears. He leaves a note for Andreia saying that he is going north, maybe to the Amazon. He leaves no contact information for her or for me. In a chain reaction, Andreia announces that she is going to return home to live with her parents. She can't do the grocery-store work anymore. The hot dog diet did not pan out and the boss has been giving her grief about her weight, trying to convince her that she can keep the job only if she sleeps with him. She has tried to make an honest income, but refuses to be put down or harassed by some grocery-store pimp so that she can earn minimum wage.

Instead, she may try to get a visa to go to Switzerland. Her sister is married to a considerably older Swiss man whom she met on the Internet, and he has some friends who would be interested to meet Andreia, maybe even marry her.

Although there is a lot of exchange between Switzerland and Northeastern Brazil, the two places are polar opposites. One is small, cold, proper, and organized while the other is large, passionate, and unstable. Everything works in Switzerland. Public transportation arrives on time. Employees are paid on schedule. Taxes go to public projects, not private pockets. The hospitals are clean and orderly. It is a safe place to raise a family. And older men who are unlucky in love, but who happen to benefit from their citizenship status, can help poor South American women get visas. Otto and Andreia had a real relationship, she says, but he is on his own journey. Otto had no interest in stability or settling down. They are finished. He is gone. She has already purchased a bus ticket back to São Paulo and will leave that evening, so we decide to start the going-away party immediately.

We round up a few of Andreia's friends and head up to the top of the hill in Olinda, the Alto de Sá. We sit in plastic furniture and sip frosty beers from the street vendors. There is a group of school-aged kids in the street. We watch as their numbers grow through the course of the afternoon. Soon it appears that the entire city is out on the streets and heading well toward intoxication before the sun goes down. The crowd continues to swell and then erupts into a full-blown street parade, with giant papier-mâché puppets on sticks, *frevó* dancers with striped shirts and twirling umbrellas, and masses of drunken revelers. The plastic chairs are stacked to make way for the crowds and we are swept along in the rivers of sweaty human bodies crushing through the plaza and out through the narrow streets.

Andreia and I walk together, admiring the spectacle, until it is time for her to leave. She says that she doesn't want to go. She doesn't want to leave the Northeast. She doesn't want to leave her new friends. She begins to cry. Returning to São

Paulo will not just mean a short-term defeat, but may mean the end of her dream to escape the city to teach. She borrowed money to make her job search possible in Recife and will now be returning home unemployed and with a sizable debt. Maybe Switzerland is the best option, but she worries that the sacrifice of personal and romantic freedom will outweigh any stability or financial gain. We trade email addresses, scrawled on scraps of paper; I instantly lose mine. She asks that I have patience with Inara as her heart is in the right place. We say good-bye on a street corner as she sobs into my T-shirt, and just like that, she is gone.

When traveling, you have to get used to this lifestyle of meeting, getting to know someone, and then promptly bidding farewell, probably forever. I can feel that my time in Recife and Olinda is coming to an end, but what I don't know is just how drastically things are about to change. After Andreia leaves, I spend a few hours in an open-air club, talking with a group of guys from town whom I've seen around before, having a few drinks and dancing with a few girls. The music switches from *forró* to an electro-Brazilian mash-up, a sort of samba-infused house. I don't usually care for house music—I prefer something a little more aggressive, with deeper bass—but the DJ is really onto something here. The music is traditional Brazilian but is set against another beat that conjures London and New York big-city swagger. I ask one of the guys from town who the DJ is and he says, "I don't know. Some gringo." I walk around to the booth to get a look at the DJ, and it is my Palestinian-Brazilian friend Azzam in a sweaty frenzy behind the decks.

We shake hands and he tells me to stick around to hang out after his set. Azzam and I end up having several more beers at the club. He tells me that this is the pre-show and that his big event is in Recife tonight. We go down to a bar in the lower area of town and continue the party. We eat burgers on the street and make plans to go to Recife. He goes on at the club at about 2 a.m. and needs to be there around midnight to meet with the promoters and get everything in order. From there he'll finish off the evening at a beach party down on Recife's Boa Viagem Beach.

"It's gonna go late," he tells me. "Last time they had me spinning until well after dawn. Let's go down there right now and you can help me set up at the club."

"I dunno, man, I'm wearing shorts and flip-flops and I've already been partying most of the day. Maybe it's not such a good idea."

"That's the Brazilian way, friend. Go home and put on some long pants if you want. Clean up. Shave, if it'll make you feel better. This is going to be a night to remember. A night for your book. I'll come by your place in forty-five minutes."

When I get home, I admire my sunburned face, neck, and nose in the mirror. I guess that's the risk of starting to drink at 11 a.m. in the tropics. I have nearly two weeks of facial-hair growth to deal with. I consider shaving it down to just a handlebar, but opt to shave the whole thing, as I've never been able to take myself seriously with any sort of mustache. The fact that I'm even considering it is a bad sign. I feel sick from all of the sun and alcohol and need to sit down. For a minute or two.

It is almost 4 a.m. when I wake up on the couch with a violent thirst for water. There's shaving cream smeared on the pillow and I am bathed in sweat.

There is a note for Azzam under my door that says:

What happened to you?

Don't be an asshole.

Call me on my mobile.

The phone number is neatly penned below. There is no water in the fridge and I am not going to risk the tap water. Ignoring the pounding in my head, I throw some clothes on and walk down the street to see if there is anyone out selling water. I find a beer vendor with a tattered Styrofoam cooler on the main street. Good enough. I decide to call Azzam from a pay phone to apologize for standing him up. I have a feeling he'll still be out.

He answers on the second ring. "Hey, where'd you go? You trying to ditch me?"

"No, I was here. I just laid down for a minute or two."

"That was about five hours ago. You must have been out cold, mate—I pounded on your door like crazy. I'm just leaving the club in Recife now. Man, the crowd was seriously wicked."

"Fuck. Sorry, man. I'll have to catch you next time."

"I'm about to spin at the beach party. Remember? You need to be here."

"Which beach?"

"Boa Viagem, right near the Recife Palace Hotel. I'll be down on the sand. Any cab driver will know where it is. It's the after-party for the club—trust me, you don't want to miss it."

"You know, I . . ."

"Listen, no excuses. Are you here to write about what's actually going on or to catch up on your beauty rest?"

"I hear you, it's just that—"

"Get in a cab. Right now. Don't go back to your apartment; you'll just fall asleep again. I'll split the cost of the cab with you and later we can split a cab back home. Now, you got any more excuses for me?"

He's right. It is my duty to the readership to check out this kind of nightlife. Maybe I can redeem Recife after all. I take a cab to the beach. Azzam is no liar—the crowd is wicked, mostly made up of the young and good-looking international set. Everyone looks a bit dazed, but they are still going strong and rocking out to Azzam's house and electro. The turntables are set up on top of a Persian rug and covered by a thin plastic tent on aluminum poles. Azzam spins for over an hour. I nod hello and hang out near the back, watching a crew of Brazilians try to samba along to the beat.

A British ex-pat who lives in Rio takes over the decks and switches to dub reggae. The sun has just broken the horizon. I wish that I had brought sunglasses out with me.

As the sun pulls fully over the water and the salty mist clears, I notice that an elderly jogger with a crisp white terry-cloth headband has stopped to listen to the music while drinking from a coconut from the nearby *barraca*. His right leg, dressed in an untarnished white sneaker and knee-high socks, starts to move to the music. He steps down onto the sand, drops the coconut, and joins the crowd.

I make eye contact with a girl who is standing with another girl and a guy, nodding her head along to the music. Her hips sway sexily and I feel my libido stir from its drunken stupor. The eye contact continues off and on for a while. As I walk up to the *barraca* to get a drink, she passes me, taps me on the shoulder, and keeps going. I follow her to the far side of a wall just beyond the *barraca*. She turns around, grabs me by the shirt, and starts kissing me. I am suddenly glad that I came out this evening. Night life in Recife is going to get a very solid review. Enough words are exchanged to learn that her name is Fernanda and my name is Thomas and we are both doing well; I am, in fact, doing very well.

After a steady couple of minutes of this, I pull away to ask if she has a boyfriend, if maybe that was him standing with her back on the beach.

"No."

"Husband?"

"No, that's my brother."

"Oh, shit, is that, like . . ."

"He's cool."

"OK." We go back to kissing. I pull away again. "But why the secrecy then? Like why are we behind this wall?"

"My mom. She's gonna kill me."

"Your mom?" I laugh. "I bet she will." I pull her closer and run my lips down her neck.

"No, really. She's back there at the party. And if she finds me, she'll kill me."

"You mean the other girl that was standing with you?"

"Yeah. We're here on vacation from Brasilia."

"She's not your friend or sister or something?"

"No, she's definitely my mom."

"OK. You're an adult. She might not approve, but she's not going to kill you, right?" I pause to breathe.

"I *am* an adult, but she doesn't treat me like one. She treats me like a little baby," she says. "I mean, I'll be seventeen in two months for God's sake."

I jump back and she shrinks back, too. I start to say something, but just then her mother rounds the side of the *barraca*, arms akimbo, with a remarkable frown furrowed into her brow. She pays me no mind and immediately tears into her daughter.

"You said that you were going to buy a Coke. What do you think that you're doing? If your father was here, I swear, he'd . . ."

"MOM, I didn't DO anything. Relax. I was just showing him how to dance. He's a foreigner and doesn't know what he's doing. Anyways, he's GAY." She pats me preciously on the head as if I were her pet cat. I stare at Fernanda, dumbstruck and confused at how I've arrived in this situation.

"Really?" the mother asks, sounding unconvinced.

"Of course, look at him. Why are you so distrustful of me?" She nods to me. My cue to play along. I can only try to force a weak smile.

Nice. I forgot how manipulative teenagers could be. The mother gives me a gaze of pure hatred and excuses me to go back to the beach while she and her daughter have a little talk. Now, of course, I had no intention to make out with a sixteen-year-old. In my defense, it's not often you see high-school–aged kids at all-night parties, and I must say that her mom's asking for problems if she's bringing her out to one.

I return to the party, sit in the sand, and have a drink with Azzam, who has finally finished packing up and organizing all of his records. The sun is getting hotter and the sand begins to lose its moist morning coolness. I can feel the rays burrowing into my sunburn. I try to avoid making squinty eye contact with Fernanda, though she does sneak some glances past her mother and send them in my direction—I think, or maybe hope, that they're intended for me. As the older of the two of us, did I necessarily take advantage of her? That is how such a tryst is generally understood. But I am unsure if it holds true in this situation. What does the fact that she is sixteen actually mean? She's only a few months younger than I was when I was rumbling around Spain in the Ghostbusters car. And she doesn't strike me as someone who is particularly defenseless or passive. I decide that she took advantage of me. And what if things had gone further? Don't get me wrong, I love that Brazil's such a hot-blooded place, but it can get treacherous rather fast. Suddenly things with Inara don't seem so compli-cated after all.

Azzam and I have a tough time finding a taxi at the beach. We walk along the *calçadão*, get turned around, and walk a couple of blocks in toward the major streets in town. He is carrying a shoulder bag full of records, so we stick to main streets to avoid get robbed. Finally, in the middle of the sixth or seventh block we see a gathering of cabs, all parked outside of a large venue called Club Sampa.

Men are walking in and out of the club, some with young,

barely dressed women on their arms. I remember seeing ads for the place on the top of taxis and on a billboard or two. It is some kind of gentleman's club—a strip club, if you will.

I am not a big fan of strip clubs. Well, not since I was sixteen myself, and in possession of a raging libido and a newly minted fake Oregon driver's license. My friends Greg and Lars and I all had them. We were suddenly adults with all of the privileges, included drinking and going to strip clubs, even if we didn't know much about either. Our first time, we made a pilgrimage up Lake City Way in Seattle to a place called Rick's.

When three strippers came over to us and asked if we wanted a dance, we paused, looked at one another, shrugged our shoulders, stood up, and started to dance with them. Then, the compassionate stripper—Tina, I believe—patted me on the head, sat me down, and showed me what she actually meant by *a dance*.

I was in love. The two of us had a connection. The ten-dollar fee was steep—a whole week's allowance—but I was willing to get a job just to be able to go back and keep dancing with my special ladyfriend. After a few mowed lawns or some shit, I returned, but the excitement had already started to wane. Tina said all of the same things to me the second time. Plus, she was dancing with any catatonic alcoholic who could cough up ten bucks. I felt disillusioned, let down by my lovely and once kindhearted Tina. That first time was as good as strip clubs would ever be for me. Then and there, I came to view strip clubs as a big tease, a way to vacuum out your pockets and end up hornier than you were before.

And yet, here I am in front of one again. Or maybe not. Azzam explains that Club Sampa isn't really a strip club, not by the American standard. It is more of a club where all of the women are hookers. Not necessarily full-time professional hookers, but women who are all there to potentially engage in transactional sex. There was no shelling out cash for lap dances. Here, you got right to the point.

"So, it's a whorehouse then?" I ask.

"Not really. It's different. More like a pickup joint. You have to take the women elsewhere, to your hotel or to an hourly-rates motel," he answers.

I am tempted to go in—to look around. I know that prostitution is supposedly wrong and bad and evil, hurts the people involved, and spreads diseases and whatnot. But I am mesmerized even watching the front door of a place where such raw human lust is bought and sold like corn at a farmer's market. Azzam and I stand there observing the action. Business is brisk.

An elegant woman dressed in a garish silver miniskirt and silver pumps and wearing silver eyeliner exits the club escorted on either side by a short, blond, Northern European man. Both men are wearing ties and speaking a strange Scandinavian language. I look at the woman, make eye contact, and nod a coy hello. She looks back at me as she climbs into the back of a taxi between the two men.

"Do you know her or something?" Azzam asks as the cab door slams.

"Kind of, I guess. She's my roommate."

Disposable
Travel Writers

Back on the coastal roads of Ceará, a few hours east of Fortaleza, the dunes have started to foreclose on the asphalt's short lease over the land. Peninsulas of sand stretch across the blacktop, straining to reconnect with each other. The driver—Washington or Jefferson or one of these English surnames that people like to use as first names in these parts—squeezes the hand brake as the road pinches to little more than the width of the motorcycle. He navigates the narrow passage with a touch of heretofore unseen precaution. The roofs of squat buildings appear at the edge of a sea of sand, backed by the gleam of sunset over the Atlantic. In any other situation I would consider this beautiful, but at this moment I am too tense to even start to appreciate it.

Call it a control issue, but I have never been comfortable on the back of a motorcycle. I can't take the speed or the leaning turns while in a passive, seated position. I am significantly less comfortable on the back of a motorcycle wearing shorts, flip-flops, a ninety-liter backpack, and no helmet.

I met the driver at a bar—or more precisely, a circle of lawn chairs around a beer cooler at the far end of the bus-station parking lot. I arrived at the station too late for my connecting bus and decided to load up on a few drinks before tracking down a nearby flophouse hostel. Three beers later, he convinced me to let him drive me to Canoa Quebrada on the back of his motorcycle-taxi. We had to leave immediately as we were losing daylight and, as he was giving me an especially reasonable price, he wanted to get it over with quickly. As for safety precautions and protection, I must make do with a pair of aviator glasses, good luck, and the courage brought on by the beers.

We lean into the curve. I grip the bottom of the seat with both hands and squeeze my knees against the frame with as much force as I can muster. While listing at this speed, even a dusting of sand on the road could put us right on our side. I don't know how Wellington would feel about me grabbing him around the waist and hugging for dear life, but it is becoming an increasingly appealing option.

Truth be told, I am not sure that I even care what happens at this point. I must be the worst guidebook writer ever. I am cruising toward bankruptcy and complete physical exhaustion. I have only a handful of introductions written and have gathered information for, perhaps, a third of the places already in the book. That doesn't even start to consider new additions to the text. I have given up on checking details of anything, except the most essential part of the guidebook. Even if it were possible to work twenty-four hours a day, I could not visit but a fraction of the places that I have left to review. I only want a couple of days of self-pity and alcohol-soaked mourning on the beach in Canoa Quebrada, until I figure out how I can best cut my losses, try to regroup my life, and triage my career—whatever's left of it, anyways.

I made the decision to leave Olinda shortly after my chance encounter with Inara in front of Club Sampa. Azzam and I eventually got a cab and I returned home to the apartment. I entered the bathroom to brush my teeth and check in the mirror to see that I was, in fact, still the same person leading this other existence. Not only had nobody bothered to tell me that I was living with, and occasionally having sexual intercourse with, a prostitute, but apparently nobody had bothered to tell me that I had been out all night with half of a beard. The only thing worse than having some drunk gringo make out with your sixteen-year-old daughter is having some drunk gringo with half a beard make out with your sixteen-year-old daughter. The areas I'd managed to hit with the razor before I had passed out earlier in the evening were cleanly shaven, resulting in broad swathes of smooth skin winding among the untouched patches, abstract hair designs along my cheeks and neck. It looked frighteningly intentional. Did this have something to do with Fernanda's gay comment? Best to just let it go.

I rummaged through Inara's drawer and found her national ID card. Her real name was Raineldes or something like that, and she was five years older than she had claimed.

Raineldes/Inara stumbled into the apartment a couple of hours later and found me asleep on the couch.

"Don't you make any judgments on me," she said, shaking me at the shoulder to wake me up. "I am not a *puta* . . . okay? I am a tourism professional."

"OK," I said, my eyes not yet open. "If you say so."

"I am trying to make ends meet here. I'm trying to help my family. Soon, I'll be a full-time model. It's just that there's this

Nokia conference in town and I know some of the managers from a conference in São Paulo, and . . ."

"Hey, you make your own choices."

"No, I don't get to make my own choices," she shrieked. "Unless you are born rich in this country, there is no chance except to work like I do. We can't all be writers, Tomas. Here, you have to go to a private school in order to get into universities. Otherwise it is modeling, soccer, music, drugs, or, maybe, some sort of tourism—whatever it takes to escape. You don't know, gringo. Don't pretend to understand."

"I hear you. Really. Do what you've gotta do. But I'd still like you to pay rent before Beatriz hires someone to break my legs or take all of my shit."

"Yeah, I've been meaning to talk to you about that. You see, I'm not like those other girls out there . . . you know. I won't sleep with just anyone. Like I said, I am no *puta* like you see walking the street. Also, I won't take it in the ass. I refuse to do any of that crazy stuff. Because I have standards, I can't make much money. I still can't pay all of the rent, but I can pay some. It's the best I can do."

"I've heard that excuse before," I laughed. My hangover radiated through my head.

"You have?"

"No, but it doesn't matter. You still have to pay Beatriz. I don't have the money to cover you."

"You bastard. I thought that we had something special. Help me out. If I have to pay all of the rent, I can't send money to help my family."

"What happened to your hair?"

"The weave was giving me a headache. I have to get it redone."

"I like it better natural."

"Thanks. So, here's what I'm thinking. You pay for part and I'll pay for part. How does that sound?"

"Of the hair or the apartment?"

"You know."

I thought about it for a second. My normal reflex would be the path of least resistance, the bleeding heart. Maybe I could rescue her from the path into prostitution. Who am I to deserve this middle-class existence, a life I was born into and don't even appreciate? Shouldn't I share the wealth?

Truth be told, I was not in a much better financial position than she was. Hell, she likely had even more money than I did. I was pretty far past the point of trusting her, and if she was lying, I'd be the one taking it in the ass while she saved up for a new hair weave. I could have said to forget the money and tried to run away from town, but I didn't, and still don't know how seriously they take those kinds of things around here. I am not an expert in Brazilian tenant law or the efficiency of regional law enforcement or Beatriz's relationships with local goons. I don't need to get my teeth knocked out while trying to sneak out of the apartment or find a cop waiting for me at the next bus station.

I thought again of Karrass. I was only going to get what I negotiated, and, under the circumstances, that was going to require a direct and determined approach. I know that implicitly he would advise me to keep the pimp hand strong.

"No. If you can't make rent, you need to get out there and make some extra money," I said in a steady voice.

"FUCKING GRINGO, *FILHO DA PUTA*, how can you do this to me?" she spat. "You *pentelho*. Are you trying to make me into a common whore? What are you, some kind of pimp?"

"Did you just call me a pubic hair?"

"Yeah. You're a *pentelho*."

I sighed. "Sorry, *bonitinha*. That's life. You should have found a less-expensive apartment. I want half the cash now and half of it by tomorrow night, or I am going to lock you out and sell all of your shoes."

"You wouldn't."

"Try me."

I was bluffing. Most likely.

I was desperate. She was desperate. And a person will do almost anything if they are desperate enough. But, I think—at least in the short run—I was in more of a bind than she was. She knew, or was coming to realize, that I wasn't just another gringo looking for a good time on vacation. Now that the stakes were laid bare, she would have to size me up and decide if I was willing to beat her to the low road. Otherwise she was going to have to restart her expansive shoe collection from scratch.

The next afternoon, Inara left the crumpled stack of bills on my pillow. It is not every day that you are paid money by a prostitute. I immediately took the money to Beatriz, who refused to let me past the gate. She spoke with me through the small slit in the metal door, peering at me like a prison guard. She wanted us to pay extra. She said that it was for utility costs and additional guest fees, though I would have been fine if she had admitted it was a penalty on late rent. I paid the small, but not insignificant, difference and washed my hands of Beatriz. She said that she wanted us out by the end of the week, that it was impossible to trust anyone these days. "Gringos are as bad as the blacks. No morality," she shouted. Moreover, she took the whole rent situation as a personal affront as she had put her trust in me and had kindly let me into her home to listen to music and translate her favorite songs with her. I hadn't even had the decency to finish the job before I left. She slammed the shutter in my face.

Inara and I spoke only once more. She asked me if I'd be interested in staying on for the next month in the apartment. She was thinking about sticking around in the Recife area for a while; some sort of soybean growers summit was scheduled for the upcoming weeks. There wasn't quite as much business here as in Rio, she chattered on, but it was certainly easier to get by.

"Don't you remember what just happened?" I asked. "The rent? Our fight? Beatriz threatening me?"

"*Nossa Senhora. Que drama.* Like I told you before, here we make do and move on. Nothing really bad happened. Nobody got hurt or died, right? I think that *I* could forgive *you*," she said.

"*You* forgive *me*?"

"I could try. Plus, it's a good apartment. I am sure that Beatriz won't refuse our money. She has all sorts of money problems; her maid told me she hasn't been paid in two months. I'll talk to her."

I wasn't sure what Inara's real name was, how old she was, where she was from, if she had tried to play me from the beginning or simply made it up as she went along. I'll take Andreia's word and assume that Inara's heart was essentially in the right place. She was trying to make it, trying to survive while standing on the edge of a precipice. That girl had gumption. That and a fantastic body. I wished her luck on her modeling career, said thanks but no thanks to a month in the apartment, and was back on the road in a matter of hours.

The subsequent trip up the coast broke me: physically, morally, and financially. It didn't take too much as I was already very close to my own precipice. For the following week or so, one place rolled into the next in a blurring series of pit stops through Brazilian coastal towns and gritty transportation and commercial hubs. I remember a lot of time in buses, in bus stations, finding my way back and forth from bus stations to city centers and back. I have a huge stack of brochures I plan to adapt for the book and lots of nonsensical notes. As I mentioned earlier, usually life on the road yields a stream of exciting and striking details that keep you in tune with each passing hour. But like anything that is done in excess, I seem to have blown past my threshold. I've never been good at moderation and have clearly inundated my senses with too much information and too much hard living.

In order to retain some sanity on the road, I tried to follow a sort of organizational pattern to give foundation to the actual process of traveling. Like soldiers who practice field hygiene just to have something that they can control in the middle of the anarchy, the incessant organizing of my backpack, folding of clothes, and stacking and reordering of brochures and collected tourist information gave me a pretense of normalcy. Otherwise, I would probably collapse under the specter of morning depression: the weight of the amount of work I still needed to do, the guilt of knowing I couldn't possibly do all of it. I further quieted the panic with a steady administration of alcohol.

I set aside time to write or, at least, enter information into my computer each evening before bed. Most of it has been data entry, learning how to order and write a practicality string for a hotel, and figuring out how that differs from the practicality string for a restaurant or a tourist site. To add insult to injury, I have not been able to afford a single room with a desk. My solution was to lean over the edge of the bed and use it as a makeshift table. I kneeled atop my flip-flops on the tiled floor in order to keep my knees from going numb.

Because of the lack of natural ventilation and lack of air-conditioning in all of my rooms, I'd have to position a fan close to my face, though not so close as to blow away all of my notes and brochures, tie my blue bandana broadly across my forehead, Axl-style, to keep the sweat from running off my brow and into the keyboard, and put down several cans of watery Brazilian beer. I knelt down like this for at least an hour every night, a supplicant in front of my LCD screen, praying that the next day I'd find the fortitude to do it all over again.

Travel writing works in a cyclical manner. We write about a place, people go there, and then we must continue to write about the place because it has become a tourist destination. Unfortunately, with success and development comes change, and the tourist-friendly places just get busier, pricier, and more touristy. They often become places where I would not want to spend my vacation time, but we have to acknowledge their popularity, nevertheless. Sometimes up-and-coming spots are added because they are listed in a competitor's guidebook, because a writer, such as myself, finds them unique and squeezes them in, or because they have become hot spots as the result of overflow from the other destinations in the book. Most cities and towns, clubs and restaurants beyond those are passed over or given a short mention in the guidebook. As such, although guidebooks give the illusion of open-ended adventure and possibility, and claim that they seek to serve the independent traveler, they are often little more than a paper arrow pointing you down an overhyped tourist route, or gringo trail, so to speak.

I hit João Pessoa and realized that the guidebook focused on the insipid city center and not on the beach area, Tambaú, which receives the majority of Brazilan travelers to the city. Rather than spending multiple valuable days redesigning the section for João Pessoa, a town that only a few backpackers on long-term overland trips were likely to visit, I had to dedicate my time and energies to more highly visited places. Over a two-day period, I made some changes to the section and even drew up a new map for Tambaú, but, considering my deadline, that was all I had time for.

I stayed in Praia da Pipa and was floored by the sheer number of accommodations and restaurants (let alone boutiques) in such a small beach town. It would require at least three days to do even a bare-bones review, but I could only allot a single night. A pleasant Swiss and Brazilian couple who owned a hostel in town convinced me to stay an extra night to attend a "locals party." I tried to refuse, but hadn't taken any time off in over a week and lost the motivation to move on when it came time to repack my bag. Attending the party, in turn, meant that I showed up in Natal so hung over and tired that I could barely walk. I found my way to a Halloween-themed hostel-slash-metal bar, built to look like a castle complete with a drawbridge, moat (of sorts), and witch-on-broomstick-type decorations throughout. I did not visit the metal bar, whose entrance was a matter of feet from my bedroom window. From my bed, however, I was able to confirm that, yes, it was a bar that played metal (suitably loud), and confirm that I would not be convalescing from my hangover or sleep deprivation at this hostel.

Natal was an important focus in the guidebook. It had a thriving city center and was a massive tourist destination, receiving charter flights from Europe and daily arrivals from Rio and São Paulo. Its visitors weren't backpackers or independent travelers, but with the new LP format, suddenly they were my audience, too. I was to explore high-end hotels and fancy restaurants here in case one of these elite tourists purchased the book. It was important to get Natal right; although considerably smaller than Recife or Fortaleza, it could have used a week or more of research in itself. I think that it got about three days.

Of course, there were some places I was not able to visit at all. In a one-day stopover, after transportation time and all of life's other practicalities, it is rarely possible to visit more than five or six restaurants and four or five hotels. Those numbers go way down if you do, in fact, visit any of the sights the town is known for. The numbers go down if transportation is delayed, the weather sucks, you don't feel well, or any of the other thousand disruptions that are bound to surface in international travel. Then there's the whole issue of trying to review nightlife, already wiped out from a day's work, with the full knowledge that the next morning you have to get up and start all over again.

I made an effort to stop in Mossoró as it was heavily covered in the *Rough Guide to Brazil* and had little detail in the LP book. I found it to be a nice-enough workaday town that would also require multiple days of research, if not more . . . and I could not justify staying more than one night. As far as I can tell, the only truly interesting thing about the place is that it was home to Lampião, the Brazilian Robin Hood, in the 1930s. I checked my email and online bank statement in Mossoró and caught the bus toward Aracati, the junction for Canoa Quebrada.

It is there, in Aracati, that I find Franklin or Anderson or whatever his name is, and we roll into Canoa Quebrada on the back of his moto-taxi, just as the sun plummets into ripe peach.

Canoa Quebrada is no longer the quaint hippie town that I visited in 1996. Once a sandy colony of New Agers and pirates, it has morphed into a commodified and somewhat sleazy notion of Bohemia. The main street, known as Broadway, has been paved with cobblestones. There are new hotels with pools, a sushi restaurant, stores selling hats with fake dreadlocks attached, and private buses preparing to return to Fortaleza with their package day tours.

There is some game in the middle of Broadway—a version of the Jogo de Bichos (animal game) lottery, with a spinning wheel and a crowd of local bettors—that is unchanged since I was last there. Otherwise, I can't identify a single building or landmark. I remember loving this place when I was first here—recommending it to others for years after, talking it up. A group of local fishermen had invited us along in a *jangada* sailboat to net-fish for prawns. We had a cookout over an open fire, drank *cachaça*, and danced reggae. The north end of town where the fishermen lived is now all hotel property. A carnavalesque scene is unfolding on Broadway, with bright lights and throngs of high-school–aged partiers and heavily intoxicated Brazilian tourists.

I don't mean to be the type of travel writer who visits a place a second time only to complain about how far down the garden path it has progressed, but it is clear that, like me, decadence has settled into Canoa. I don't know that there is any way to turn it all around.

My deadline looms. My failures haunt me. I am lost and disillusioned; all of my great plans for the book and for this trip have disintegrated. Am I the only person who has failed so badly at this type of project, or was I unrealistic in what I believed that I could accomplish? I would like to justify it as an industry-wide phenomenon, but it is only safe to assume that it must be me. They should have selected someone more prudent, more organized. Someone who would get to bed on time and get a fresh start to each day. Someone who can get past their idealistic bullshit and who has no compunction about contributing to mass-travel homogenization.

I have never met any of the other writers, but I imagine them to be a sort of legendary beast equipped in head-to-toe Ex Officio safari gear with the built in SPF, the kind of clothes with tons of pockets for notebooks and rolls of film, digital voice recorders, compasses, GPS devices, and waterproof highlighter pens. They wear sensible sun hats, carry duct tape and carabiners (just in case), don't shack up with prostitutes, and always live up to the demands of the readership. They get all of the details right and look professional doing it.

Soon I will find out that these beasts only roam the lands of my personal mythology. But for now, I have no perspective to see this. And I didn't get much direction from my editor—who is my only real tether to the company. Long ago, I wrote her with questions about what I was supposed to be doing, and how I was supposed to be doing it. These were questions that would put my situation into context, carefully worded so as not to betray the poor job that I was doing, but clear enough to help me determine if I could turn in my material with a straight face or if I should go ahead and commit career hara-kiri. I assumed that she was laboring over her response, making sure to cover all of the angles. Only that would justify such a long delay.

The email finally arrived while I was in Mossoró. I opened it with some trepidation. I read through the email. It was not just sent to me, but to many of people. There were a number of things in it. Pleasantries. How good it had been to work with all of us. Thank-yous. Something about a new job in music or technology or music technology or something that I didn't understand.

All I really learned is that she is leaving the company. A publishing manager will be stepping in soon to help guide the book along until another editor can fill in, but, until then, I am truly on my own.

The editor's abandonment gave me cause to check my online bank account while I was in Mossoró. Banking was something that I had studiously avoided for the last few weeks. It registered at $283. I checked it multiple times to be sure. With no apartment back in the States, no income, and the next portion of the advance not due for some months, the number took on an especially foreboding significance; $283 might be enough to get back to the U.S. if I drop the rest of my research and don't eat for the remainder of the trip. A multiple-day bus trip back to Rio could cut costs, too. Fuck it, though, I may as well go out in style. I opt to spend a couple of days in Canoa, belly up to the bar, and admire myself in my death throes. Then maybe I'll actually feel like a real writer, if only in a Malcolm Lowry, *Under the Volcano* kind of way.

Once settled into my hotel room in Canoa, I split my existence between drinking at the bar and trying to sleep for as many hours as possible in my room. Sometimes I regain some hope, and fantasize about various schemes to get out of this mess—but my options are limited. Perhaps I'll be able to work out some sort of a deal with the hotel owner where I send him money later, or trade some of my personal belongings for the accommodations. That would help with the whole getting-home part of this trip. My camera's not a digital and it's pretty old, but it is a Leica and still takes decent photos. It was one of the few things that I had with me the day that my apartment was broken into. I sit at the hotel bar, trying to numb my guilt, my financial situation, and my failure as a travel writer.

One morning I manage to befriend a guy at the hotel who starts drinking at 10 a.m. and wants nothing more than for me to join him. I find a version of this guy every day, in every town. Today my friend is Nils: baggage handler at the Copenhagen airport by day and singer in the grunge band Synthetic Jesus by night. As a native Seattleite, I am happy to know that even if the music is dead at home, it is still big somewhere in Europe. Nils's round forearms are tattooed with black Gothic lettering that says something about mind slavery and thought control; long dirty-blond hair falls over his shoulders, obscuring half of his cherubic face. He is here on vacation to get some perspective after an overdose killed his bassist and a car accident killed his drummer.

"These things happen to any good band. It's all part of the creative process," he says.

I wish I could maintain that level of optimism.

We play the Synthetic Jesus CD on the bar's stereo system and I promise him that if he ever makes it to Seattle, I will take him to visit Kurt Cobain's house in Leschi. I haven't lived in Seattle in a while and don't know when I'll be back, but Nils considers this to be the best news he has heard in years.

Morning drinkers tend to become fast friends. Nils and I are no exception. I tell him that I have $283 to my name, less now that I owe the hotel for the room and bar tab. I tell him that I still have nearly 500 of my initial 1,000 miles of Brazil's northeastern coastline to cover by boat, bus, and dune buggy. That I have no editor. That I'll never get rehired by LP, and might never write again. I ask him what he thinks the chances are of me staying in Canoa, marrying a cocoa-skinned beauty, and opening a souvenir shop, or maybe a small bar.

"You know what you should do?" he asks.

"What?"

"Go to Roskilde."

"What's that, Danish rehab or something?"

"Kind of. It's a music festival. You never been?"

"No, but I recognize the name now. Isn't that where all the people died at the Pearl Jam show?"

"Yeah, in 2000. But fuck that. If you've never been to Roskilde, you've never lived, man."

"Roskilde?"

He takes a long drink from his beer. "In 1992 my mom died, I dropped out of school, and I got arrested. That summer I went to Roskilde for the first time. Three words for you: Nirvana, Megadeth, and Pearl Jam. All the greats. Talk about perspective on life, man. No matter if I ended up homeless, as a baggage handler, or as prime minister, I'd never be a failure—right there, I dedicated my life to rock." He looks at me without a hint of sarcasm.

"Roskilde?" I ponder.

"Yeah."

"Yeah." Why didn't I think of that before?

As Nils blathers on about the current state of Scandinavian speed metal, I drain my bottle and consider my options. A souvenir shop could be limiting, particularly as I don't like souvenirs, and owning a bar would be suicide. Maybe I'll just say fuck it all and head to Roskilde. I could replace the drummer or bassist in Synthetic Jesus and get a Danish state job with ten weeks of paid vacation. But first I have to figure how I am going to get out of the country. And even before that, I have to figure out what I am going to do about my tab at the hotel.

I already know from past experience what it's like to dedicate yourself to a romantic goal and then watch your life crumble around you. Some years back, I gave up everything and moved to London for a woman, imagining that love would trump all other obstacles or some such cliché. Within a matter of weeks, she had spent the night with some banker dink, told me to move out, and sent me into a tailspin that caused me to lose almost a year of my life before I washed up as a retail sales associate at Club Monaco in Manhattan.

I had promised myself that I would never let anything like that happen to me again. I would not be so vulnerable. I would fight. I would improvise.

I think back to all the time I wasted feeling sorry for myself after that fiasco. And here I am again, wallowing in self-pity because my romantic and unrealistic notions of travel writing have all been demolished. I cannot let it happen again. I will heed my old promise to myself and not sit back like a turkey staring up toward the clouds, mouth open while it drowns on rainwater. *Sempre tem jeito.* There is always a way.

And then the idea, the master plan, comes to me. Like stepping on a rake, it hit me in the face; it had been in front of me all along, I just needed to remind myself that it was there. I look at Nils. He is still talking. I interrupt him by raising my bottle and making a toast. "To the creative process," I announce.

"To Roskilde," he toasts, and promptly orders another round.

First things first. I approach the hotel owner, a jovial Scandinavian sailor who set anchor here in the 1970s and simply never left. I explain my situation, asking him about accepting my camera as payment or partial payment for my debt. I am hoping that he'll be flexible, as I don't have much of an alternative. He laughs at me and says he likes my sense of humor.

"This is your first time working for Lonely Planet, huh?"

"How'd you know I work for Lonely Planet?"

"What do you think, I'm stupid? I know who you are. Any of the decently smart hotel owners in town know you're here. I'm just happy that you decided to stay with us."

"You had a good recommendation in past guidebooks," I offer.

"Yeah, that's because ——— [an LP writer who formerly worked on this section of the book] stayed here every time that he came to town, and I always took extra good care of him. I'll take extra good care of you, too." He laughs hysterically. "I've got your bar, food, and lodging bill covered."

"Are you sure? I mean . . ."

"Look kid, you're easy. You're so easy that I almost didn't believe that you worked for a guidebook. When ——— was here, he drank twice as much as you, ate twice as much as you . . . you name it. The *malandros* from the other guidebooks are much worse, always demanding the best suite in the hotel or trying to get me to set them up with some girl. You've cost me nothing compared to them."

"Drank twice as much as me?"

"At least twice. ——— was a good guy, though. We still keep in touch by email."

"Do you think that you could give me his email address?"

"Of course. You should talk to him. You're in Brazil, kid, learn to be a little more Brazilian. I mean, I'll take your camera, but fuck . . ." He cracks up again.

"I was kidding about that."

"Yeah, well, listen, you can go ahead and use the computer in my office this afternoon; if you like, I can drive you around to the best hotels in town. You'll take care of all of your research in a couple of hours. I own the main bar on Broadway, too, so you should check that out later tonight. All of your drinks there are on me. I'll let the bartender know."

"I really appreciate it, but I should let you know that I can't . . . I can't trade you for positive reviews in the book. You know, policy . . ." I state awkwardly.

"Sure, whatever kid, I'm confident that you'll like it all. I'll make sure of that. I just want you to spend your time getting to know my places a little better."

"Why didn't you mention any of this to me before?" I wonder out loud.

"You seemed like you were trying to be so serious or something. I didn't know how to read you. I've met a few of these really serious writers who come through with big poles up their asses, but they never last very long. I've never seen the same one of them come back twice."

I sit in the hotel owner's air-conditioned office and email the former writer, digging for sagacious advice, some nugget of wisdom handed down from the guidebook writers of yesteryear. Then the owner drives me around in his dune buggy and I am able to hit a cross-section of the town's accommodations in three hours, chatting up the hotel owners, flaunting my card, and graciously accepting just about anything that anyone wants to send my way. Of course, I probably end up visiting all of his friend's places, but that is the price that you pay for free room and board. And, I guess, the subsequent loss of complete objectivity is the price Lonely Planet pays for not giving writers enough money to do comprehensive research.

When I return to my hotel, I check my email for a reply from the other writer.

My Svengali has spoken. His counsel is:

> "remember that if you are in your room at night writing, you aren't doing enough bar research."

He also directs me to LPA (Lonely Planet Authors), the Yahoo! Group and private online community for Lonely Planet writers. I spend some time trolling the site and find it to be a virtual water cooler of sorts, where nearly three hundred of the old curmudgeons who got the axe from LP, the lifers, the dabblers, and the newbies can meet and talk shop, discuss strategy and voice their complaints about travel writing. It is not my place to share their private conversations outside of the group, but I will say that I read all sorts of entries from all sorts of people on the same shit that I'd been experiencing. The impossibly large projects and the impossibly low pay are frequent topics of conversation. Some of the threads go on to discuss "desk updates," which mean not paying to send the author to the destination at all.

While many rail against the company, they hold their tongue about their personal techniques for getting the job done. Apparently, what happens on the road stays on the road. No one will write anything self-incriminating, but rumors do swirl about others who are no longer associated with the company—writers who subcontracted other hacks to do their research for them, blowouts and meltdowns with editors, alcoholics, burnouts, prima donnas, psychos, con men. I start to get the sense that I am not alone. Maybe I'm not even the worst of the bunch.

While I may not know how to report on things and am clearly an ineffective researcher, the real me does know how to travel and how to have fun. I used to think so, anyway. As exercise guru and Gazelle Glider spokesman Tony Little says, "Always believe in yourself." If Tony's physique and fitness empire are any indication, he is a man who knows the path to success. I will finish my research trip, except now I will travel for pleasure, and will do my best to convey that in the writing. Lonely Planet can do what they will with it.

I will not lose any more time fruitlessly knocking on front doors. I will allow friends and contacts to let me in through the back. No more spending money I don't have, dealing with hotel and restaurant owners who have never heard of Lonely Planet or beating myself up over obscure details. I will not waste more time trying to follow updates to the style manual. I can figure that out after the rest of the trip. If the previous book was built on comped hotels and bar research, I don't see why I can't continue in that tradition.

I realize now that I just need to play the game. I need to pinpoint more hotel owners like this guy, who will act as my patrons, and maybe then I'll be able to squeeze out the rest of this trip. Unfortunately, such tactics won't fully remedy the financial situation. My finances need serious, immediate life support, and that is where my master plan comes into play.

I am a kept man for as long as I stay in Canoa. I enjoy free drinks at the bar in town that evening, and on a whim walk over to the neighboring sushi joint to get an idea of the menu and see if I can swing a free sampling. The waitress suggests that I come back after she closes down the restaurant, around midnight. We can talk more then.

I don't eat any sushi, but we end up having sex in a chair and then on one of the tables in the back corner of the restaurant. I pen an observation in my notebook that I will later recount in the guidebook review, saying that the restaurant "is a pleasant surprise . . . and the table service is friendly."

For the first time, success seems within my grasp.

The Hustle

In order to truly appreciate travel, a person must relish the quirks, the setbacks, the annoyances that make up an average day on the road. A missed bus? An opportunity to soak up the frenzied culture of a foreign bus station. Giardia? Malaria? Dengue fever? Given the right perspective, these are all opportunities to learn about anachronistic medical systems and, if nothing else, gain a go-to story that'll outclass anyone's tale of traveler's diarrhea. You don't just take the punches; you must revel in them.

That said, when it comes to work, it is nearly impossible to revel in the quirks, the setbacks, the annoyances. Working implies predictability, productivity. So if your work is travel, you are in a precarious situation; at least that's how I figure it. It stands to reason that treating travel writing as work could only be a path to frustration and burnt-out oblivion. There's little room in the travel guidebook—writing industry for the tired, the middle-aged, or the infirm. Pitch them over the side. This ship is for the young, the idealistic, and the malleable.

In the words of Peter Tosh, "I am going to pick myself up, dust myself off, and start all over again." But I'm going to head in the opposite direction. I will use just enough of a framework of occupational exertion to get the job done. If I'm actually enjoying myself, I should be able to write some decent introductions and establish a sense of the place that conveys why a traveler might actually want to visit a destination. That'll have to be enough—even if I don't get all of the mundane opening hours and hotel prices right. When it comes to those details, what I can't plagiarize, I can always make up.

The time has arrived to put my plan into action. In what appears to be a converted garage, I find a narrow Internet café lined with tight rows of nicotine-stained monitors. Backpackers smelling of bitter sweat, brick weed, and bus-seat vinyl sit shoulder to shoulder with hyperactive kids playing shoot-'em-up video games in their bathing suits. I take my place at the single available computer and wait as the connection opens lethargically. I type out an email to unamoscaenmisopa@_____.com.

It reads:

> Hey man. It's your travel writer friend from Rio. Remember me? I'd like to discuss some business opportunities with you.
>
> Will be at this café for another hour, so hit me back soon if you can.
>
> T

I kill some time reading an email from Knute. He says that he's traveling with Karla, the Israeli girl that he met at the Villa.

They have been traveling north with Max Buckman and Mr. Yay. Yay got beaten up by cops while trying to buy coke in Porto Seguro and has decided to leave Brazil. Max met a Brazilian girl in Trancoso and decided to stay with her. Knute and Karla are now in Morro de São Paulo, practicing yoga and partying. He is thinking about following Karla to Australia. They are considering saving some money and building a future together.

I busy myself writing emails to other friends and family members, and within a half hour I have a reply from unamoscaenmisopa, also known as Robert Fishman.

> Good to hear from you. Let's not get into details here. We'll open a clean stream of communication. Open a new account with the name of the best team in the history of the NBA (and the world) combined with the name of the beach where we met. One word. At _____.com.
>
> From there we'll make no references to these emails, names etc.
>
> Gotta go find a coffee right now and I'll hit you up at your new email in about 20.

Fucking Lakers fans. I have always said that rooting for the Lakers is like cheering for Microsoft or the De Beers Cartel or, on a bad day, like supporting Nazi Germany. Lakers fans say it is actually more like being a fan of the Yankees (which is still kind of like cheering for Nazi Germany), but I'm not wholly convinced.

I begrudgingly open a new account at lakerscopacabana@ _____.com and use the name Jeff Renner: Seattle's beloved weatherman, once known for his beige suits and formidable mustache. I like to think that back in his bachelor days he threw some insane '80s coke parties, seducing big-haired, shoulder-padded female reporters and studio interns with his baritone amorous advances. These days, he is a thicker, filled-out version of his earlier self. The mustache has been tamed and he's a family man who has lost much of his swagger, but in my mind he'll always be a wild man, showcasing his feathery mounds of exposed chest hair, a Newport Menthol dangling nonchalantly between his fingers.

I receive an email at the new account from someone named Victor Maitland:

> What up?
>
> How's it going man? Are you interested in getting some photographs or what?
>
> Victor

Victor Maitland? A quick Google search confirms that Maitland was Axel Foley's nemesis in *Beverly Hills Cop,* a coolly crooked LA businessman. I notice that at some later point in his career, the actor who played Maitland, Steven Berkoff, also played John Roebling in a TV miniseries. It must be a sign, an auspicious moment to embark on a new business venture.

I reply:

> Mr. Maitland,
>
> Am up north. Still working or, at least, trying to. I've reconsidered your offer. I was wondering if you could send me some doubles of the photographs from the trip. How about 4 shots? I am in a very tight way right now. Any chance that you could front them and I'll get you back ASAP? Sincerely,
>
> The Weatherman

To my right, a teenage boy sits chain-smoking and looking at soft-core porn. To my left a group of three European backpackers crowds around a monitor, apparently trying to make online hostel reservations. Their guidebook lies closed next to the keyboard. Smoke hangs dully under the fluorescent-tube lighting, sandwiched between painted cinderblock walls. As I do every time that I use the Internet, I write an email to my family, tell them I'm doing well, working hard, living the dream. My folks are supportive when it comes to my travel, though always wary of my impulsive decision making. I write an email to my ex-girlfriend Sydney. I have sent her a few emails during this trip, but haven't received any response. She is probably just too busy to get back to me.

Bobby's reply eventually arrives:

Renner,

Have you seen what a good deal VHS is these days? I am stocking up on all of the classics for a steal. Am watching Rambo II right this moment. That movie is so sick dude. The don't make em like that anymore. Did you know that Steven Berkoff also plays the Soviet Army guy who tortures Stallone? I also realized that he was General Orlov in Octopussy, remember the one with the circus and the Faberge eggs? That was the last great Roger Moore film. Remember the place where Octopussy lived with all of that hot ass laying around, the two knife-throwing twin brothers? Man, I'm gonna have to go out and buy that one too.

But I digress. I can front you two photos. I don't usually do this, but sometimes make exceptions for friends who seem trustworthy. You are smart enough to know that not getting me back for two little photos now will cut you off from an endless supply of photos in the future. And maybe buy you an old fashioned ass-kicking, too.

How long you plan to be up there?

Mr. Maitland

Two photos are obviously not four, so that would be fifty instead of one hundred if I remembered his photo scheme correctly. But again, I am negotiating from a weakened position. I am desperate. I ask him how much we are talking about per pill. Bobby is slow in his response—things always become awkward when you discuss money. I eventually receive an email that states simply:

> Sorry that took so long. I've got the shits. Am sure you know how that goes. We're gonna have to do twelve dollars each because this is the first time and I am fronting them. Ten normally. Eight for greater numbers of photos. Pay me in dollars or euros, not reais. Exchange rates are your problem. Absolutely nothing smaller than a Jackson. Franklins are preferred. When you have the money, get in touch and we'll open new accounts. I'll give you a PO box to send the money to. Put it between paper or cardboard in the envelope and it'll be no problem. Never lost a penny in the mail.
>
> Where and when do you want me to send the photos?
>
> Victor

I open my trusty *Lonely Planet Brazil*, or at least the pages that I have razored out and put in my notebook. I scan through them, looking for a reliable hotel. In the end I decide to go with the business hotel that I'd stayed at the first night when I arrived from Fortaleza. It's not reliable, but at least I know that the night man will be bribable—reliably so.

I send him the hotel name and address, and he responds

that he'll FedEx the envelope that day, and email me the tracking number.

Fifty pills are better than nothing. I need to make up for all of the cash I hemorrhaged while slamming my head against the wall and trying to do this project by the book. If I can unload them all on the Dutch and Israeli backpackers up and down the coast, I could possibly stretch my two-hundred-and-something-thing dollars through to the end of the research.

Now, if I only knew the first thing about dealing drugs . . . but, shit, I used to be a PhD student. How hard can it really be?

I pull out my journal and do some quick accounting.

> **Fifty pills**
>
> $12/each to Victor
> 50 × $12/each = $600 overhead
>
> 50 × $20/each = $1000 gross
> Profit = $400

On one hand, that works out to be a measly $400 of profit for breaking untold numbers of laws. However, if I play the game correctly, I think that $400 can get me through the rest of the trip. Or the $400 could be seed money and I could build from there. With that $400 I could purchase forty more pills, or hopefully fifty at $8 apiece. I could resell those for another thousand dollars. I then go up to $600 in profit. With $600 I could purchase seventy-five more and gross $1,500, which will work out to about $8 profit per pill. I could make some real cash at that point.

Fortunately and unfortunately, my life does not take place in an economics classroom. Nothing is a given and the price isn't constant, especially in a market like this. I can't assume that I'll be able to sell them for $20 apiece. If I start to sell in threes, fives, or tens, customers will surely ask for discounts. Moreover, making that whole scheme bear fruit would require me to sell a total of 175 pills. That is a lot of work. Maybe if I run into a big Israeli trance party or something, it'd be possible, but those tend to be way down the coast in Trancoso or in Morro de São Paulo.

I feel like the Successories Essence of . . . motivational collection would definitely have something for this occasion. Maybe a photo of a soaring bald eagle at dawn. The word *Resolve* inscribed below it. An Essence of Determination mousepad would tell me: You must above all, believe in yourself, face your goals and then fight as if your life depended on it. OK, that is the first part of the equation, but I can't think of a Successories that focuses on the second part: restraint. Does restraint fit anywhere in our accepted definition of *success*? Without restraint, such attributes as determination, resolve, and audacity eventually become plain fucking stupidity, or worse. I should know.

Audacity can range from popping your collar on your hot-pink Polo shirt and driving a neon yellow Nissan X-Terra to pulling a Teddy Roosevelt—taking a bullet to the chest and still making your stump speech before going to the hospital. I must find moderation. At this point, I am no longer simply risking credit card debt, getting fired, or pissing off an uppity boss. I must mind the precipice. There are no protective fences, no BEWARE OF CLIFF signs, and nobody to sue if things go wrong. I don't even have an editor to blame. As an American, I am disoriented by the utter lack of potential second- or third-party liability in this situation.

I make a clear decision within myself. This will only be a stopgap, something to make the rest of this trip possible. I will unload this first batch of pills and will use the profits to finish the projects as best I can. I will be audacious, but quit while

I'm ahead. I open my notebook and write out my own self-styled successory about restrant. It reads ALWAYS PULL OUT BEFORE IT'S TOO LATE. I underline it, and then color in the letters. Below it I sketch a man peering out from the window of a country jail, gripping the bars with clenched fists. My family would be pleased to know that I am showing such moderation and balanced decision making.

Picking up the pills is more straightforward than I had imagined. I am able to ride along with a friend of the Canoa Quebrada hotel owner to get back to Fortaleza and, once in town, stay for free in a place that belongs to one of his contacts. Close to midnight I find my way over to the hotel where I spent my first night in Fortaleza, the place where I was tossed out to make way for the business travelers from Teresina. As I had hoped, my favorite night watchman, Mr. Gratuity, sits behind the counter. The glow of late-night music videos from a small television flicker across his face.

"I need to pick up an envelope for Jeff Renner," I say with trembling hands. He wipes his teary eyes, battered by the television tube, and says that he is not allowed to give out mail. He is jut the night watchman and could get in a lot of trouble if there was a complaint. I tip him a few reais and guarantee that nobody else will ask about the mail. He rummages around in a closet for a minute and comes out with the envelope. It is addressed to Jeff Renner, PhD, from a Señor Victor Maitland in Chile.

I slide the envelope up my shirt and am out the door, into a waiting cab, and across town in a matter of minutes. Back in my room, I open the envelope and find two sheets of heavy photo paper. One of the pages has double-sided contact paper on it. Stuck to the contact paper are fifty pills, each off-white with a spade logo pressed into the top face. The pills are arranged in five rows of ten, all of the little spades facing neatly in the same direction. I peel each off of the page and put the lot of them in an amber pill bottle which had once been for Allegra. Shortly after sunrise, I am off to Jericoacoara.

Sitting on perhaps my hundredth bus of this trip, I am sandwiched between the window and a spongy Swiss-German guy suited in a Titleist hat, white Reeboks with short socks, and rimless glasses that slide down his beak. He works in international currency sales, or at least he did until some recent changes in the company. He's the proud alumni of an American business school, the name of which I immediately forget.

He points out to me that the Brazilian real just fell against the euro and the dollar, so my money will be worth more here in Brazil. Just like that. I have gone from about $200 in net worth to approximately $215 in net worth.

He tells me that when he found out about the change in rates, he immediately went out and slept with a high-end hooker in Fortaleza—a much-deserved gift to himself. "A good deal too, the equivalent of approximately sixty-five dollars for the whole night," he explains, as casually as if it were a discussion about hotel rates. It was a much better deal than the $110 that he spent at Help in Rio. Now is the time to purchase goods and services in Brazil, he tells me. It'll be a tough time to buy foreign products, though. "Tough for Brazilians, but better for us," he laughs. As we are to record the prices for everything in the guidebook as U.S. dollars, I am going to have to recalculate the price of every hotel, activity, and restaurant item that I've researched thus far. I'm sure I'll have it all in order just in time for the currency to change again.

The bus crawls six hours from Fortaleza to the beach town of Jericoacoara. I watch out my window and the suburbs transition into towns and eventually devolve into bushes and sand.

My seatmate shows me photos on his digital camera of the women that he has recently compensated to have intercourse with him—forced smiles and coquettish poses, a plethora of soapy shower shots, fortunately none of them exhibiting his bar of Toblerone.

When the road ends and the bus can go no farther, the passengers get out and switch to an awaiting four-wheel-drive flatbed that takes us across the dunes to the little global village of Jericoacoara. I ditch the Swiss guy and sit on the truck's long benches next to a sociable Brazilian couple from Praia do Forte, Bahia. They explain to me that there are no roads into or out of Jericoacoara, except along the beach or over the dunes. This is their eighth time coming back to Jeri over the years, and they have fallen in love with this hamlet wedged between a sierra of dunes, the sea, and the imposing *pôr-do-sol* (sunset) dune at the edge of town. Jeri gets bigger and crazier and more packed with visitors every year, they tell me.

Upon arrival, I go straight to a hotel recommended to me by my patron in Canoa Quebrada. He assures me it will be "friendly to my cause." I show them my shiny blue business card with the Lonely Planet logo and I am told that they have a free room set aside for me. I check in, lock my laptop to the bed frame, hide the pills and my passport in the bathroom, and head out to explore this trendy destination on my terms, with a renewed sense of confidence and purpose.

A 1991 *South American Handbook* (hardcover, 67th edition) that I lifted from the book exchange in a hostel in Natal says Jericuacuara [*sic*] is one of Brazil's most secluded, primitive beaches . . . increasingly popular among travelers and Brazilians. It is so quaint that "pigs, chickens and donkeys roam the street at will."

The last edition of *Lonely Planet Brazil*, the 5th edition from 2002, calls Jericoacoara a small fishing village popular among backpackers, hip Brazilians, and windsurfers . . . "a beautiful spot where dozens of palms drowning in sand dunes face *jangadas* (traditional single sailed Brazilian boats) stuck on a broad gray beach. Goats, horses, cows, bulls and dogs roam the sandy streets at will."

That is exactly the same thing that the 4th edition, from 1998, says about the town. The only change is that there is a warning in the 4th edition about *bichos de pé* (foot parasites), and in the 5th edition things seem to have improved on that front. It seems to me that quite a bit more has happened to this *small fishing village*.

These days, this town, built off of four or five main streets of sand, has more free-roaming cokehead hotel owners, Israeli kitesurfers, and Argentinian playboys than goats, horses, cows, bulls, or dogs. The locals have watched the place mushroom from a charming yet soporific outpost that didn't even have regular electricity until 1998 to an international hot spot, complete with beach yoga and crêpe restaurants. Locals are sidelined as undesirable obstructions to Jeri's development, living farther and farther from the central part of town. Some have bought into the growth and become restaurant owners, souvenir salesmen, hotel staff, or professional girl-friends. However, the majority of the Brazilian business own-ers are from larger towns in the region or the big cities to the south.

A creature weaned on grassroots tourism, Jeri is now hit-ting a stage of maturity at which package tours are starting to arrive and it is poised to become the region's tourism center. The backpacker vanguard may have trampled and stamped down the trail, braving inconveniences and the unknown to get here, but now the tour operators have taken over with their buses and block hotel reservations. It is my job to open the aperture a bit more: to write about the guy who is building up his fleet of motorcycles to do bike tours of the region, the kitesurfing classes, to write about the new soup restaurant, or the new Italian restaurant with mushroom risotto and rich chocolate desserts.

It would be misleading to say that all of this growth has been spurred by Lonely Planet, though its impact is undeniable. Lonely Planet's seal of approval means that the little fishing village gets a booster shot of global publicity, whether the town wanted it, needed it, could handle it—or not. It is hard to make it through a meal without seeing a copy of the book on one of the other diner's tables, or to see a group of sunbathers without at least one of them flipping through the guidebook's pages.

While the guidebooks come first, hand in hand with the backpacker front line, the newspapers and magazines are not too far behind in the feeding frenzy. Other travel publications have been on the Jericoacoara story for a decade. The *New York Times* travel section had its first piece on Jericoacoara in 1994. The same year, *Washington Post Magazine* upped the ante with an article that claimed Jericoacoara had one of the "top ten most beautiful beaches in the world." While the overall location is undeniably gorgeous, the beach itself is not even a top ten in Brazil. The travel-writing hype machine was already in motion.

The first luxury hotel has just opened its doors. Plans are in place to redo most, if not all, of the beachfront property, to get rid of the hostels and cabanas and replace them with higher-end hotels with swimming pools and bars. Earlier this year in Manhattan, I had a pseudo-Brazilian cocktail of rum, ginger, and honey called a Jericoacoara. It was served at a French-named Lower East Side bar for something like $7 or $8. Even there, about 4,000 miles away, I knew it was already over for the little fishing village. Because of its remote location, Jericoacoara is still less developed than Canoa Quebrada (which according to that 1991 *South American Handbook* "has been discovered and is becoming a major tourist attraction"). The land also has protected status, which is supposed to limit development, but it is clear that hard currency always wins in the end. The next steps will be paved roads and direct bus tours, an official website in English, ATMs, spring breakers, *Girls Gone Wild* videos, timeshare condos, and Teva-wearing Canadian retirees. I can feel it in the air. I can see it in the rapacious eyes of the Milanese and Paulistano hotel and restaurant owners. I am conflicted about my role in all of this, but the process was under way long before I got to town.

I sit on the corner of the sandy plaza fronting the beach with Junior, the owner and inhabitant of the town's single surf shop. Long and wiry, with clear eyes and a laugh that borders on hyperventilation, he spends most of the day in a navy Speedo with white zinc oxide on his nose, drinking tall bottles of Antarctica beer insulated in Styrofoam cozies. He drinks with friends and passersby, engaging the odd shop client and listening over and over again to the popular song of the moment, "Zóio da Lula" (Squid Eye), by the reggae and hip-hop influenced Brazilian band Charlie Brown Jr.

The song repeats again. Junior stands up from the table and sings along to the chorus, flecks of saliva springing from his lips:

> *Meu escritório é na praia*
> *eu tô sempre na área*

It loosely translates as:

> *My office is on the beach*
> *I'm always around*

It sounds a lot better in Portuguese, and it rhymes, too, but in either language the sentiment captures Junior's ideals and my own. The beach is his office. That's where he's at, so deal with it. Exactly.

While having your office on the beach sounds appealing, it doesn't seem to be the most predictable or steady line of work. After a few drinks, I try to edge into a conversation with Junior about the business climate in Jericoacoara—feeling out my sales potential. This is my office, too, in a way, so I figure I should be doing some market research. Before I fully broach the subject, he is already asking if I can pay to buy more beers. It is low season, I am told. Money is running short throughout the town. "It's not like everyone keeps extra money in their savings account or something here. We don't even have a bank in town. We make it, we spend it, and we need more to keep going. This time of year we are very poor."

Even for low season, there seems to be a fair number of visitors in town. I hear English, French, Hebrew, Spanish, Japanese, Dutch, and Portuguese with distinctive Rio and São Paulo accents. "Hotel capacity is around ten to fifteen percent right now, but we need things to be around fifty percent or more to really start making money," Junior explains.

A group of three gringos walk by. They all look reasonably tough, tattooed, and sun baked. Definitely partiers. Maybe I should strike up a conversation with them. A fourth trails a few paces behind the others, listening to a large gray MP3 player of some sort and bobbing his blond, ponytailed head along to an unknown music.

"Otto," I shout.

No answer.

"OTTO."

"Thomas?" He pulls off his headphones and walks over. "Oh man. I can't believe it. This is the first time in my life I think that I am happy to see an American. Brother, I can't wait to get out of this town. It's so Lonely Planet here," he smirks. "What are you doing? Let's go up to São Luís tomorrow."

"I just got here, man. I can't leave yet."

"C'mon. We can get a Land Rover up the coast and go up along the beaches to the Sand Dunes National Park."

"Sounds epic, but . . . I've got business to attend to before I can go anywhere. Give me a few days, all right? And then we'll head up the coast."

"OK, but hurry up, because I've already closed this town."

"What do you mean?"

"You know, just like Olinda. I am all locked up with a girl here. The town's closed, there are no more female opportunities, no future for me here. You can't switch horses in the middle river, or whatever you say. Especially not in a town of this size. And I'm not settling down here for eternity. So, it is time to move on. This place is closed."

"How long have you been here?"

"Three days, I think. A long time."

"Right. Well, you're going to have to sit it out a few more and let me figure some shit out. After that, I'm game."

My days revolve around sandboarding on the dunes, driving in dune buggies, and living the culture of the town, making mental notes for the guidebook while I try to meet buyers to fund the rest of my research. It's nowhere near as easy as I had hoped. Moreover, I am embarrassed about what I am doing and even keep it a secret from Otto.

The research, particularly the restaurant research, is much easier when everything is networked and prearranged. The owner of a hotel will put you in touch with the owner of a restaurant, and once things are in motion it is no time before you end up with a full schedule of lunch and dinner plans, menu samplings and free cocktails. I get to meet the managers, chefs, and owners; tour the kitchens; and chat with some of the guests. A pizza restaurant that is closed for the low season is opened and the wood oven is fired up so that I may give their food a try. The manager, a Canadian and a bit of a cougar, even joins me as a dinner date.

I'm learning as I go, and it is increasingly clear that this game has its own set of rules. Some of the owners try to bad-mouth other establishments or steer you away from them, so it is important not to take everything they say at face value. You smile, you speak ambiguously, you show that you are thankful (but never overly impressed), and, most important, you accept their assistance without making any promises. A big part of the job is learning who you can trust and who you can use but never trust. Yes, I accept freebies and hookups, but that only helps to make the research possible. I swear that I would never write something untrue about a place, simply because they gave me a free room or a plate of pasta. However, I do recognize that researching within such a network inherently limits the scope of the research to more tourism-savvy establishments, likely those that are already in the guidebooks. I'd like to think that the whole process frees up some money for me to attend unpaid meals at a few more obscure places, but there is not much money to free up at this point, either way.

I run into the Swiss-German guy from the bus a couple more times. He has stayed at three hotels in four nights and gives me his quantitative rundown on the differences in values of the rooms and bathrooms. He is not satisfied with any of them and will be moving to another hotel this afternoon. He does recommend a restaurant that gives a "fair portion of meat, at three hundred twenty-five to three fifty grams or more along with the rice and beans." I am learning to pick up research from others and suss out whether they know what they are talking about or not. I try to feel out if he would be interested in ecstasy with a story about "a friend who has some," but he assures me that he already has enough vices.

Four nights become five and I am still in possession of exactly fifty pills—my fifty little spades. I may not be a good salesman, but I've lived the life of a traveler in this town and now have a feeling for what attracts people here, why they stay, what makes the town move. As for my incipient sales career, I am too self-conscious about the whole thing to initiate the conversion. I am like a virgin trying to convert from foreplay to penetration. Should it be discussed outright? Should it come up organically? Will I offend someone if I bring it up, and scare them off?

The closest that I got was when I overheard a mixed crew of Aussies and Dutch in my hotel talking about DJs and clubs in Rotterdam and Melbourne. It seemed to be the perfect entrée for my sales pitch. But they claimed to already have a bunch of pills. They said they would purchase a few of mine for $5 a pill—just to restock. Unfortunately, it wasn't worth my while.

The little fishing village is in constant flux. The bus carries away dozens of travelers during the day and replenishes Jeri with a load of new conscripts every evening. This has to work out sooner or later, I preach to myself. Someone will bite. Something will happen.

It is a late-night town that doesn't get going until around midnight. As I shave and clean up prior to going out to Planeta Jeri, the town's main nightclub, I hold counsel with myself in front of the bathroom mirror. "You need to get out there and make some money. Just like Inara. You have the same needs as everybody else. You must, above all, believe in yourself, face your goals, and then fight as if your life depended on it." I dig for more motivational clichés. "Tonight's your night."

Planeta Jeri is a partially open-air club, with crowds of locals and travelers sitting at and dancing on the outdoor tables below a painted rip-off Planet Hollywood logo. Carts line the packed-sand street just off of the premises, selling caipirinhas, rum-and-Cokes, and all sorts of fresh fruit cocktails that undercut the drink prices at the bar. The DJ spins everything from the Jackson 5 to Roni Size to something that I can only define as bad acid trance. I need to gather some resolve and ask people if they want to buy some ecstasy. I have to get things moving. This is a business and requires work just like anything else. Before I am able to approach anyone, I am cornered by an apparently inebriated French girl.

"I heard that you write for *Lonely Planet*," she says in accented but impeccable English, teetering backward.

"Really? From whom?"

"I heard it around."

"OK. Maybe it's true." Is this my chance at my first French groupie?

"You know what?" she hiccups.

"No, what?"

"I was traveling with some friends. We split up for a few weeks, but made plans to meet up at a bar in Salvador on a specific date. We picked the bar out of the *Lonely Planet*. It was highly recommended. When I got there, I found out that it closed down. MANY YEARS AGO. Somebody told me that it has been closed for ALMOST TEN YEARS. I have not seen my friends SINCE. YOU RUINED MY TRIP, *Meestair Fucking Lonely Planet*," she shouts, staggering back against the people sitting at the table behind her. At least a dozen people are staring at the two of us. So much for being inconspicuous.

I try to explain that I didn't work on the last edition, nor did I cover any of the information in Salvador, but that is of no consequence. I ask her to give me the name of the place and promise to pass it along to the appropriate person. Within minutes I am mobbed by random travelers, asking about what it's like to work for Lonely Planet, how to apply for the job, if I really visit all of the places, if I've met Tony Wheeler or the guy from the Lonely Planet television show. Working for Lonely Planet is a dream job. Lonely Planet is ruining independent travel.

My cover is blown. And once again, I have no luck talking to anyone about my business proposition. But I do meet three members of an Australian windsurfing company and their two Brazilian windsurfing pro hosts. We make our way out to a small bakery that is open to the public only during the baking hours of 2 a.m. to 6 a.m. There are exactly three things on the menu. The bakery is full of partiers from all over the world trying to put down a few calories and calm their stomach with something solid before heading back to their hostels and *pousadas* to crash. Aside from fornicating with a stranger under the stars, the early-dawn bakery offers the quintessential late-night Jeri experience. I can't say that I would have ever found the place had I passed through the town in one evening or spent the night in my room writing rather than doing bar research.

Being a drug dealer is a much more difficult job than I had imagined. I was always led to believe that it was fast money and low stress, the kind of job that delinquents fall into when they can't play it straight at Wendy's or whatever "real world" servitude that they might have access to. No. Drug dealing is hard work. I'm not saying that it's a noble profession, just that it's not easy money. In fact, it probably takes a lot more organization, entrepreneurial skills, independent thinking, and intelligence than most jobs. Working in the black market is the truest form of capitalism. There is no support network. No rules. No regulation. No recourse. No HR ombudsman to complain to. The competition is unbridled and, at least in the early stages, you are single-handedly in charge of protecting your business interests.

I am a reluctant salesman and am even worse at driving a hard bargain. Karrass would be ashamed. DB Cooper would be mortified. Roebling would consider me pathetic. I am embarrassed for myself. I am not a drug dealer. I am not a businessman. Audacity? I couldn't even sell clothes at Club Monaco.

If this whole experience were a *Choose Your Own Adventure* book, say *The Lost Jewels of Nabooti* or *Deadwood City*, I would have a choice of thirty-seven endings. I would realize that I had selected the wrong page and would flip back to the earlier choices, do it differently until it worked out. But I cannot go back. This is on-the-job training—spontaneity, action, and adventure, exactly what I had desired once upon a time back in my office cubicle. Or course, back then my romantic vision didn't include potential incarceration or death and/or dismemberment as additional consequences beyond getting fired and going bankrupt. Now I don't even have the money to scrounge my way back to Rio and get home. All I have are the spades.

I wonder if the towns of Jericoacoara or Canoa Quebrada ever feel the same way; do they wish that they could go back to a more innocent, less compromised time? But now the hotels and restaurants have been built and need to be filled over and over again. Minimum 50 percent capacity. They need to sustain themselves, need to compromise, bend and evolve. They need to just get on with it, regardless. Copacabana was once a remote beach community, too, on the periphery of Rio de Janeiro city. Then came the weekend visitors, the tunnel, fancy hotels, Orson Welles, the favela, Carmen Miranda, cocaine, Michael "Blame it on Rio" Caine, and that was that. Sometimes there is no looking back.

After several days of the game-playing circuit, I become sick of it all. Sick of drinking. Sick of eating in restaurants. Sick of being politic. Sick of being around travelers. I keep running into the owner of one travel agency in the street near my hotel and I am convinced that he is stalking me. Research is going well but I am seething with anxiety over my financial problems. I need to get away from the traveler scene and slow things down so that I can think more clearly. I need perspective, so I wander up the beach and out of town. I am still broke, and all that's changed since my travel-writing epiphany is that I now owe a bunch of money that I don't have to a drug dealer in Chile. I recently checked my email to find a firm message from Bobby, devoid of his typical garrulousness, telling me that he expected to see his money soon, very soon, or we were going to have problems. First Beatriz, and now this.

Some twenty minutes north of town on foot, I see two men, both in their mid-forties, sitting cross-legged on the beach next to a blue dune buggy. One is a deeply, almost professionally, tanned European man with a blond pageboy cut; the other, a fair-skinned Latino guy with a conquistador beard, mustache, and short midnight black ponytail. A couple of beer cans lie spent in the sand between them. On closer inspection I see that the cans are not beer, but black cans of Pitú brand *cachaça*. I wonder momentarily why the aluminum can of hard liquor never caught on elsewhere in the world. A liter bottle of orange soda appears to be the chaser.

A beat-up touring motorcycle is partially tethered to the back of the buggy. Its front end has broken free and—judging by the long sandy rut trailing behind the parked buggy—it had been dragged at least fifty yards before they came to a halt. Suddenly, the black-haired man springs back and gets to his feet as the blond man starts vomiting violently into the sand. A stand of scrawny palms waves soothingly in the breeze. The sun is stretched into a silent mushroom cloud of nuclear orange, hanging low on the liquid horizon.

As I walk past, the standing man, the one with the conquistador, looks at me and shouts in my direction, "WHAT'S UP,

BRODER?" The other tries to wash out his mouth with orange soda, which only triggers more vomiting.

"Can't you give us a hand? We gotta get out of here, fast," the conquistador pleads. Then he reconsiders. "You ain't a cop, are you?"

"Look at him," the other takes a break from his vomiting to offer. "He's just another gringo, he's no cop."

"You ain't no CIA then, are you, gringo?"

"I don't think so, man." I don't know much anymore. I do know one thing, though: I am about as good at selling drugs as I am at travel-guidebook writing.

Dream Job

Don't talk to strangers is about the worst advice that I received in Seattle Public Schools—that, along with *Just say no*. Not talking to strangers makes sense if you are ten and some bearded naked dude pulls up next to you in a cargo van, but otherwise such spoon-fed paranoia has long-term negative effects on a person's psyche and, in my opinion, on our national character. Increasingly, off-line North American social interaction is limited to work functions or some sort of purposeful activity, like sports or a religious organization. Otherwise people tend to stick to friends that they made before the age of twenty-one, and their only spontaneous social interaction comes in various states of intoxication in dimly lit bars.

In my seventh-grade Spanish textbook, we were introduced to Marisa Jiménez and Elena Ochoa, two Spanish-speaking *estudiantes* with wide smiles who enjoyed reading, cats, and spending time in the plaza. I never cared for cats, but I wanted to go to the plaza, too. I was sick of after-school television and organized team sports. I wanted to get to know Marisa and Elena and hang out in the town square with its cobblestones and palm trees, where people had casual contact with broader society. Thus began my interest in Latin America.

The two drunks, the pageboy and the conquistador, aren't as alluring as Elena or Marisa, but I am in Latin America and they are strangers in need.

"What are you celebrating?" I ask, nodding toward the demolished man in the sand.

"We're leaving town. My friend Micky is having a going-away party and I'm trying to tie his fucking motorcycle back on my buggy," he says in English with a light Spanish accent. "I'm called Arturo."

"Where you off to?" I continue.

"Top secret."

"Top secret?"

"Yeah, bro. *Tip-top* secret. You sure you're no CIA?" He cackles and drinks from the can of *cachaça*, sending a spastic shiver though his body. He has the gaunt, high-metabolism look of a man who is nearly impervious to alcohol and sedatives.

"We're foogitives. . . ." The blond man, Micky, again raises his head to chime in. He clears his hair from his eyes and wipes his mouth with the back of his bronzed forearm. He recovers from his dry heaves enough to brush a few handfuls of sand over the vomit and assemble a drooling smile in my direction. In spite of his state of inebriation, he has a perfect set of laser-whitened teeth.

Arturo interrupts, "I ain't no fugitive, man. *Him*. He's the fugitive. I'm just the—how do you say?—the accomplice, the fucking getaway driver, mang."

"I hope it's worth the hassle, 'cause it looks like that bike is smashing the shit out of your buggy. That's no Vespa you're trying to put up there, man."

"You're right. CIA is smart, no, Micky? That *is* a problem.

SEE WHAT I'M FUCKING TRYING TO TELL YOU, MICKY?" Arturo shouts at his fallen comrade. The back end of the huge BMW motorcycle, the part that is still lashed to the roll bar, has buckled the rear deck of the buggy and is sending white cracks chasing out toward its edges.

"Yeah, well, it is notta situation of worth it or not worth it. My Dutch buddy here can't keep it in his pants and now he's looking at spending a few trips around the sun in the clink. They were coming to arrest him and he tried to ride off on his bike. Drunk bastard crashed it into a sand dune. And since I've known his stupid fucking ass forever . . . well, you know how it goes . . ."

"Can't he pay a bribe?" I say, digging a hole in the sand with my bare feet.

"He already paid two bribes, but now they want another. It's all a scam. They've got the whole thing planned from the beginning. I know this one well because my cousin used to run it in Isla de Margarita on foreign businessmen. It's an old trick for when money runs short in the low season. If he pays another bribe, they'll just want another until he escapes or goes to jail. We're going to the border."

"Venezuela?"

"Can't say."

"You're Venezuelan, though?"

"Yeah, CIA. I am. You ask a lot of questions, mang. I've been in Spain for most of my life, though. Went to school in Miami for a couple of years, too, when my dad was working in the States. Got kicked out of the school first, and then I got kicked out of the country," he laughs. "Me *and* my dad. That enough information for you, gringo?"

"Hey man, you called me over."

"Right." He has another drink, followed by the same fierce shivering. "This is my friend Micky. We've known each other since, like, fucking forever."

"You already told me that."

"Just making sure you're listening, kid."

Micky starts to recompose himself and says, "Hey man . . . my name's Micky." He spits some rusty phlegm into the sand. "From Amsterdam. I've known this bastard forever, we used to run Ibiza. Don't truss [*sic*] anything he says."

"All right . . . I'm Thomas. What's up with the motorcycle?"

Arturo starts back in, "It took us forever to try to tie that fucker on the back of my car. It's breaking the whole back. Too fucking heavy. The buggy's made of fiberglass, you know? We made it about ten minutes before the rope broke, and the front of the bike fell down. If you can help us get it back up on the thing, we can get it to the next town, at least." Arturo lowers his voice. "Micky's not much use at this point."

We set about lifting the bike back onto the buggy. The fender bends, buckles, and cracks under the weight. The busted rope is too short to properly bind the bike frame to the roll bar. We make a few attempts to knot the pieces of rope together. I dig deep for Cub Scout knowledge. The bowline knot: the bunny runs around the hole, up through the hole, whatever; fuck the bunny method.

Arturo swears to himself under his breath in Spanish as the two of us try again to hoist the bike into place. Micky does not lift a finger to help, but gently nurses the liter bottle of orange soda and ponders out loud how things went so wrong. He used to own Ibiza. Own Mustique. Own New York City. Own Amsterdam. Now this. Why does he now have to flee some poor fishing village in order to evade provincial police? He should own them, too. "I know European royalty. And American celebrities. I used to party at the Playboy Mansion with Jon Bon," he reminisces.

"You never told me that you knew Le Bon." Arturo exclaims.

"No, *Bon Jovi*."

"Shit, I was about to say, I remember Simon Le Bon. He was the fucking man. . . . I never understood all the dudes with lipstick, but, you know."

Micky then subjects me to the résumé version of his life, how he arrived in Mustique as a deckhand on a yacht, met Mick Jagger and David Bowie at Basil's Bar, befriended the inventor of some oil drill bit and helped him build private Formula 1 tracks in Southern Spain. At some point, either earlier or later in his CV, he also devised new revenue streams for television, including the text messaging interface that became the foundation of shows like *Big Brother*. He paused to vomit again, now as orange as the sunset. These days he lives in a loft in SoHo "during New York's only two bearable months of the year, April and November." He has a beach house in Formentera and also stays with an associate on an unnamed island in the South Pacific. He lives on the open road the rest of the time.

Micky was in the process of covering the entire northern coast of Brazil by motorcycle. He made the point again that he was friends with Jon Bon Jovi and that most of the world-class creativity that was coming out of the Netherlands was the direct result of the high-grade weed that was being grown there.

"Me, I'm just family money." Arturo cackles again, "That's the South American way to do it."

"What are you doing here? Vacation?" Micky asks me.

"I'm trying to write. I think."

"Yeah, cool. I'm a writer, too. I'm writing a screenplay called *Tatajuba Heat*. Or, at least I have this idea for a screenplay." Tatajuba is a small town up the coast that is taking some of the spillover from Jericoacoara. "I mean the setting is based on Jericoacoara, but I figured that *Tatajuba Heat* sounded better than *Jericoacoara Heat*." He starts back in on a small sip of *cachaça*. "It's about the beautiful daughter of the hotel owner who makes every visitor believe that she is in love with them."

"Sounds intriguing."

"Then she seduces the men, encourages them to take Polariods with her camera, and then gives the photos to the guys. Her father goes to the police, who, of course, find the Polaroids in the man's room the next day. The cops and the father then try to extort money out of the man because she is actually fifteen even though she looks like she is twenty-three and is ferocious in bed."

"Good story. Fiction?"

"Yeah. What are you writing?"

"No *Tatajuba Heat*. Just a guidebook."

"Guidebooks. Shit, someday I'd like to meet a Lonely Planet writer and tell him what rubbish those books are. I mean, I still use them, even though I am very rich, but their good hotel recommendations are very bad. I stayed at one place in Fortaleza that was in Lonely Planet and they didn't even carry my bags to my room."

"Jesus. How bourgeois."

With a crash, the motorcycle again falls from the back of the buggy, almost taking my arm with it. Arturo is exasperated and starts kicking the tire. He repeats to himself "Fucking bullshit, Micky . . . worse than having fucking enemies . . ."

"Hey, Tim, you ever been to Ibiza?" Arturo asks. "I met this bastard here in San Antonio, Ibiza, decades ago."

"It's Thomas. No, I've never been. Seems a bit hectic these days."

"Oh dude, the place sucks now, or, at least, San Antonio does. Full of overweight, drunk English girls with their tits flying out of their shirts. Let me tell ya though, bro—back in the day, the late seventies and early eighties—it used to be paradise." He sticks two cigarettes in his mouth, lights them with a single match, and passes one to Micky. "Now it's all cheap flights and weekend club multipasses. We were there when that shit was starting, when the first girls arrived from the Netherlands with a half kilo of MDA and a pill press. I'd never seen anything like that in my life. Get this, the girl said, 'Do

you want to try the drug that will make you love your enemy?'
How could I say no to that?"

We untie the remaining bike tire that was still successfully
lashed in place and set the motorcycle down on the ground.

"Tim. Why don't you ride this bike behind us to the next
town? Micky is too drunk to walk, let alone ride it. We'll pay
you. We can mail you some cash in the future or something."

"Dude, honestly, I don't know how to shift on a motorcycle
or ride on the sand. And, you know, it's getting dark."

"You could drive the buggy and I could ride it."

"It's not that. It's that, you know, you guys seem cool and
all, but I'm not sure that we're tight enough yet for me to be
helping you run from the cops."

"OK, CIA. I see your plan. You want to buy Micky's motorcycle, don't you?"

I try to force a laugh. "I don't have any money and I don't
even know how to ride it. I don't even know if it works."

"OK, I'll make you a special deal then," Micky interrupts,
suddenly clearheaded, "How about you trade it to me for a
thousand dollars and your U.S. Passport. Then just go to the
embassy and tell them that someone stole your passport. That's
the best deal that you'll get on a BMW in your whole life."

"Sounds like a hassle to me, man. And when I said that I
don't have any money, I meant no money . . . I could trade it to
you for say . . . for fifty hits of ecstasy."

"And the passport?"

Think: Karrass. "No passport."

They look at each other and laugh. Arturo jumps back in,
"This ecstasy that you kids take, this MDMA, is like M&Ms
compared to real MDA. Let me tell you, I remember taking
MDA with Harrison Ford at Roman Polanski's kimono party in
Ibiza back in 'eighty-three . . . or was it 'eighty-one, fuck, what-
ever man."

"As in everyone was wearing kimonos?"

"Exactly. Harrison was just sitting there at the table with a solid kilo of weed in front of him rolling joints. That was a classic party. There's nothing like that anymore. I seen him, Harrison that is, I seen him around since then, you know, he was with his family flying a helicopter to Canaima, you know, to go to Angel Falls in Venezuela. Well, man, I got a chance to talk to him and I say, 'Hey, Harrison, you remember me?' and he says, 'No, should I?' And I say 'Yeah, I was hanging out with Carmelito at Roman's kimono party back when you was Han Solo.' And he looks at me sideways with his face all screwed up like he does in the movies, you know, he's got that crooked nose, just like you. And he says, 'Please do me and my family a favor and let's just say that that never happened.' That fucking guy. He knows about real MDA, even if he won't admit it. Me and Micky know it real well. You kids don't know shit. Fuck, I personally introduced ecstasy to Miami when South Florida was still full of Cocaine Cowboys." He smoothes down his conquistador mustache and goatee with his thumb and forefinger.

The sun has almost set and the wind is picking up. "Well, look guys, I need to get out of here. You want to try to get the bike up there one last time?

"Are they pills or caps?" Micky asks.

"Pressed pills."

"What's on them?"

"Spades."

"Whats?"

"*Spades*. Like hearts, diamonds, clubs, *spades*."

"Ah *Schoppen*. Nice. From Amsterdam?" Micky questions, still seated in the sand.

"Dutch, yes. Or so I'm told. Globalization, I guess."

"I think I know who makes them. Not worth much back home, but I can sell them in Caracas or the Caribbean for a few euros. Art, maybe you can give me the address of your cousin in Margarita?" He spits up something dark and thick that looks like more like blood than orange soda. "Maybe I'll just take them myself, I'm about done with *cachaça*."

"I have to run back to my hotel. Go park the buggy over there behind that dune so no one sees you. I'll be back in less than a half hour," I say. "I'll be with a friend, an Israeli guy. Don't mind him." And with that, I have made my first business deal. It isn't exactly a sale, more like bartering or laundering, but it is heading in the right direction.

I return with the pills and Otto in tow, my unassuming body-guard and motorcycle appraiser. Arturo is already sitting in the driver's seat, chain-smoking and kneading the steering wheel. Micky is prostrate in the sand to the side of the car, breathing heavily. Fortunately for them, there are somewhere between zero and two police in town on a given day. Besides, no one would expect them to head in the direction that they did, as there is no town of size for half a day's drive.

Otto gives the bike a once-over, fires it up. "I think it could use a new spark plug and you could stand to clean out some of the sand, but otherwise it seems fine," he says. Then he pulls me aside and whispers, "It's a nice enough bike and I think that you can get it for less. What else are these fools going to do?"

"I don't know, hide out, sober up, and drive in a few hours? I don't want anything to do with these pills. Let's just get this thing done and get out of town."

"Your choice."

Micky asks from the sand, "Do you guys have a cassette or something to throw in to sweeten the deal? We need some decent music for this trip. I don't want anything from the Israeli, but, you, Yankee, do you have any Detroit techno, some San Francisco or Chicago house or anything?"

"Sorry, man. Haven't owned a tape in a while now." I hand Arturo one of the pills for inspection.

Arturo looks closely at both sides of the tablet, bites a little flake from its edge, and rolls it over with his tongue. He spits, nods, and asks to see the full amber prescription bottle. I quickly pick off the parts of the prescription label with my name on it and pass it over. He tosses the bottle along to Micky, who is on his feet and climbing stiffly into the passenger seat. Arturo then throws me the keys to the bike and says, "Tell the CIA and the Mossad that you never met us. We're just gosts."

"Ghosts?"

"Gosts. Yeah, *fantasmas*, like Casper . . ."

"Would the CIA trade you pills for a motorcycle?"

"They'd trade you RPGs, planes loads of cocaine, child slaves, stuffed ballot boxes. . . . I seen 'em do it. So, I don't see why not. This is chump change, no?"

"You guys know where you're going?"

"No. North, maybe. We'll figure the rest out." Arturo revs the buggy.

"Art's right, these are like M&Ms," Micky shouts. He then proves his point by knocking back a pill with a slug of *cachaça*. He throws the can over his shoulder and they peel out onto the moonlit beach, kicking up a low rooster tail of wet sand.

Otto and I are left standing at the edge of a dune, silent except for the crashing of waves. He shakes his head disapprovingly as I hold the heavy motorcycle under a sky of a million stars.

The next day, I take a seat across from a small desk governed by a swarthy, stocky man with a black goatee and a black beret. His coffee-colored eyes are narrowed by the stinging light that cuts through the window behind me. Stacks of papers—order forms, deeds, and service forms—cover the computerless desk. Otto stands with the motorcycle just outside the window. It is a fine piece of Bavarian engineering, I tell the man. Maybe a bit beat up, but fitted for distance travel with knobby tires to deal with the sand, I continue.

I had flirted briefly with Otto's idea of riding the bike up the coast. But there is too much open ground to cover. A motorcycle adventure would require planning, maps, information on river crossings, extra gasoline, a compass, rain gear, perhaps a new spark plug. Two people on a single bike with two backpacks doesn't strike me as a good time, especially as I would be on the back. Most important, I need to liquidate my assets as soon as possible.

Dudu, the pirate across the desk, is one of the few locals who has ascended to business ownership in the Jeri tourist economy. I try to explain to him that I am working for the guidebook, but he is not familiar with guidebooks or the larger tourism system outside of Jericoacoara. Publicity and marketing, things that might not earn him cash now but would potentially benefit him in the long run, are alien concepts. He knows about his little business and that's about it—there will be no freebie here.

As for the motorcycle, he says, "It's too big. I need smaller, lighter-weight dirt bikes—the kind that are comfortable for tourists on short afternoon trips."

"Trust me, this is the best deal you'll ever get on a BMW," I argue. "If you don't want to keep it, you can trade it to someone else for two smaller bikes and build up your fleet. How about you give the two of us a ride up the coast to the dunes at Lençóis Maranhenses National Park in your Land Rover, stopping so that I can check some things out in some of the towns along the way? That, and a thousand dollars for the bike."

"You're crazy. This isn't Beverly Hills, gringo. I don't have a thousand to throw around."

"OK, so what can you do for me then?"

The evening before we depart Jericoacoara, I confine myself to my room and attempt to write. Tonight there will be no distractions. I am prepared with the flip-flops, a fan, the bandana properly tied to my head. I have responsibly replaced the usual cans of beer with a liter of cool water.

Otto knocks at the door. He met a girl from town. He bought some beers. She and her friend want to go to the beach with us. The girls are waiting down the road. All that is missing is my presence.

I tell him that I appreciate the invite, but I have important business to attend to. Beyond that, I can't even think about drinking. "Suit yourself, asshole," he says, adjusting and retying his ponytail. "*Adventure travel* writer, huh?" He sulks and walks off.

My knuckles are cracked one by one, notes are organized, pages are formatted; I am finally ready to write.

There is a brutal pounding on the door. Otto enters with the look of a hardened mercenary in his eye. "You know what? I thought about this and this is BULLSHIT. I told you that this town is already closed for me. I am making a delicate tactical maneuver here. You're coming with me, RIGHT NOW." He lowers his tone, "The girls are waiting for us and I need your backup."

"*I just . . .*"

"RIGHT NOW." His fists are balled.

"*But . . .*"

"I helped YOU before. Now it is YOUR turn to help ME. You can write another day." He hurries me toward the door and hands me a six-pack.

"I appreciate your help, but you have to understand that I'm really trying to not drink and my deadline is getting close and I finally have a chance to—"

"I helped you break all sorts of laws and all I want is for you to have a couple of beers on the beach, keep this girl company and maybe have sex with her, so I can spend some private time with her friend."

He is right. I could never let down a friend in need. I am

just that kind of guy. Plus, he is scaring me. As for the drinks, I could always call ahead and reserve a bed in rehab for when I get back. It would be a soft landing, at least.

Fortunately, I am able to return to my room with just enough time to finish packing and wash the sand out of my crotch and off my back and out of my hair before our dawn departure in Dudu's Land Rover.

We drive north along the coastline in the same direction as Arturo and Micky. Within minutes we are on desolate stretches of beach, wedged between the sea and heaving sand dunes. Shrubs, the odd tree, a dead giant sea turtle, and a random misplaced head of cattle are the only interlopers in the landscape. Dudu, his beret turned backward, chain-smokes filterless cigarettes while speeding along the hard-packed sand near the water's edge.

Part of the deal with Dudu was that we needed to get three other passengers before we could depart, and so we had to wait in Jeri an extra day. Fortunately, the group materialized quickly and consists of an expat British couple who live in Rio and a Brazilian woman who spent last high season working in Jeri and was now moving farther north to avoid the tourism onslaught. Daniela, or Dani, as she is called, is looking for someplace more relaxed. She had worked at a restaurant in the south, in the beach town of Paraty, for a number or years and had moved to Jeri in search of a slower pace. She wanted something more raw and less developed, but found that even Jeri was too far on its way.

Half of the $500 worth of reais that Dudu and I settled on is in my front pocket, and the other half hidden in my backpack. Including the value of the ride up the coast, I grossed approximately $600 out of my ecstasy-for-motorcycle-for-transportation-and-cash deal. At first Dudu offered me just the

$500, but he tracked me down later and threw in the Land Rover trip. He said that a tour agency owner in Jeri had partially subsidized the trip as they wanted me to have the opportunity to "get to know and write about" the town of Atins at the national park. I owe Bobby $600 for what he advanced me. I'll pay him half, $300, when I get to the next major city and half later from the States, if I ever get back there. That leaves me with about $200 in pocket. It's not much of a gain (none at all, really, as I'll still owe Bobby the other half), but I did temporarily double my net worth and make some progress traveling up the coast.

We stop off in Tatajuba, Camocim, and Parnaíba so that I can jump out and quickly see a hotel or grab menus from a restaurant or two. I mention to the rest of the passengers that I am doing some research, but keep it vague, not wanting to let on about my exact job. The Brits are reading aloud to each other from the old Lonely Planet book—the "Bible," as they call it—and keep quoting the ever-dependable last writer. I bite my tongue, lest I get cornered into a Q&A session.

I just do quick run-throughs at most of the stop-offs, but still manage to finagle a free crab pie at one restaurant, a beer or two at another, and a few liters of water and soft drinks to share with the other passengers. We could do worse.

The towns end and the dunes reappear. We ford smaller streams in the truck, but wheel it onto rafts in order to cross the larger river mouths that cleave the beach. These simple wooden barges, equipped with an outboard motor or two and manned by crusty old ferrymen, don't look like they can take the weight of a large British 4×4. But they get us across without any setback. We pass churches and old villages that have been consumed by the dunes, leaving only a bit of steeple or peak of a roof protruding from the mound of sand. We kill a few hours in the frenetic market town of Tutóia and help elderly shoppers pack bags of rice and grain into trucks for the long, slow ride back to their remote villages.

Dani rolls and smokes a joint every time that we make a stop. Her laugh is infectious. She only wants a tranquil job in a tranquil town. Clear, fair life goals. Something I respect. I might be in love again.

The dunes gradually increase in size until they appear as a shining mountain range on the horizon. We must be getting closer to the town of Atins and Lençóis Maranhenses National Park. *Maranhenses* is merely a reference to the park's location, in Maranhão state, but *Lençóis* means "bedsheets," a metaphor for the nearly 600 square miles of rumpled sand dunes that rise and fall across the coastal landscape. I am sitting next to Dani and am pleased when she falls asleep with her head on my shoulder. The Brits, still reading from the guidebook, tell us that after the rains, water filters down through the sand and creates small crystalline pools in the troughs between the dunes. Perfect for swimming. Access to the park is impeded by rivers and marshes that cut it off from most of the mainland, and the entire northern side borders the open Atlantic. It is a moonscape of sand, a small Sahara carried across the sea by the trade winds and deposited here in this lost corner of South America.

We are approaching the park from the east and are planning to stay in the small neighboring town named Atins, from which you can enter the park on foot. The east side of the park is almost completely undeveloped. Most visitors enter the park from the other end, through the larger town of Barreirinhas, which is linked by a highway to the regional capital of São Luís. I have heard that Barreirinhas has a decent-size tourism infrastructure, but is actually pretty far from the dunes and requires a tour boat to enter Lençóis Maranhenses.

"I wonder if we'll be able to find a place to stay there?" the man asks the woman.

"Ask Thomas. He is a world-renowned expert on the re-gion," Otto suggests. I slouch down in my seat and pretend that I, too, am asleep.

"What do you mean?" the man asks in my direction.

I mumble, "Nothing. I just . . . I'm sure that there'll be places in Atins."

"Well, I know that the Land Rover can only take us as far as Caburé. From there we have to take a boat to Mandacaru and on to Atins. Or maybe we can get a boat that goes straight from Caburé to Atins. I'm not sure. The LP only has one sen-tence on Atins."

"Right, of course," I say. Truthfully, I have only ever heard of Atins, and don't recognize the other locations he mentions.

"Yeah, I don't know, mate. What if there's nowhere to stay in Atins? The Bible here only mentions one place, Filhos do Vento. I guess we could try to call, but I'm not going to count on finding a phone out here."

"Looks like you should be writing the new Lonely Planet, not Thomas," Otto laughs.

"Lonely Planet? Yeah, right," he laughs. "You're taking the piss, right?"

I give Otto my best shut-the-fuck-up stare, which includes raising both eyebrows and clenching my teeth.

"Taking the piss? I don't follow," Otto plays along.

"Yes, you know, bullshitting me."

"Oh, I see. I never understand you Britons, you should speak English better . . . like Americans."

"Now I'm onto you, mate." He chuckles and turns back to me. "But really, do you work for LP? Is that why you ran into those hotels back there?"

Otto cuts in, "Look at him, do you really think *that guy* would be writing *the Bible*?"

"Right. Funny, I always took you Israelis for a stoic lot," the Brit says, and goes back to reading the book.

We arrive in Caburé, which consists of a small group of thatched huts, a couple of sheds, and a small, vacant hotel on the sandy shore along the river's edge. It is the end of the line for Dudu and his Land Rover. We spend the night in the hotel and are the only guests. There are limited menu options, so we order dinner and spend the evening chatting on the patio, drinking beer, and smoking Dani's joints under the stars. Our voices are the only sound in the entire town. When clouds roll in and black out the night sky, the others head to bed. The sensory deprivation brought on by total darkness and the complete absence of background noise gives me mild vertigo as I stumble to my room.

Dudu returns to Jeri the next morning. The others clamber into a *jangada* and head off for Atins. They cannot fit all of us in, so I volunteer to take a smaller *jangada*, piloted by a local kid. The sail is made out of black plastic garbage bags stitched together with twine. I tie my backpack inside of another garbage bag as the wind lashes water over the low edges of the boat and soaks the interior. I bail water with the top half of an old Clorox bottle for most of the trip.

We stop off in Mandacaru and grab a couple of supply boxes off of the pier, which further weigh down our boat, but we do creep along the river and eventually arrive outside of what, I am told, is Atins. There is nothing to see beyond a bit of collapsed dock and a flooded marsh. A man meets me as I wade ashore in knee-deep water and guides me to a dusty road. Here, the fringes of the town have started to blossom with new structures; there are three hotels, according to my walking partner, who tells me that he was already notified that a writer would be arriving. The core of the town appears to have remained unchanged by tourism, but there are PARCEL FOR SALE signs everywhere, with small, thorny fences woven together and strung up to divide properties. I am told that all of the property in and around Atins is being snatched up, especially by business owners who were successful in Jericoacoara. "That one over there belongs to the lady who owns the chocolate restaurant in Jeri," he points out. I ask if he has ever been to that restaurant, hoping to get a local opinion for the book. Never, I am told. He has never even been as far as Tutóia, let alone Jericoacoara.

I decide to stay by myself at the hotel closer to the town. Dani is there speaking with the owner about some part-time work. It seems that in the last hour she already got a job on the far side of town, working at the hotel where the rest of the people from the Land Rover are staying. She's hoping to pick up a few extra hours here, too. She knows some English, Spanish, and Italian from her time in Paraty and Jeri. It'll come in handy—it is just a matter of time before Jericoacoara becomes a resort full of package tourists and Atins evolves into the new backpacker hot spot, before it then becomes a resort itself.

After having spent the past couple of days locked in the Land Rover, I feel the need for some time alone. I ask Dani to pass a message along to Otto that I'll catch up with him in a day or two. He'll understand, I'm sure. I spend the first evening walking by myself along the beaches on the edge of town, feeling pleasantly solitary, but unusually intimate with the stars and galaxies in the distance—feeling as if I understand the interconnectedness of the millions of grains of sand beneath my feet and the vastness of the Milky Way above. I breathe the scent of sea salt, marsh, and sand. My hard-won sense of relaxation returns.

The next day, I arrange for a guide and, together, we enter the park on foot. We hike on trails through brush and around lakes until the land opens into a rolling desert punctuated only by the clear pools of rainwater. We stop to drink from green coconuts at the house where the guide grew up. His microscopic village, tucked away in a valley inside the park, consists of nothing but a few one-room houses, a stand of palm trees, half a dozen goats, quite a bit of sand, and a pool table. The town is permitted within the park's limits only because it existed before the park was established, and no new residents are allowed to move there. We forge on and the landscape opens up again. It appears as if we are on the high seas, the sand undulating out to the horizon in every direction. As we crest a band of tall dunes, the ocean reappears in the distance: navy, almost black when contrasted against the pale sand.

We hike at a steady clip and in the late afternoon the guide leaves me at a small, three-walled restaurant on the edge of the park. I am told that it is an easy walk back to Atins. The proprietors here laze in hammocks and send for provisions only when a customer arrives. I order a fried fish with rice and sip on coconuts while waiting for the food to be purchased and delivered, the kitchen to be activated, and for the food to eventually be prepared.

I use this time to think, to clear my head of hotels and bars and backpackers. I relish the opportunity to not speak a word for hours. As I am finishing my meal, the Brits appear with a guide and greet me joyously.

"Thomas, I'm on to you."

"What do you mean?"

"The owner of our hotel told us that a Lonely Planet writer is here in Atins. Is that true? Is it you?"

"What?"

"Someone from Jeri told him that the writer was coming. I thought that the Israeli was joking. Do you really write for the Lonely Planet?"

"Yeah, well yes, but, you know, this is actually my first time through this part of . . ."

"My God. You really do. That is my bloody DREAM JOB, mate."

"It's not all that you might imagine."

"Oh man, I wish I'd known. Hey listen, I've got a couple of questions for you. Logistical questions. You know how long it is to take the bus to São Luís from the other side of the park? Three hours, or four? We're going to take it in a couple of days."

"Uh, three and a half?"

"Are you asking me?"

"No, telling you. Three and a half," I say, averaging out his two guesses.

"What about the price of flights from São Luís to Fortaleza, or back to Rio?"

"Uh, that really depends. You know, on schedules and seasons and such. I'm going to be doing some more precise research on that soon." Ari Fleischer would be proud of my tactics.

"Hey, do you know how I can I become a travel writer?"

"No idea, man."

"Listen, we've got a plan for this afternoon and you should bloody well join us."

"What is it?"

"You like to party?"

Maybe he wants me to bang his wife in the sand dunes while he watches. I'm never sure with Brits: proper on the surface and feral after a drink or two. I give a hesitant nod. "What do you have in mind?"

"We actually bought some pills down in Morro de São Paulo. We were going to take them in a club down there, but the music was shite everywhere, so we saved them for the dunes out here."

"E?"

"Yeah," he says, and holds out an open palm with four little off-white pills, each stamped with a little spade.

"Where did you say that you got those?"

"Morro de São Paulo, off some Norwegian nutter. We met him and his Israeli girlfriend in a yoga class."

It comes on slow at first: a need to clench my hands, a warm trembling in my lower jaw, a looseness in my thighs and knees. We are running up and down the sides of the dunes, cartwheeling, jumping into the pools below when it hits.

And when it hits, it hits hard. This is not the kind of ecstasy where you are chatting and bouncing around to music, but the kind of ecstasy when your stomach quivers and waves of orgasmic pleasure surge from your lower abdomen and roll upward, making you rock your shoulders forward, tighten your sphincter, and shut your eyes. Sweat streams down my temples; the movement of others is masked in tracers. I can hear, taste, and feel the sunset. I can see my sense of contentment. These are no M&Ms.

I float on my back in the pool between the dunes, staring up at the sky. Atins is paradise. It is the perfect tranquil place. I can see why Dani would want to move here. I do not want to include Atins in the book. All that will do is bring in more tourists, and 90 percent of the profits will go to foreign investors. Beyond that, there'll be a whole bevy of other problems. The world is good in its natural and perfect state, from the sand up to the stars. I simply need to strike a balance between myself and nature to discover true harmony, the perfect, pure form of being. I just have to change my own mental approach to the universe. I must try to remember this.

The Brits have twisted themselves into a knot of an embrace, kissing desperately and lying on their sides in the sand. A very improper display of public affection by English standards, I think. Though I can't say that I'd mind being in their situation. I thank them for the party favors and make my way back to town.

I start to even out, and my vision clears, although my pupils are still wildly dilated. In the face of all of my other thoughts, it slipped my mind that ecstasy and tropical heat are a perfect recipe for dehydration. I need drinking water, urgently. On my way back through the core of the small town, I walk into the single open-air bar. I ask for a bottle of water and am told that they only serve beer and *cachaça*. Beer will have to do. The beer is mostly water here, anyway.

Men are hanging around the periphery, shooting pool and drinking from tall bottles. I get to talking to a few of the locals: authentic, hardworking salt of the earth. I want to talk to everyone, know their stories, their desires, their ambitions, their understanding of the universe. Know what it is like to live in this oasis of paradise. They are all fishermen, their hands broad and muscular. Some are remotely welcoming, some are clearly indifferent, but even the friendly ones are taciturn. The biggest of the group, Bonitão (Big Pretty), has the look of a young, backwoods Cassius Clay. He is the obvious alpha male and acts as the cultural ambassador.

"Are you from São Paulo?" he asks me.

"No, I'm a foreigner. Can't you hear my accent?"

"Yes, but people from São Paulo are white and have accents, too."

"I'm from the United States," I say, and instinctively hold my breath as you never know what kind of reaction that'll elicit these days.

"Mmmm, yes, I know about it. It's not *so* far from São Paulo though, no?" There is only one adult woman in the bar. She is visibly intoxicated and is dancing with what appears to be her teenage daughter—I don't let these things slip by me anymore.

Bonitão shares a beer with me. He talks about fish. He asks how many children I have. He asks if it is true that there is a new cassette player that can play a hundred songs. I attempt to describe an iPod, but give up when he asks how it works. After another drink, he drifts over and starts dancing with the woman. Her daughter, no more than fourteen, meanders off to the street in front.

Suddenly, a shorter, shirtless man in his mid-twenties with a smooth indigenous complexion staggers into the bar and does a double-take when he sees the woman—his woman—dancing with the huge fisherman. He screams drunkenly, "WHY ARE YOU DANCING WITH MY COUSIN, *PUTA*?" Though only a few people were talking before, the bar now becomes as silent as a tomb. The man next to me says under his breath, "Her husband . . . bad drunk." Bonitão, who is twice the cousin's size, steps away from the woman as if he has nothing to do with the situation, and walks to the bar.

As the woman turns to face her husband, he takes a step forward and drives the full weight of his fist into her mouth. Her head snaps backward. A ribbon of blood—tar-black under the bare lightbulbs—arcs over her head and lands in a long spattered streak on the sandy floor. He advances again, sustaining scratches to his face and neck, and wrestles the now shrieking woman into a headlock.

I survey the bar; some men are watching, some aren't. No one is doing anything or looks like they are going to do anything, including Bonitão, who has his back to the commotion. The man continues to yell and choke his wife. She, of course, continues to scream.

Quiet conversations begin again in the bar. I hear the cue ball ricochet around the pool table. Personal matters, I guess. But shouldn't I do something? I am certainly bigger than the assailant. He's about my age, maybe younger. It could lead me to getting jumped by the rest of the bar. Half of these people are probably related and would stand up for the guy, no matter what. I learned that lesson the hard way in a beach town in Montenegro, where as a teenager I wound up getting my ass kicked in front of my own mother by some poor man's Dolph Lundgren, who probably went on to work in a Bosnian ethnic-cleansing camp. Maybe this sort of spousal-abuse shit happens every night in Atins. Still, no matter how much I've learned about the merits of cultural relativism, this is wrong.

Then the daughter streaks back into the bar through the main entrance. Using both hands and all of the strength she can muster in her small body, she brings down a tall bottle of beer on the man's—her father's? her stepfather's?—head. He falls to his knees and lets go of the woman, blood and foam tumbling from his scalp down his bare back. A deep cut has opened above his ear, matting his hair with thick, shiny blood. The girl cries hysterically and runs from the bar.

"Let her go," someone says from the back of the crowd, although no one was poised to try to stop her.

The bloodied man screams, "Never mess with me," over and over again into his wife's face. She pleads with a mouth full of red teeth to any man who will listen to her. "What did I do to deserve this? Did I deserve this?" One by one, each man turns away from her. It is her issue. She has no audience here, except maybe the feckless, tripping gringo in the corner, who may have thought about doing something but didn't. No one wants to get involved.

She staggers out of the bar and into the night, clutching at her battered face. The husband goes to the bar and orders a beer. The man to my side leans toward me again. "Women shouldn't be out at night," he says. "And, she *knows* how he is when he drinks."

Perhaps Atins *could* benefit from a little development. I must have fallen into the old noble-savage fallacy, imagining there was something exceptional about this traditional lifestyle. What just happened seemed quite a bit more savage than noble. Who am I to decide whether to put this town on the map or not? While I'd hate to come back in five years to find a nightclub full of hookers, hotels replacing houses, and the locals living on the edge of town, God knows, it may happen with or without the guidebook hype—surely my contribution would only be speeding along the inevitable.

Moreover, who am I to say that it should always stay the same, like some exhibit in the zoo? I am sure that there are many people here who would like nothing more than to see the arrival of development, particularly in the relatively pleasant form of tourism rather than the standard forms of smoke-stacks, soybean plantations, cattle ranches, or strip mines.

The world never stays in balance for very long.

I lie awake in bed that night mulling over work. I decide to take the middle road—I'll give Atins its own little heading in the book, but I won't overhype it. I'll mention that it is the only place where you can stay the night and enter the park on foot. I'll avoid the "colour and flair" that I am supposed to use to talk up a destination. Maybe this way, it'll draw more intrepid travelers. If I avoid the hyperbole that it's "slated to be the new Jericoacoara," maybe I will contribute just slightly to development, without overdoing it.

The next day, Otto and I meet up and take a motorboat from Atins away from the park and upriver to the larger town of Barreirinhas. Bonitão drives the boat and no mention is made of last night's blood-spattered incident.

Barreirinhas lacks the proximity to the park that is enjoyed by Atins and lacks many of its secluded charms, particularly the desolate beaches that appear like lost desert islands under the night sky, but it does have a decent foundation of hotels and restaurants, with a river promenade of sorts, bustling streets, banks with long lines waiting to use the ATM, kiosks selling tours to the park, and, most importantly for us, a direct bus to the capital of the state of Maranhão, São Luís.

At a restaurant on the river walk, Otto and I enjoy a long

and much-appreciated lunch of broiled robalo fish fillet swimming in a creamy yellow passion-fruit sauce flanked by glasses of fresh cashew-fruit juice on ice. The cashew nut is actually the seed of a tiny fruit that is attached to a larger, yellow apple-like "accessory fruit." This cashew apple, as it is known, can be pulped and made into a refreshing juice with a somewhat chalky flavor. As the fruit is highly perishable and is a bit of an acquired taste, it is rarely seen outside of areas where cashews are grown. That is a shame as it goes particularly well with a dash of *cachaça*.

The restaurant was recommended by the lady who owns the Atins hotel, who happens to be related to the hotel owner in Jeri, who knows the hotel owner in Canoa Quebrada, and so forth. When the time comes to settle the bill, the restaurant too is friendly to my cause.

I don't have a personal contact for a place to stay in São Luís, so I buy a phone card and call a hotel that I found in the LP book, in order to confirm a discounted room for the upcoming night. The call is a follow-up to an earlier email that I sent from Jericoacoara. Leading with an email gives the information some time to makes its way to the manager. I now know that if you show up at the desk and surprise the clerk with a discount request, they may not be in a position to offer it to you, or may not know what you're talking about. A phone call to follow up the email usually does the trick.

Once I am firmly ensconced in the room, I will contact the manager and ask for suggestions of restaurants and other hotels that will be of some help to me. I will delegate from there, find people who've been to those places and pick their brains for information. The days I spent hustling to try to make it to all of the places, to see them with my own eyes, are far away. Now the most important part of the job is determining who does and doesn't know what they're talking about and figuring out how I can best stretch my money to keep going until the end. The game is being played, and possibly even being won.

I revisit the Publisher's Note, the hallowed creed of guidebook writing in the front of each book that claims that writers don't take freebies in exchange for positive coverage. On closer inspection, this is a carefully worded loophole, as it allows for acceptance of freebies, just not in exchange for positive coverage, as in "if you let me stay here for free, I'll give you a good review." Any hotel owner with an ounce of business savvy would prefer the writer to stay, eat, or drink at their establishment rather than not come at all. By staying the night or enjoying a free meal, the writer can get to know the place better and write about it with a greater degree of detail.

So freebies are kosher in the sense of "if you let me stay here for free, I'll know your place a lot better." The ends are the same, even if the means are slightly more nuanced.

There is a huge gap between what is required of the author and what the author can realistically do with the allotted time and budget. Is this due to weak editorial direction, or willful ignorance on the part of the travel publishers, who choose to disregard how underpaid and overstretched the writers are in order to keep production costs down? I cannot say. A little of both, I guess. A successful guidebook writer must keep up appearances and play the game correctly behind the scenes. There is not enough time and not enough cash to do otherwise. We are to get the book done and not expose any of the folks in the office to the gory details. It's a classic "don't ask, don't tell" policy.

The sad truth is, travel writers are disposable and can easily be replaced by new writers for cheap if they don't learn how to play the game, or ask for too much cash. This is a "dream job," after all, and there's always someone else in line.

In the long run, however, forcing writers into a situation that makes them dependent on the existing tourism infrastructure only contributes to the further entrenchment of a narrow Lonely Planet Trail. This trail not only shortchanges the readers and the quality of the product, but fundamentally alters and frequently corrupts the small, underdeveloped towns that fall in its path, not to mention the people who live there.

Paid Vacation

São Luís marks the beginning of the end of my maiden voyage as a travel writer. Otto and I arrive from Barreirinhas in the airy bus terminal outside of São Luís. It took three and a half hours, just as I had predicted—my faux-authoritative guesswork is getting better all the time. We take a cab to the edge of the historic center, which we then enter on foot.

Originally founded by the French, the city's old quarter brims with dilapidated colonial splendor. The city is now in the process of reshaping itself into a tourist ghetto; some of the colonial architecture has been converted into hotels fronted with al fresco dining options, while neighboring buildings have succumbed to climbing vines and tree branches reaching out from the windows, searching for sunlight. The unmistakable reggae *one drop* beat pounds from little grocery stores, beer bars, tourist restaurants, street vendors, and squatter dwellings in vacated colonial townhouses. The bass sounds from every direction, shaking the cobblestones and loosening azulejo tiling.

The old city is where travelers come when they visit São Luís. The other São Luís, the living city with the HSBC building and the housing projects, newly constructed condos, favelas, and car dealerships lies just across the bridge. I check into my comped room and negotiate a considerable discount for Otto. Next, I email Bobby and get the address of a Chilean PO box. I put half the money that I owe him between pages of newspaper and cardboard in a courier envelope and send it off. I assure Bobby that I am good for the difference and will have it in no time. His email response asks where and when I'd like my next batch of photographs. I say thanks for the opportunity, but, at heart, I am a writer, not a businessman. I wish him the best in his endeavors and promise to be in touch with him down the line.

I set about researching São Luís and the neighboring city of Alcântara, which must be visited by boat. São Luís is not quite as large as Fortaleza or Recife, but it is still a major city and is deserving of the multiday treatment. I follow one verbal recommendation to the next, seeking out hotels and restaurants that are willing to work with me.

I've finally let go enough and can appreciate the trip without fear of debtor's prison. I attend street parties, enjoy discounted meals at restaurants, and party my face off at a live reggae show at the Bar do Porto. I wake up with stacks of flyers, business cards, notes on napkins, and other scraps filling my pockets. I finally start to strike a balance and find time to scope out a few new hotels, restaurants, and other venues to add to the text. I am discovering that elusive functional middle road, just as I near the end of my trip.

I start the night like any other, with some friends from the hostel at a bar on the Beco Catarina Mina. However, it is not any other night. This will be my last in São Luís, one of my last nights of the trip. My deadline is approaching and I must re-treat to a safe haven where I can do my writing. The flight hasn't been arranged quite yet, but I have stashed away just enough cash to get me back to Rio on a domestic airline, and from there I already have a return ticket home.

Beco Catarina Mina is a colonial alleyway consisting of a staircase of long, low steps, each one big enough to accommo-date a number of tables and chairs. The passage is lined with a few bars and restaurants with vines grappling their way up and over the deteriorating masonry. I take note of the names of the bars, grab a card from one, and write the price of drinks on the back of it.

The crowd grows, street musicians arrive, and people start dancing between the tables on the stairs. I am taking in the carefree vibe, legitimately enjoying myself for a change. Otto and I pile into a car along with four Brazilians from the bar and drive across the bridge, past much of the city and out to São Luís's beaches. We arrive at Bar do Nelson, a smaller yet popu-lar outdoor reggae club across the street from the beach.

It is still early and the dance floor is empty. Musicians are setting up their equipment, plugging in amps, and tuning gui-tars as a DJ plays roots reggae in the background. Otto and I grab a drink and start talking to some Argentinian travelers who, in turn, invite us to walk out onto the beach to smoke a joint. There had been some sort of protest earlier in the day and we had seen a significant number of police during the ride over from the old city. They were stopping cars and messing with people, doing whatever the police in these parts do. Whatever it is, I am fairly sure they aren't interested in us, so we agree to the spliff. You simply can't go to a reggae bar in remote South Amer-ica and not smoke a joint—it's all part of the traveler experience.

We meander across the street and out onto the sand, near a closed-down restaurant on the beach's edge. One of the Ar-gentinians produces a sizable joint and a lighter. He passes it to me and asks me to do the honors.

I get the thing going, take one full hit, and offer it to the other Argentine at my side.

"Is there something wrong with it?" he asks, noticeably concerned.

"No. Not at all, why?" I cough.

"Why did you only smoke once?"

"Common courtesy, I guess." My vision shifts, imperceptibly at first, then begins to flatten out. We are all standing rather close to one another in semidarkness. The air is thick and brackish, still hot enough to cause me to sweat uncomfortably.

"In Argentina, we smoke for as long as we like. Smoke more. You must appreciate this *porro* that we're sharing with you."

I try to figure how I can explain that I don't smoke very much without seeming rude—in Spanish. It took me about ten years to finally understand that heavy marijuana use and social interaction do not mix well for me, especially when I have to communicate in a second or third language. Light drinking can help with foreign language skills by lowering inhibitions, but even a small bit of weed heightens self-consciousness and makes it difficult to fumble your way through foreign syntax and verb conjugation. Furthermore, my Spanish and Portuguese seemed to be mutually exclusive and after this many weeks in Brazil, my brain is favoring Portuguese. As I try to assemble the words, my awkward slide into the languageless abyss between Spanish and Portuguese is interrupted by the arrival of a small armored paddy wagon that parks itself alongside the streetlight on the road at the back of the beach. "Hey, check *that* out," I say half in English, half in something close to Portuguese.

"It is BLITZ." One of the Argentines shouts. Before I can even ask what a blitz is, they are off and running toward the darkness of the water's edge. I, of course, am left holding the joint, smoldering between my fingers.

"Shit, man, it's a roundup," Otto tells me. "It's my professional recommendation that you run as fast as you can."

Blue-uniformed military police begin to pour out of the

truck like clowns out of a circus stunt car. They emerge with guns and nightsticks already drawn.

"Take it easy, man," I say. "I'm putting the joint out. They didn't see anything."

"It doesn't work that way here. There is just NO WAY that I'm letting these fucking fascists put their hands on me. LET'S GO."

"Hold on. They've got guns. Don't be stupid, they're just gonna chase you." The Argentines have already disappeared into the darkness near the water. I look back in time to see the cops roughing up a couple of young Brazilians on the edge of the beach, hitting them with nightsticks in the shins.

"Suit yourself," Otto mutters over his shoulder, already in a full sprint toward the restaurant.

They are on me within a matter of seconds. I don't even have the opportunity to move my feet, though I am able to toss the joint into the sand. There are no thoughts of probable cause, due process, or fair arrest procedure. It is straight to restraining my arms and cramming a .38 revolver in my mouth.

The gun tastes of oil, steel, and sweat. I am taken back to childhood: the bitter smoke in the alleyway after shooting Roman candles at each other on the Fourth of July; the metallic smell on my hands after playing with wrenches and tin snips in my grandfather's workshop.

"ARE YOU HIGH, FAGGOT?" the teenage cop yells, staring down the length of his arm and over the hammer. His eyes are black and watery, and the sparse facial hair gathered on his upper lip and jawline would be comical if not for the blue military police uniform and the firearm in my mouth. Were he American, he wouldn't be out of place in a high school shop class or ringside at a pro wrestling match.

A bead of perspiration trails down from his blue cap, curling to the tip of his fist-sculpted nose. Sweat soaks through my T-shirt and trails down my back and sides. It streams between the inside of my knees and my pant legs. Pools in my shoes. Climbs between my toes.

"ARE YOU HIGH, YOU FAGGOT GRINGO?" he shouts again, the words garbled in such a thick provincial accent that I wonder if he can read or write. Meanwhile, someone behind me starts to conduct a prison-style body search, groping toward my prostate through my jeans, emptying my pockets of all of my money. I squirm and rise to my tiptoes. The gunman raises the pistol so as to keep the barrel firmly hooked under my palate.

This is hardly what you would call an organized police roundup. It is more of an opportunity for a gang of weapons-toting adolescents to do as they please. The man giving me the suspiciously thorough body search notices something in the sand and recovers the nearly extinguished joint. He comes around to face me. This one's slightly older, pockmarked, and sporting a clipped black mustache. He looks like the kind of guy who grew up admiring Franco, Pinochet, and Norris.

The other police have spread out along the beach. I am all alone with my two new friends. Otto has evaporated into the night. The cops gave chase, but have lost the trail. A couple of them are dispatched in the general direction that Otto ran, and are searching around the pitch-black area below the restaurant deck that cantilevers out over the beach.

Officer Mustache holds the remainder of the joint between his callused thumb and middle finger. It is still smoking lightly from the edge of the paper. With a look of tired, try-hard sadism, bordering on indifference, he blows on the ember of the joint—heating it back to a cherry red. In this world, justice is not a protracted legal process of paperwork, courts, and bureaucracy. Here, they get right to the point.

Otto always said that when confronted with a group of assailants, you should single one out and take him to the ground.

They will not be expecting you to take the offensive. No matter the size of your opponent, he said, cut out the distance between the two of you and tackle him hard at his center of gravity. Once you gain the upper hand, do something so gruesome, so audacious that it shocks the others into temporary inaction: bite his nose off, crush his windpipe, gouge his eye out. The nose bite possibly has the best visible gore effect.

But I am not feeling quite that brave. I'm not feeling so brave at all. I am feeling pretty damn high. I try to explain the situation, to talk my way out of it. This is a blitz, after all: a horde of cops playing off of one another's energy, feeding off the mob mentality. Maybe if I can just reason with one of them, this leader guy . . . I can tell him that I am here doing essential work for the development of local tourism infrastructure. . . .

The younger officer secures me by my wrists while the little dictator grabs the fingers on my right hand, extending them downward and exposing my palm. He doesn't make any threats, doesn't build any suspense or fear; he simply brings the joint down—stubbing it out—on the soft skin on the inside of my middle finger. The joint hisses on my sweaty skin, the ember darkening to black. My skin bubbles and sears: a power drill twisting into my flesh. My knees go out from under me.

"You rich gringos think that you can do anything here, no? We have laws in Maranhão." He starts to blow on the ember again. No luck. He produces a lighter from his pocket, cranks the flame, and holds it under the crushed tip. "You're going to have to pay for your crime. What was in your pockets does not cover your fine."

My brain and right hand pulse simultaneously with pain. I hold my breath and try to lower myself toward the ground, wanting only to play dead, pretend that I am not here, that this is not happening.

Suddenly, I hear a hollow thud at about thirty yards. One of the men sent to track down Otto is lying on the ground, flat on his back, gripping at his chest and wheezing, struggling for a breath of air. For a moment, we all stare in silence. We then look at each other as if to ask, "What the fuck was that?" and, "What do we do next?"

They make the decision for us. The first punch is buried straight in my stomach, followed by a flurry of punches and kicks for good measure. I drop to the ground. All I can see are the jackboots goose-stepping on my head. I scramble to cover my face, neck, and ears. Pain is an afterthought—there is so much adrenaline coursing through me that I hardly feel the kicks. Yet they keep coming, each accompanied by a flash of light—or perhaps a flash of darkness, it is hard to determine.

The world, the beach, this fight . . . they all start to drift farther and farther away. Quieter and quieter. My vision narrows and my tenuous grip on consciousness loosens. I'm going . . . going . . . and, then, as fast as it started, it is over.

I lay there panting, throbbing, clearing sand from my eyes, mouth, and nose. I can see them off and running, trying to chase down the mysterious Israeli assailant, whom they'll never catch. I am alone on the edge of the beach, the sound of the waves breaking gently in the distance.

As it's not in my best interest to wait for them to return, I struggle to get up and make a limping dash for the club back down the street. I lose myself in the crowd, eventually slipping into the fetid bathroom to recompose. The pain arrives and surges through me like a cattle drive, pummeling me with a crushing pressure on the back and top of my head. My hands shake uncontrollably. I am blindsided by nausea and dizziness and, as the adrenaline subsides, an overpowering fatigue.

Have I become the kind of traveler that I originally abhorred? Am I no different from Mr. Yay? Here I am smoking weed on the beach with a group of privileged international travelers, with no regard for local laws, thinking that the whole world existed on my little tourist trail, catered to it, in fact. I suppose we felt that being outsiders, we were not subject to the same realities as everyone else. Was I on *The Real World Brazil?*, consumed by the supposed reality of house drama, ignoring the fact that I am in a country where the homicide rate qualifies as a low-intensity civil war; a country where crime, corruption and a pervasive fear of violence are frequent visitors in most people's day-to-day lives? I think that I may have just gained some much-needed perspective, and also some incentive to leave town, quickly.

I find a ride back to the hostel, where I discover a note scrawled on a paper napkin and slipped under my door. It was written quickly, in an almost unintelligible script. I can make out the words *amateurs, solar plexus, hand,* and *should have run.* It says something about making sure to include all of this in the "piece of shit guidebook" and is signed "stay out of trouble, OTTO."

He doesn't leave his email address or any of his contact information. One more good-bye—although I suspect that he would be able to find me again if he wanted to. He could probably break into my house, hogtie me, and kidnap me if he pleased.

I want to be home with my family. Home and comfortable with a full refrigerator, a clean shower, a nice girlfriend, a dog. Safe. Normal. Regular. Calm.

I look at myself in the bathroom mirror. There are fortunately no visible marks of the fight except for the ballooning red blister on my hand. The rest of the swelling is covered by my hair or is internal. I run my hands back over the top of my head and map out the irregular landscape. I am not pissing blood, so I take that as a sign that all of my essential organs are intact.

I doubt that the cops are looking for me, but considering that my friend clocked one of them, it is a definite possibility. I toy with different long-distance bus ideas, but don't have extra days to waste in transit. I don't have that kind of patience at this point, anyhow.

My clothes are changed and my bag is packed in a matter of minutes. Of course, all of my belongings were already folded and stacked nearby, just in case such a situation were to arise. My field hygiene routine finally pays off. I settle up a few extra charges at the front desk, take a cab out to the airport, and check into an unnamed hourly-rates place right down the road. I ask for ice at the front desk, but am only able to come up with three cold cans of beer. I lie in bed still trembling from the ass-kicking I received, battling with a looming fatigue, but not at peace enough to sleep. The cans of Brahma are positioned around my head on the pillow to help with the swelling. At least I can be inconspicuous in this little room of whitewashed bricks. I stay this way for hours, breathing in, breathing out, daydreaming of home, wherever that may be.

As soon as the airline ticket desks open for business, I walk down to the airport and purchase a flight to Rio. I sit quietly in the corner of the airport restaurant, waiting for the boarding call. I also haggle over the phone with my international airline and am able to change my return ticket to standby for the flight later today. I am retreating. Pulling out before it's too late. I have come as far as I need to come and it is time to go—that much is clear. Now the primary question is; *where to*?

I won't kid myself, my parents' home is no place for a man in my condition. Now is not the time to test the limits of un-conditional love. No, I decide that I only have one realistic choice, only one person who would truly understand my condition.

Gateway Substance

New York, under normal circumstances, is an inhospitable, unforgiving place. New York without the key to an apartment or money for a hotel is like being a wayward peasant locked outside of the keep during a siege.

I stand in front of the house and remove my backpack. It is the only freestanding house on its block in Washington Heights. Neighbored by a narrow lot of tall grass pushing forth from fissures in the asphalt and a couple of overflowing Dumpsters, the three stories of blue-green vinyl siding is more appropriate to residential Queens than this bustling top finger of Manhattan. The house itself looks like something that grew up between the cracks in the pavement, an interloping species, a rogue dandelion or Norwegian rat.

Three teenage girls sit precariously close to broken beer bottles on the stoop, already busy sending text messages and braiding each other's hair just before 9 a.m. They speak in Spanglish at a fast Dominican clip.

The minivan is still parked in front. It is a good sign that things haven't changed that much since I've been gone. Electrical cords run out of the van window and are spliced into the base of a streetlight, its metal cover pried to the side. Through the tinted windows of the van it is usually possible to see the flashing light of a TV screen as the young proprietors do battle at Mortal Kombat between selling twenty sacks of hydro to foot traffic and cars coming off of the Cross-Bronx Expressway. The screen appears to be off right now, probably too early for business hours.

I knock on the door of the house. There is no answer. The bell, like the rest of the house, is broken. I ask the teenagers if they've seen anyone leave the house this morning.

"I ain't seen nobody today. They had a big-ass party here last night, though." I walk up to the corner store with the big lottery poster in the window, stacks of the *Post* nestled among plantains, limes, and tall cans of beer on ice. The bananas, even in this misplaced concrete-and-brick corner of the city, are huge, fluorescent yellow, and completely unblemished compared to the fruit that I have seen in the tropics.

Metal gates are lifted from storefronts as the neighborhood begins to come alive. One of dozens of barbershops named after a town or province back in the Dominican Republic takes its first client of the day, just in for a quick line-up before work. You can feel that the crowds of hysterical pedestrians are just minutes from impact.

I return to the front of the house and knock again, repeatedly. I hear a fumbling with the deadbolt. The door swings open and a guy staggers out, straight into my shoulder, and keeps going.

"Terribly sorry," he says in some sort of English accent, his breath a bubbling cauldron of last night's alcohol. He pulls his hat down over his eyes and walks briskly toward the corner, head down, knees locked. The front door is ajar.

I enter the darkened front hallway, stepping past a keg in a blue plastic tub and a scattering of red plastic cups on the stained wood floor. The soles of my shoes peel off the floor with every step.

I walk down the staircase and arrive at the basement bedroom. I knock. Again, there is no answer. I take a deep breath and enter. I will make my case, plead for asylum. The worst that can happen is that I'll get turned back out onto the street.

My eyes focus straight on a girl's bare nipples, her hair swept over her face. Not what I was expecting to see. I turn my head away and decide to step out, shut the door, and knock again, but take a quick second look before closing the door.

"Yes?" says a meek voice from behind the door.

"Hey, it's Thomas. Can I come in?"

"Who? Uhh, OK, just a second . . . OK."

I wait a moment and then reenter the room. She has pulled the sheets up to her neck and looks at me with perplexed hungover trepidation.

"Sorry," I begin to explain. "I just . . ." I stop myself when I realize that I have no idea who this girl is. I have never seen her before and she is definitely not who I thought she was. I start to think that maybe I am in the wrong house or wrong room. But a quick glance around reveals familiar surfing posters on the wall, a snowboard still hanging from the rafters, and a beaten-up surfboard leaning against rows of polyester Hawaiian shirts in the open, sliding-door closet.

"Sorry, I've been out of town for a while. Does the Doctor still live here?" I ask.

"Who?"

"The Doctor. Does he still live here?"

"Never heard of him."

"This is all his stuff on the walls here. You sure this isn't his room?"

"No. It *could* be. It's just . . . well, I'm not really sure what I'm doing here myself," she says.

Well, what do you know? A woman after my own heart.

Before I have a chance to inquire of her further, we hear weighty footsteps creak down the wooden basement staircase, landing powerfully on the heels and reverberating through the basement.

"WHAT THE FUCK ARE YOU DOING HERE, YOU SADISTIC LITTLE LOUSE?"

I turn around to see the Doctor standing behind me, wearing a white coat with a stethoscope protruding from the pocket. He looks back at me, disheveled and red-eyed, glances at the unknown naked woman in his bed, and at my backpack, which is on the floor next to us. He grabs the folding chair next to the door and raises it back over his shoulder, ready to strike me with it.

"Hey, Doc, nice to see you, too," I say.

"You leave me drunk, bleeding, and half knocked out in the middle of the street, don't even CALL TO APOLOGIZE, and now here you are, a month and a half later, fornicating in my bed with some trollop. I'M GONNA BEAT THE LIVING FUCK OUT OF YOU."

"No, dude, you don't understand, I thought this was your girlfriend. . . ."

"YOU THOUGHT YOU WERE CRAWLING INTO BED WITH MY GIRLFRIEND? You're even sicker and more devious than I imagined," He raises the chair higher.

"No, I mean, I thought it was Sandra and maybe you were in the bathroom, or maybe you have a new girlfriend. I mean, I *just* got here. I don't even know her name. DUDE, I SWEAR."

He lowers the folding chair, but doesn't change his expression. There are a few seconds of silence. "So who are *you* then?" he bellows at the girl.

"I'm Sara." The duvet is now pulled up to the base of her nose.

"Oh, OK. That makes perfect sense then." He stares at her uncomprehendingly and then recasts his glare on me. "And what the hell are you doing here, Thomas? I mean, I can guess what you are doing here, but what the hell are you doing *here*?"

I look at the Doctor and shrug. From the corner of my eye, I spot her bra, shirt, and pants mixed in with his clothes, papers, CD cases, and piles of used food containers on the floor. "I know that we had a little altercation, but I was hoping . . ."

"*Altercation*? First you gave me a black eye, you fuck, and then you attacked me later that night and left me with soft spots in my head."

"It was a matter of bad timing," I plead. It is not in my best interest to make a you-started-it, you-literally-asked-for-it, or you-deserved-it argument. "Water under the bridge. Old friends, right?" I look at the girl, "I don't look like a bad guy, do I?"

She shakes her head nervously, only her eyes and fingertips visible about the sheets. "Can you pass me my clothes, please?" she asks.

The Doctor shakes his head and stares at me, wild-eyed. "Look at how trashed this house is. I work all night at the hospital and have to return to this shit."

I ignore him. There are more important things to attend to. I locate the girl's shirt and hand it to her, but she seems to have misplaced her bra and can't find her panties. The Doctor's anger starts to subside and he remembers that he is talking to a naked woman in his bed. He softens to his bedside-manner tone. "So what, may I ask, are you doing here, young lady?" I notice the Doctor gently nudging her bra and panties under the bed with the tip of his shoe. I continue to search for them in the far corner.

"I came out for a graduation party last night. I . . . I just graduated from NYU. My friend knows your roommate. I think his name's Ali, right?"

"Beats me," he says.

She continues, "Ummm, did you happen to see a Welsh

guy around here by any chance?" Once her shirt is properly in place, she lowers the duvet back to her neckline.

"Did he have a cap on like one of the characters from *Newsies*?" I ask.

"Yeah, he had a hat."

"I saw him running out the front door," I say before I can catch myself.

"You had a one-night stand with a Welsh guy in my bed? Jesus-motherfucking-Christ," the Doctor says.

Sara bursts into tears. The duvet now covers her entire face. Muffled sobs emanate from the lump under the sheets. The lump rises and falls with the crying.

"*Nice one*," I mouth in his direction.

"*Fuck off*," he mouths back at me and taps a forefinger against his own chest. "*This is my house.*"

He tries to make it up to her. "You look pretty good to me. I definitely wouldn't run out on you in the morning. I mean, this is my bedroom, you know, so I couldn't anyways, but you follow what I'm trying to say, right?"

"*Much better*," I mouth again in his direction.

"What are you so upset about? I thought that you just graduated from NYU," he continues.

"Yeah," I add. "It's not like you just stepped off the bus at Port Authority. People—you know, like this Welsh guy—can be sleazy."

The lump under the covers speaks. "I know, it's not even so much that. I just finished school and I don't have a job yet. My roommates are starting in a few weeks as paralegals and I-banking analysts. My ex is a consultant." She pauses to cry for a few long seconds. "And I am apparently unemployable. I go out to cheer up and now this *motherfucker* runs out on me."

The Doctor, who has spent much of the past year working in a trauma center, has no patience for this kind of quotidian drama. He stands there limp, looking befuddled. At least it takes his focus off of me.

"I just don't know what to do with myself," Sara moans from under the duvet.

"No structure, huh? Do you have school debt?" I ask, trying to keep the conversation going so he doesn't throw out both of us.

"No."

"*No*? Are you kidding me?" the Doctor blusters. "I'm gonna be paying off medical school until you hit menopause. I even bought this asshole a three-hundred-dollar bottle of rum as a departure gift . . . with my *school* money. You don't have shit to worry about."

"Actually, I paid for that bottle, dude. I still owe Master-Card for it."

"Whatever. You still went and smashed it before you smacked me around. . . . Total disgrace."

This is going nowhere good. I turn back to the lump on the bed. "Maybe you should try to enjoy some different aspects of life while you have the freedom to do so. I just screwed up my whole existence to be able to do that. You're jobless, so it'll be much easier for you to do at this point."

"That's easy for you to say, you have a career to come back to," she replies.

The Doctor counters, "No, actually, Thomas doesn't have a job. Not really. He's here to beg to sleep on my floor. Aren't you?"

I nod.

He continues, "And he likes that, I guess. But, you know, I'd kill for a little time off. A day. A week. Fuck it, maybe a year or two. I've barely slept three hours a night for the last four or five nights. I sure as hell haven't been getting drunk and having sex with strangers in that bed."

I try to clarify. "I'm not exactly happy to be begging to sleep on your floor, but, you know, I'm excited or, at least, I'm cool with not knowing what's next. About having open possibilities. You've got to take hold of the random craziness and own it. Right, Doc?"

"So what you're saying is that you've found a way to justify the fact that you're an irresponsible douche bag?" the Doctor asks.

"Something like that. I mean, maybe I haven't chosen the easiest or most sensible path in life, but it works for me. And, now that I have a taste for it, I look forward to doing it bigger and better."

"Well, you know, that's what we call a gateway substance at the clinic."

"Which clinic?" asks Sara.

"The substance abuse and dependency clinic. I finished my rotation there a few weeks back."

"*Rotation*? Is that what they call it these days?" I push.

"No, DICK. I did a rotation in the clinic for med school and now I'm on to pediatric psychology."

That makes even more sense. "Shit, if you can work in substance abuse and dependency, I don't think it should be a problem for me to pull off something like this guidebook."

"Did you find my panties yet?" Sara interrupts me.

"No, sorry, still looking. I can't seem to find the bra, either. I could have sworn it was around here somewhere."

"You two need get out of here," the Doctor says. "My girlfriend will be here in half an hour to take a nap between her shifts. I've got to run back to the hospital. . . . Don't be here when she gets here."

"Wait a sec, you're leaving?" I ask.

"I only came home to grab my Palm Pilot."

"You're really kicking me out?"

"No, my little parasite. You can leave your bag here and come back later, after her nap. There's a sleeping bag in the closet. You can have that corner of the floor." He points to the few feet of space to the side of the bathroom door. He's always been a softie at heart.

"Thank you, benevolent one."

"If you two decide to hook up, do it in the sleeping bag, not in my bed, please."

"Dude, I knew you were crass, but really. How can you say that?"

"Yeah, I'd never stoop to having sex with a stranger in a sleeping bag," Sara laughs.

I sit across the room from her in the chair by a dusty, translucent blue-and-white iMac. The Doctor leaves and I try to comfort her. I think that she feels better by the time that we discover her underwear and she walks out the door toward the 1 train. We don't hook up. OK, kind of, for a few minutes, but that barely counts. I flip over the navy duvet and make the Doctor's bed, so he'll never notice, anyhow.

I now have eight days to finish writing this guidebook. If I properly utilize every hour of every day, I might be able to make the deadline. Maybe. I will sleep only enough to keep my body from giving out on me. Eat only while continuing to type. I must be focused. I must move forward. I will not think of Sydney or how I could ride the subway down to her apartment and beg her to start all over again. I am a writer now and must become a miserable, surly, sleep-starved hermit to have any realistic chance of success.

For the next week, I subsist on a diet of Gatorade, coffee, Pepperidge Farm Goldfish (cheddar flavor), Red Bull, and Ritalin. Sometimes I allow myself a break to walk up to the corner store. I purchase the melted-cheese-and-cold-cut sandwiches on French bread that are popular in Dominican delis. The sandwiches are for special occasions, when I finish a chapter or write a particularly good boxed text.

At night I work on the floor while the Doctor works at his desk and his girlfriend works in the bed. Sometimes I work at the sticky table upstairs, if I can find room among the pizza boxes, beer cans, and old copies of the *Times*. But it is poorly lit, drafty, and full of noise from the street. I prefer the floor in the basement bedroom, one foot folded underneath me with my chin on the other knee, hunched over the laptop. The Doctor treats me to what he calls his "specialized outpatient program." Sometimes he prescribes a tall bottle of Presidente to bring down anxiety levels, other times a two-liter of Mountain Dew, a Ritalin, or the occasional bump of coke. These are all approved to increase my mental focus and productivity. He calibrates the optimal levels of medication by thoughtfully pretesting them all on himself. Anything to get through the project.

I write from my experience. I write from my research. I write from my imagination. I write about the Brazilian space program. I write about the history of *forró* music. I write about hotels and restaurants and towns that I never visited. I write about hotels and restaurants and towns that I feel guilty about not visiting. I write about hotels and restaurants and towns that I never visited and could care less about. I write about nudist beaches, recipes for traditional salted meats, anaconda mating habits, and the two-inch-long *candiru* catfish that swims up your urethra (the requisite Amazonian horror story that every travel writer must pen about Brazil). I write about things that I learn about as I am putting them down on the page. I write about things that I still don't understand, even after I've written about them.

Some of the writing is good. Some of the writing is appalling. I discover that there are only about seven or eight ways to describe an attractive beach. At points, the writing degenerates into fill-in-the-blanks reviews like: the _____ (gorgeous/splendid/beautiful) beach of _____ (white/powdery/perfect) sand and _____ (sky blue/crystalline/aquamarine) water is backed by _____ (palm, mountain, rain-forest) fringed *whatever*.

Distilling a Brazilian bus station into a 250-word transportation table is alchemy at best. There is no making sense of some of them. If I were to come up with a set schedule for the guidebook, I'd basically be making it up, lying to fit Lonely Planet's standards. And that's exactly what I end up doing. I use a lot of estimating, averaging, and faux-authoritative decision making. How many buses a day from Fortaleza to Aracati. Twenty? Twenty-five? Forty-five? Who knows? Who gives a fuck? They come all the time.

I don't sleep. I lose weight. I lose sanity.

I vomit millions of tidbits of information from my brain, passing them through my fingertips into the keyboard and into the electronic memory of the computer. I arrange the information in sentences that sometimes make sense, that give a sense of place, and that are properly formatted according to the Felix template guidelines. A helpful assistant regional publishing manager (ARPM) is put in charge of the book until a new editor is selected or recruited or picked up off the street or whatever it is they do. The ARPM looks at one of my chapters and notifies me that all of my practicality strings are misformatted, that I need to relearn Felix. It is a very steep learning curve, I am told.

I connected the Doctor's Internet cable to my computer and seem to have contracted a computer virus while attempting to follow up on restaurant and hotel information online. A similar virus has appeared on the Doctor's iMac. I am sure that it has something to do with the endless research of low-grade Brazilian tourism sites and tourism clearinghouses, what with their cornucopia of pop-ups, spyware, and adware. Or maybe it has something to do with the Internet porn I repeatedly stumble across during personal breaks, while the Doctor and his girlfriend are in class or at the clinic. Either way, my invincible Toughbook has been felled by a nasty little computer STD.

The Felix template refuses to load and the computer crashes every time that I used the Internet. I have to reformat all of the pages using the drop-down "style" and "font" menus in Word. For those who don't waste their time knowing what that is, it means that I have to format the whole thing line by line, highlighting a word or group of words and then searching through the menu, selecting whether it is to be body text, intro text, POI, list B, icon, box heading 2, heading 5, or whatever. I resist the urge to smash the Toughbook on the floor. I trudge on.

As I near the end of the book, it feels similar to running the last couple miles of the New York City Marathon: hobbling along the edge of Central Park, being tempted to lie in the grass or stagger into a nearby bar, but too close to the end to give up— on principle. Some auxiliary supply of ego pulls you through in the end. In eight days, I somehow complete 112 pages of writing and editing.

Putting the finishing touches on the manuscript is rather anticlimactic, as I am stuck with all of the pages on my ailing computer and have no way to send it in to the company. I also still have to do clean mark-ups of all of the maps, fill out dozens of map keys, and fix up the front-of-book environment chapters, but I will have to deal with that situation after my deadline.

I try to use the iMac. I try to get the information off of my computer and onto a computer at the medical school library. It is to no avail. A nervous breakdown looms like a squadron of B-52s on the horizon.

I share a quasi-celebratory drink with the Doctor. We toast

to getting by while making sure to remain ridiculous. He tells me I need to find a new place to live, quickly. My recovery is almost complete and now it is time to leave the nest. Plus, my presence on the floor is not good for his sex life. Traveling is a fantastic opportunity to get to know some interesting and unique characters, but there's nothing quite like the charms of an old friend.

Fortunately, my friend David works in computers and tells me to come down to his work on lower Broadway after office hours. It takes me nearly an hour to get down to the edge of the Financial District. David is working late as usual, trying to get everything up and running for the next workday.

He tells me that the computer is crawling with viruses. It must be completely overhauled. He sets about backing up my manuscript and then wiping and reinstalling my entire operating system. Once that is done, it will be possible to submit the manuscript.

I gaze south out the window and catch sight of my old office building. I count the floors down from the top and see that the light is still on in my little conference room on the corner of the fifty-seventh floor. I imagine that someone is pulling a late night, putting documents in chronological order or maybe milking a client for overtime. To the east of the building, I look out toward the Brooklyn Bridge and reflect on my admonishment to myself that I should make life changes and decisions at a prudent, responsible pace—to not resurface too fast.

I look back down at the blackened scab, the burn, on my right hand and laugh. I never was particularly good at following advice, especially my own.

Performance Anxiety

A year later, I am researching Patagonia and Tierra del Fuego for Lonely Planet in the dead of winter. Bundled in a ski jacket and hat, I am allowed fifteen minutes of Internet use at a small Chilean government outpost office near Cape Horn.

Yes, that's right. I did it again. And again. And then, a few more times. I must be some kind of sick masochist. But in the end, I really loved all of it, every triumph and every setback—at least in retrospect. Experiences were had. Repertoires were expanded. Boundaries were pushed. Beverages were consumed. Ladies were bedded. And several hundred pages were written, all of which potentially affected some local economies and several thousand travelers' itineraries.

For a while, I figured that I was receiving more travel book contracts only because the feedback from my first book had been stalled in bureacracy. I imagined it would all catch up to me soon enough. Once the feedback landed on the desk of the powers-that-be, I would be discovered as a hack and a third-rate pretender.

With my breath hanging in the cold air between me and the monitor, I open my email to find that I have finally received my Author Performance Feedback Form (APFF) for *Lonely Planet Brazil*. I open it with some hesitation, anticipating a bloodbath. Such is not my fate. The review reads:

> Thomas is an excellent writer and researcher with a deep knowledge of Brazil. This was his first project for LP, and he did a fantastic job. Thomas is a hard worker who's willing to go the extra mile to make sure his text is right. He added a lot of great new material to the chapters and substantially revised everything that he did decide to retain. He fits well with LP tone and style, and is a delight to collaborate with. I look forward to working with Thomas again. (_____ Coordinating Editor)

What can I say?
I'm a natural.

Acknowledgments

├ ─ ─ ─ ─ ─ ─ ─ ─ ─ ─ ─ ─ ─ ─ ─ ─ ─

Thanks to my astute agent, Mr. Byrd Leavell III, for being on board from the minute I first spoke with him and telling me over a round of Guinness, "I am definitely going to sell this book." His proactive handling of the project took this from a few draft chapters to a reality.

Many thanks to my talented editor, Brandi Bowles, who also believed in my writing and in the book. She fought to make it happen and make it the best book possible. Much gratitude goes to my other talented editor, Adam Korn, who saw early promise in the story and nimbly carried the book through to the end. Jay Sones also deserves thanks for his hard work on the publicity front. Thanks also to Carrie Thornton for overseeing the project, Min Lee for the legal review, and everyone else at Crown/Three Rivers Press.

I must also thank my friend Mark Eisner (buy his books) for his support and editing; Shari Goldhagen and Anthony Doerr (buy their books) for guidance and advice in the early stages of this project; Anthony Chatfield, a solid up-and-coming writer and fellow former QFC deli employee, for his tech support; Zohar Lazar for the cover art; and my friends Becky and Billy Austin, who were always excellent hosts whenever I needed to come to NYC for work.

A final thanks goes out to the usual suspects: Ed and Linda Kohnstamm, James Kohnstamm, Joanna de Velasco, Dani Silva, and Tábata Silva. Thank you for the support and foundation that, regardless of what I'm up to, always keep one of my feet in the realm of sanity.

About the Author

Thomas Kohnstamm was born in 1975. The United States government saw fit to pay for him to get an M.A. in Latin American Studies from Stanford University, where he studied Portuguese among other things. He has since gone on to write for Lonely Planet, *Travel + Leisure*, *Forbes*, *Time Out New York*, the *San Francisco Chronicle*, the *Los Angeles Times*, the *Denver Post*, the *Miami Herald*, and numerous other publications.

When not traveling, Thomas lives in walking distance of where he grew up in Seattle, Washington.